★ AMERICAN ★
CONSTITUTIONAL HISTORY

HARPER TORCHBOOKS

A reference-list of Harper Torchbooks, classified by subjects, is printed at the end of this volume.

★ AMERICAN ★
CONSTITUTIONAL HISTORY

ESSAYS BY
EDWARD S. CORWIN

EDITED BY
ALPHEUS T. MASON
AND
GERALD GARVEY

HARPER TORCHBOOKS *The Academy Library*
HARPER & ROW, PUBLISHERS
NEW YORK, EVANSTON, AND LONDON

American Constitutional History: Essays by Edward S. Corwin

Printed in the United States of America.

Harper & Row, Publishers, Incorporated
49 East 33rd Street
New York, N.Y. 10016

First HARPER TORCHBOOK edition published 1964 by
Harper & Row, Publishers, Incorporated
New York, Evanston, and London

Contents

Editorial Note

Students of the Supreme Court are struck by Edward S. Corwin's insights. They are equally impressed by the range of his scholarship. We have tried to capture both the penetration and sweep of his thought.

Corwin touched every area of constitutional inquiry, but one subject bears his indelible mark above all others: the theory and practice of judicial review. The twelve essays included here have been selected as representative of Corwin's "best"—a contribution to the story which runs from Coke's *dictum* in Dr. Bonham's case to applications of judicial review on behalf of free speech and religion.

The essays are arranged in accordance with the logic of the subject matter, rather than in the order in which they were first published. To increase the number and variety of pieces, cuts have been made, hopefully without violence to the integrity and literary quality of the selection. In certain instances—"The Supreme Court and the Fourteenth Amendment," "Statesmanship on the Supreme Court," and "Bowing Out 'Clear and Present Danger' "—the tightness of Corwin's scholarship demanded editorial forbearance; these essays appear as their author wrote them, complete and unabridged.

For each piece included, others perforce had to be excluded. Choice, though never easy, was facilitated by the knowledge that certain of Corwin's best known works are easily accessible. The " 'Higher Law' Background" article is available in paperback; *The President: Office and Powers* came out in 1957 in a freshly revised edition. Those interested in "the complete Corwin" may consult the bibliography of his writings.

A final aim has been to present Corwin as a participant in public affairs as well as the scholar and exegete. Along with that exacting and eminently scholarly workpiece, "The Basic Doctrine of American Constitutional Law," we included his impassioned plea for judicial self-restraint, "Curbing the Court." His forthright testimony on behalf of President Roosevelt's "Court Packing" bill complements rather than contradicts the heavily documented, influential study of "Due Process before the Civil War."

From this collection, though severely abridged, we can derive something of both the flavor and method of a distinguished scholar. Hopefully also, there is in these chapters a compelling logic that owes nothing to the choices and groupings the editors have made.

A. T. M.
G. G.

Introduction to the Torchbook Edition

Edward S. Corwin stands among the giants of American constitutional commentators—with Kent, Story and Cooley. More than any other scholar of our time, he justified and illustrated his own incisive observation: "If judges make law, so do commentators."[1]

Professor Corwin was a man of broad culture and profound learning—in history, politics, and legal philosophy. For him these were not isolated disciplines, nor were they ends in themselves. All were intertwined manifestations of the basic principles of a functioning, evolving society. He took especially to heart Aristotle's admonition: "If you would understand anything, observe its beginning and its development."[2] Realizing that this advice applies to law as to few other subjects, he followed it rigorously in every aspect of constitutional interpretation.

Corwin had a penchant for arresting comment and devastating wit, particularly in the medium of a book review. He took pride in his literary style. Use of italics and the exclamation point fell only short of mannerism, while his gift for the homely epigram verged on the other extreme. The elegant phrase, the rustic analogy livened his pages as well as his classes. "Linch-pin of the Constitution" was his graphic expression for the Supremacy Clause. He stamped enduringly the label Dual Federalism on the theory that the states, by their very existence, limit national power. Judicial review, he told his students, was "American democracy's way of covering its bet."

Corwin was a scholar's scholar. Yet the reluctance that restrains many academicians from joining the debate of public issues never deterred him. His second-floor study at 115 Prospect

[1] Review: *The Law of the American Constitution,* by Charles K. Burdick. 22 *Michigan Law Review* (November, 1923), 84.

[2] Review: *A Selection of Cases and Authorities on Constitutional Law,* by Oliver P. Field. 25 *American Political Science Review* (May, 1931), 459, 460.

Avenue, Princeton, and the "Old Stone House" of later years were sources of relevant comment and counsel. Refusing to remain in his ivory tower, he served as an adviser to the Public Works Administration and to the Department of Justice. In the 1930's, he was special assistant to the U. S. Attorney General on Constitutional issues and actively supported Roosevelt's "Court-Packing Plan." From 1949 to 1952 he was editor for the Legislative Reference Section, Library of Congress, directing a research project that resulted in the massive volume: *The Constitution Annotated: Analysis and Interpretation.* In 1954, he became chairman of a national committee opposing the ill-fated Bricker Amendment to restrict the President's treaty-making power.

The single, monumental work he planned was never written. But the corpus of Corwin's writings advances every frontier of his subject. His ideas, including the phraseology in which they were couched, have entered the mainstream of constitutional thought. But in scholarship, as in other matters, it is the most familiar that least deserves to be taken for granted. These selections from Corwin's voluminous publications support the belief that his work should be more readily available to teachers, students, and the public generally.

I.

Edward S. Corwin was born on a farm in Plymouth, Michigan, in 1878. He did his undergraduate work at the University of Michigan, and subsequently presented himself (along with a dissertation on the French-American Alliance during the War for Independence) for the Ph.D. at the University of Pennsylvania. The decisive year was 1905, when Woodrow Wilson, then President of Princeton University, picked young Corwin as one of the new band of teachers in his famous preceptorial system of instruction. The apprenticeship ended in 1911, when at thirty-three he became a full professor.

The outstanding development in American constitutional inquiry during Corwin's apprentice years was the preoccupation of scholars and of the Supreme Court itself with the "rights of property." That "stern arbitress of historical scholarship—the economic interpretation of history"[3]—enjoyed wide appeal. Beard and his disciples had made judicial review seem a mere device of Federalist robber barons

[3] Review: *Life of John Marshall,* by Albert J. Beveridge. 4 *Mississippi Valley Hist. Review* (June, 1917), 116, 117.

who had somehow managed to get a good press until "economic interpretation" appeared to set matters right. The Court, moreover, did little to dispel the resulting picture of the judiciary as an anti-democratic institution. By tortured construction of the Due Process clause, the "nine old men" championed property against all comers, and in so doing called into question the Framers' intention to authorize judicial review in the first place.

"How are we to know what was the intent of the framers of the Constitution in this matter?" Beard asked. "The only method is to make an exhaustive search in the documents of the Convention and in the writings, speeches, papers and recorded activities of its members."[4] Beard concluded that the Framers unambiguously, consciously, and decisively intended the review power. He added, for good measure, that his documentary evidence was confirmed by the "spirit of the Constitution"—which was, of course, the spirit of property-holders resolutely determined to protect their rights against the minatory forces of democracy. These findings did not go unchallenged. Charging "usurpation," Dean William Trickett of the Dickinson School of Law flatly denied the legitimacy of any such power. "There are a few considerations," Dean Trickett insisted, "that persuade that the Framers and enacters of the Constitution did not grant the power to the federal courts to annul federal statutes. It was as to existing courts a disreputable and disputed power. They could have made their intention . . . clear with a line. . . . *Why did they not write that line?*"[5]

Corwin agreed, in general, with Beard's conclusions. But he pointed out that what is *historically* correct is not for that reason necessarily relevant, especially if the question is framed and answered in the context of an overbearing, *contemporary* predilection. What Corwin wrote of the "economic interpretation" in general applied to Beard's research in particular: "Had Professor Beard been less bent on demonstrating the truth of the socialistic theory of economic determinism and class struggle, his own performance would be less open to criticism."[6] Returning to the subject in 1925, Corwin added: "No one denies that the concern felt by the Fathers

[4] Charles A. Beard, *The Supreme Court and the Constitution* (1912; Englewood Cliffs: Prentice-Hall, 1962), p. 46.

[5] William Trickett, "Judicial Dispensation from Congressional Statutes," 41 *Amer. Law Review* (Jan.–Feb., 1907), 65.

[6] 5 *History Teachers' Magazine* (Feb., 1914), 65.

for the rights of property and contract contributed immensely to impart to American constitutional law its strong bias in favor of these rights from the outset." *But* the concession only serves to throw certain unanswered questions into a higher relief. For, what warrant had these men for translating any of their *interests* as *rights;* and why did they adopt the precise means which they did to advance their interests or secure their rights—in other words, why did they choose the precise system set up by the Constitution to do the work which they put upon it?[7]

In certain respects, Trickett made a greater contribution than Beard. Of him it could have been observed what Sherlock Holmes once said to Watson: "It is true that you have missed everything of importance, but you have hit upon the method!"[8] Those who charged judicial usurpation drew the wrong conclusion, but at least they drew it from the right premises. For Corwin, judicial review was one of those cases in which the silence of the Constitution spoke more loudly than any number of the 3,500-odd words written into it.

Consider, he reasoned, the theoretical prepossessions of the Framers' generation. The Fathers were heirs to the British tradition of Fundamental Law. Since the time of the enterprising Coke, this notion implied the existence of a "higher" law capable of controlling the legislature. From here it was but a short step to the concept of Higher Law, with capital letters. This step had been taken long before the Constitutional Convention by American intelligencers of John Locke's natural law: by James Otis in *Rights of the British Colonies Asserted and Proved,* and by Thomas Jefferson in the *Declaration.* When embodied in the Constitution, this Higher Law tradition automatically produced a control over any conflicting law of mere men. Sanction for judicial review existed wholly apart from any combings for the expressed "intent of the framers."[9]

[7] "The Progress of Constitutional Theory from the Signing of the Declaration of Independence to the Meeting of the Philadelphia Convention," 30 *Amer. Historical Review* (April, 1925), 511, 512.

[8] Arthur Conan Doyle, "A Case of Identity," I *Works* (New York: Appleton, 1902), p. 89.

[9] See *Twilight of the Supreme Court* (New Haven: Yale, 1934), pp. 103-04.

II.

Corwin went on to unravel the dialectic whereby the right to interpret "Higher Law" had become the peculiar province of judges. "The Courts were at once the authors and interpreters of the common law," he wrote, "the most usual source of individual right; . . . were ancient defenders of the Rule of Law against prerogative; . . . *were occasionally willing to invoke Natural Law.* Not only were judges the traditional defenders of individual rights; they were also the only persons competent to discharge the task." As Coke had explained: "Causes which concern the life—or goods—of . . . subjects are not to be decided by natural reason, but by the *artificial reason and judgment of the law.* . . ." The translation was all but complete: "From being the universal inheritance of mankind, its distinctive inheritance, because attesting man's participation in the divine reason, law had become a professional, nay, an official mystery."[11] As rationalized by the judges during the formative stage of American institutions, judicial review invoked a miracle.

It supposes a kind of transubstantiation whereby the Court's opinion of the Constitution, if pertinent to the decision of a case properly before the Court, becomes the very body and blood of the Constitution. This dogmatic assumption of the identity of the law with the judicial version of it is not, however, coeval with the Constitution, but long antedates it. It is fundamental to the common law, and has a dignified place in legal history.[12]

Why did the Framers not "write that line" which Dean Trickett demanded? Because judicial review "rested upon certain general principles which in their estimation made specific provision . . . unnecessary."[13] It was a creature of logic—the logic of an age—not of the intent of the Framers.

"The 'Higher Law' Background of American Constitutional Law" explained not only judicial review, but also the existence of certain rights *qua* rights, entitled to the special guardianship of

[10] "The Supreme Court and Unconstitutional Acts of Congress," 4 *Michigan Law Review* (June, 1906), 616, 626. Emphasis supplied.

[11] See *Twilight of the Supreme Court.* p. 109. Emphasis deleted.

[12] *Court Over Constitution* (Princeton: Princeton, 1938), pp. 68–69.

[13] See *Doctrine of Judicial Review* (Princeton: Princeton, 1914), pp. 14–17.

courts. *"A priori,"* Corwin pondered, "it is difficult to see how judges, having set out to be defenders of 'natural rights,' were in a position to decline to defend, and therefore to define, all such rights whether mentioned in the constitution or not."

The difficulty is disposed of, however, the moment we recollect that our judges envisaged their problem not as moral philosophers but as lawyers, and especially as students of the Common Law. "Natural rights," in short, were to be defined in light of common law precedents.[14]

The property right, in this tradition, was inviolable against "interested and overbearing majorities" not merely because it was proprietarian, but because, as "the old Dialogue of Doctor and Student informs us, [it] was protected by 'the law of reason' by which term those 'learned in the law of England,' were wont to designate the 'law of nature.'"[15] Property was protected by natural law—that is, by "the law of reason." Simultaneously, it enjoyed the cherished guardianship of the common law—that is, of what Coke had called "the artificial reason and judgment of the law."[16] The same theory which underlay judicial review, as a putative bulwark against arbitrary government, furnished a no less arbitrary bulwark than the "right reason of the judges."

The doctrine that the Court was the Constitution's unimpeachable mouthpiece met its first real test in the political upsurge taking shape as the Jacksonian revolution. Under Jackson's theory, enforcing the Constitution meant upholding the people's will as manifested at the ballot box—the theory of judicial power must change accordingly. Under this new dispensation judicial review was transferred

from its original foundation on the law of nature to the basis of the written constitution, and so is transferred from an obstacle to the realization of popular sovereignty, to the indispensable instrument for that realization.[17]

[14] *The Basic Doctrine of American Constitutional Law,* p. 8. Offprint from 12 *Michigan Law Review* (Feb., 1914).

[15] *Ibid.,* p. 9.

[16] 8 Coke 118a (1610).

[17] "The Establishment of Judicial Review, II," 9 *Michigan Law Review* (Feb., 1911), 283, 306. Cf. Review: *The American Nation,* vols. 16–19. 2 *Amer. Pol. Sci. Review* (Nov., 1907), 110, 117.

Yet prevailing notions during the early years of Corwin's scholarship were in outright contradiction to the theory that courts should serve the popular will. In 1908, Arthur Twining Hadley could declare without risk of contradiction, "Democracy was complete as far as it went, but constitutionally it was bound to stop short of *social* democracy. . . . The forces of democracy on one side . . . [were] set against the forces of property on the other side, with the judiciary as arbiter between them."[18] Thus, if the "economic interpretation of the Constitution" was a gross oversimplification, the judicial application of constitutional phrases like Due Process of Law to social and economic problems of the day was a misguidedly over-complicated gloss on the Framers' document.

Initially "due process of law" referred only to the kind of procedure which a legislature observed in passing a law.[19] Later on it began to be interpreted as declaratory of the truism that the legislature can act only in a legislative capacity, *i.e.,* not as a Court. Then the doctrine emerged that any deprivation of property was a penalty. But only Courts—and, a *fortiori,* not legislatures—could impose penalties, *i.e.,* punishments, within the prohibition against attainders, and hence within "due process of law." The conclusion followed directly: "Once it was recognized that to define 'legislative power' finally and authoritatively lay with the courts, the power of judicial review became limited only by the discretion of the judges and the operation of stare decisis."[20]

Thence came the final irony. The only limit on the "discretion of the judges" was the same "judicial right reason" of the Higher Law tradition that the Jacksonian revolution's emphasis on popular will and the written constitution had ostensibly replaced! "Natural rights, expelled from the front door of the constitution, are readmitted through the doctrine of separation of powers."[21]

III.

Pre-Civil War attempts to enforce "natural rights" under the guise of enforcing written constitutional limitations were climaxed

[18] *The Independent,* LXIV (Jan.–June, 1908), 838.

[19] "Due Process of Law Before the Civil War," 24 *Harvard Law Review* (March, 1911), 366, 368–70.

[20] *The Basic Doctrine* . . . , p. 6. Emphasis deleted.

[21] *Ibid.*

in *Wynehamer* v. *New York* (1856). Here the New York Court of Appeals boldly invoked the State Constitution's Due Process Clause as a substantive limit on the state legislature. "I entertain no doubt," Judge Comstock wrote, "that, aside from the special limitations of the constitution, the legislature cannot exercise powers which are in their nature essentially judicial or executive. . . . There is no process of reasoning by which it can be demonstrated that [the prohibition law at issue] is void upon principles and theories outside the constitution, which will not also and by an easier deduction bring it in direct conflict with the constitution itself."[22] The Court promptly fulfilled its own prophecy by vetoing the statute before it as violating Due Process of Law.

One year later, Chief Justice Taney, in the *Dred Scott* case, applied the *Wynehamer* reasoning to the Due Process clause of the Fifth Amendment with the portentous effect of striking down the 1820 "Missouri Compromise" as unconstitutional. Then, with ratification of the Fourteenth Amendment in 1868, the way was clear for the Supreme Court to carry over this entire pre-Civil War tradition to the Due Process clause of that amendment.

This translation, beginning in the 1880's, was completed in the *Lochner* case of 1905, when the "test of reasonableness" made its twentieth century debut as a limit on all state legislation affecting "property."[23]

Widespread popular protest indicated that if judicial review were to survive, the Court must keep pace with the advancing needs of the time. In 1912 the voluble "Teddy" Roosevelt, who apparently wanted the judges to meet at Armageddon along with everyone else, proposed a modified popular recall of judicial decisions. "Truculent leaders of Labor," as ex-President Taft dubbed them, joined the crusade.[24] The most far-sighted protest came in 1913 from Brooks Adams: "Capital finds the judicial veto useful as a means of at least temporarily evading the law. And the Bar, taken as a whole, quite honestly believes that the universe will obey the judicial decree." "No delusion," Adams cautioned, "could be profounder and none, perhaps, more dangerous."[25]

[22] 13 N. Y. 378, 390–92 (1856).

[23] See Corwin's complete account in "The Supreme Court and the Fourteenth Amendment," 7 *Michigan Law Review* (June, 1909), 643.

[24] William Howard Taft, *Justice and Freedom for Industry* (Pamphlet), Address to the National Assn. of Manufacturers, May 26, 1915, p. 4.

[25] Brooks Adams, *Theory of Social Revolutions* (New York: Macmillan, 1913), p. 219.

Corwin's lesson was to similar effect. The significance of his early writings—indeed of all his writings—lay in his conviction that the continuing viability of the Court's supervisory function depended on whether it facilitated or impeded operation of implacable social and political forces. Yet the judges refused to moderate their decisions or to temper their views. Two major decisions—*Hammer* v. *Dagenhart* (1918) and *Bailey* v. *Drexel Furniture* (1922)—strikingly illustrated the Supreme Court's apparent determination to save democracy from itself. In the former, the Justices set aside the then-pioneering national Child Labor Law on the ground that the Interstate Commerce clause gave Congress no power to lay a direct prohibition on interstate transportation of goods manufactured by children.[26] A few years later, in *Bailey* v. *Drexel Furniture*,[27] the Court voided a special congressional tax levied on goods produced with the help of child labor—this time, on the ground that the Taxing Power could not be used as a means of *in*direct regulation.

The practical upshot was to invest the Court with censorial powers not only over the *types* of legislation open to Congress, but also over the *purposes* for which national legislation could be passed. Thus the earlier-won judicial pre-eminence under the Fourteenth Amendment suddenly bulked to new and more dangerous proportions. The Court now could apply the Fourteenth Amendment against the States, thereby preventing local regulation of the nation's expanding industry on the ground that it interfered with "liberty" or "property" without Due Process of Law. At the same time, the Justices were doctrinally equipped to overturn congressional regulations of industry by virtue of their supervisory—indeed, super-legislative—activity on the national level. *"And the total result of this kind of reasoning,"* Corwin emphasized, *"was the appearance of a no-man's land in which interests organized on a national scale at all times escape all regulation."*[28] In terms of the power to govern, the consequence was *reductio ad absurdum*. "The States, which, without challenge, originally possessed this power [to regulate commerce] have now lost it by virtue of having delegated it to Congress, but Congress never received it: 'Dual Federalism' thus becomes triple federalism—inserted between the

[26] 247 U. S. 251 (1918).
[27] 259 U. S. 20 (1922).
[28] *Commerce Power versus States Rights* (Princeton: Princeton, 1936), p. 153.

realm of the National Government and that of the States is one of no government—a governmental vacuum. . . ."[29]

IV.

Corwin promptly turned to an exploration of the resulting paradox. Interpenetrating and underlying the "constitutional law" which the Court was bound to apply, was "constitutional theory," meaning "the sum total of ideas of some historical standing as to what the constitution is or ought to be."[30] The most striking example of constitutional theory was Dual Federalism, the doctrine "of two mutually exclusive, reciprocally limiting fields of power [state power and national power], the governmental occupants of which confront each other as equals."[31] Palpably, it was a judicial creation at odds with the constitutional law of John Marshall; moreover, erection of the "powers reserved to the states" clause of the Tenth Amendment into a substantive limit on congressional power ran counter to the logic of the Supremacy Clause—the Constitution's "linch pin."[32] Yet Dual Federalism fitted into Corwin's definition of constitutional theory. It had, moreover, gained historical standing in the writings of the "Father of the Constitution" himself, James Madison.[33] Constitutional theory had developed out of controversy "as to what the constitution is or ought to be." Emerging from a debate as old as the document itself was a set of *mutually contradictory* ideas: National Supremacy versus Dual Federalism; strict versus loose construction; Marshall's idea of the "adaptive" Constitution versus Taney's fealty to the views of the Framers.[34]

Constitutional law, in the sense of a "rule for decision," must logically prescribe one outcome for a given dispute, and one

[29] "Congress's Power to Prohibit Commerce," 18 *Cornell Law Review* (1933), 477, 498.

[30] "Constitution v. Constitutional Theory," 19 *Amer. Pol. Sci. Review* (May, 1925), 290, 294.

[31] *Commerce Power versus States Rights,* pp. 135–36.

[32] *The Constitution and What It Means Today* (Princeton: Princeton, 1958), p. 178.

[33] See especially "Congress's Power to Prohibit Commerce," *loc. cit.,* p. 481 and *passim.*

[34] Corwin's further development of the "constitutional antinomy" theme appeared in *Twilight of the Supreme Court,* pp. 115–17, and *Constitutional Revolution, Ltd.* (Claremont, Calif.: 1941), pp. 11 ff., 108 ff.

only, or else it is not law. From this it followed that the hallmark of law must be the *mutual consistency* of each decision with those on the same point that went before it—a hallmark that obviously disappeared when constitutional law gave way to constitutional theory. In overthrowing Marshall's nationalist precedents in favor of Dual Federalism, the Court elevated to the status of law a legally and logically discredited element of constitutional theory. Nor was this all. For the Justices simultaneously invested themselves, as regards both national and state legislation, with freedom to choose from antinomous constitutional doctrines so as to insure arrival at politically predetermined goals. The consequence Corwin called "Judicial Review pure and simple."[35]

As a corrective to the judicial license which the Court had permitted to supplant judicial review, Corwin urged a return to the jurisprudence of Chief Justice Marshall:

> . . . [L]et the Court, abandoning the by-paths of contradictory doctrine and speculation regarding the relation of national and State power . . . , retrace its steps to the highway of the clear-cut, straightforward, logically clean, historically authentic principles which are associated with the name of Marshall.[36]

V.

Yet Marshall no less than his successors had enjoyed a rendezvous with the myth of judicial infallibility. "Courts are mere instruments of the law and can will nothing,"[37] Marshall had asserted. Unfortunately, as long as judicial legerdemain thus transfixed both the Court and its critics, there could be no attack on judicial review, either in principle or in application. "It is not possible to disprove such a theory of plenary inspiration, any more than it is possible to disprove that Moses was—as Coke asserted—God's amanuensis."[38]

Corwin was among the first to demonstrate that the myth of judicial aloofness screened the fact of judicial power. He instanced

[35] *The Constitution of the United States: Analysis and Interpretation* (1953), p. xxvii; *Twilight of the Supreme Court,* pp. 180–81.

[36] *Commerce Power versus States Rights,* p. 267.

[37] *Osborne* v. *Bank,* 9 Wheat. 738, 866 (1824).

[38] "Curbing the Court," 185 *Annals of the Amer. Academy of Pol. and Soc. Sciences* (May, 1936), 45, 50.

the following theory—so often professed by the judges themselves, and so frequently contradicted in the very terms of its application:

. . . no legislative act may be pronounced void by a court on the ground of its being in conflict with natural justice, the social compact, fundamental principles, etc.—in short, on any other than strictly constitutional grounds. This is because the supremacy of the Constitution—its claim to be considered higher law by the courts—is today traced to its quality as an ordinance of the people rather than—as originally—as due in part to its content. . . .[39]

On more than one occasion he dilated on the implications of the correct theory. "As a *document*," he wrote, "the Constitution came from its framers, and its elaboration was an event of the greatest historical interest, but as *law* the Constitution comes from and derives all its force from the people of the United States of this day and hour."[40] Hence the conclusion:

The proper point of view from which to approach the task of interpreting the constitution is that of regarding it as a living statute, palpitating with the purpose of the hour, reenacted with every waking breath of the American people, whose primitive right to determine their institutions is its sole claim to validity as law and as the matrix of laws under our system.[41]

As a final thrust, Corwin's argument concluded: "What gives the *coup de grâce* to the idea that . . . 'courts are mere instruments of the law and can will nothing,' is the simple fact that most so-called 'doubtful cases' could very evidently have been decided just the opposite way to which they were decided without the least infraction of the rules of logical discourse or the least attenuation of the principle of *stare decisis*." Underscoring the point, he concluded: "In short, *decision is choice; the very circumstances which produce doubtful cases guarantee the Court what Justice Holmes has termed 'the sovereign prerogative of choice' in deciding them.*"[42]

[39] "Judicial Review in Action," 74 *U. of Pennsylvania Law Review* (May, 1926), 639, 644.

[40] *The Constitution and What It Means Today,* 3rd ed. (Princeton: Princeton, 1924), p. 2.

[41] "Constitution v. Constitutional Theory," *loc. cit.*, p. 303.

[42] *Twilight of the Supreme Court,* pp. 114–15.

At the 1937 Senate Judiciary Committee Hearings on Roosevelt's Court-Packing Bill, Corwin pointed to the judicial record. Our system had become, he told the Senators, "not a government of laws, but a government of chance."[43] The very process by which the judges attained supremacy proved that they were not acting on behalf of any true constitutional legality.

The implications for judicial supremacy were clear. Once it was granted that the changing voice of the people was supreme, the judges were unjustified in enforcing as law anything but this popular will. To do so would be to set up an oracular legality, archaic at best and spurious at worst, as an obstacle to, rather than as the instrument of, the Constitution's supremacy.

VI.

The basic premise in the argument against the then dominant opinion that Courts are "the only agency that must be assumed to have capacity to govern"[44] turned on the supremacy of popular will. On this premise Corwin made his final contribution to the theory of judicial review: "By the political or departmental conception of it judicial review, considered as an instrument of constitutional interpretation, is not the outcome of a power peculiar to the courts. . . ." Rather,

> Finality of interpretation is . . . the outcome—when indeed it exists—not of judicial application of the Constitution to the decision of cases, but of a continued harmony of views among the three departments. It rests, in other words, in the last analysis on the voting power of public opinion.[45]

This shift in Corwin's jurisprudence required rethinking as to the role of the Court in post-New Deal America. If the judges were to serve a useful purpose, they must become participants *in*

[43] Part II, Hearings before the Committee on the Judiciary, U. S. Senate, 75th Congress, 1st Session on S. 1392, p. 174.

[44] Justice Stone dissenting in *United States* v. *Butler,* 297 U. S. 1 (1936), 87.

[45] *Court Over Constitution,* pp. 6–7. Cf. Review: *The Constitution Reconsidered,* Conyers Read, ed. 16 *New York University Law Quarterly Review* (May, 1939), 674, 676.

the political process. In 1940, he predicted: The Court "will no longer play States Rights against national power and vice versa as it often did throughout the half-century between 1887 and 1937. It will no longer be the make-weight . . . of economic power against political power. It will not, in brief, play the role that it has done at times in the past of shaping governmental policy in the broad sense of the phrase." Having abandoned guardianship of property, the Court would be free to play a new role in support of the political processes: "it will be free as it has not been in many years to support the humane values of free thought, free utterance, and fair play."[46]

At first sight, advocacy of this new brand of judicial guardianship seemed to identify Corwin as a libertarian paladin, championing judicial activism in free speech and procedural rights cases. But Corwin himself repudiated this interpretation in his commentary on the Pennsylvania *Flag Salute* case of 1940.[47] The Court's spokesman, Justice Felix Frankfurter, argued that judicial power to intervene on behalf of children's religious convictions must be severely restricted, if not actually repudiated, because judicial review is itself "a limitation on popular government."[48] If performance of the Court's function is to be "great and stately,"[49] it must be confined so as to make room for popular laws, whether in the civil liberties area or elsewhere.

The scope of judicial review should be narrowed, Corwin agreed, but *not* willy-nilly. Nor did the new role embrace special judicial protection for any particular constitutional rights. In contrast with "Bill-of-Rights absolutists," he pointed to a distinctive responsibility with respect to *all* types of legislation. Judicial review "still has its uses, and important ones."

Especially does it present an admirable forum in which to rationalize and clarify, to authenticate in terms of broad principle, the determination of political authority, and to articulate them with the more durable elements of tradition.

[46] "Statesmanship on the Supreme Court," 9 *American Scholar* (Spring, 1940), 159, 163.

[47] *Minersville* v. *Gobitis,* 310 U. S. 586 (1940).

[48] *Ibid.,* p. 600.

[49] The quoted words are from James Bradley Thayer's classic article, "The Origin and Scope of the American Doctrine of Constitutional Law," 7 *Harvard Law Review* (1893), 129, 152.

Judicial review was not, as Frankfurter contended, necessarily a "limitation on popular government," but only "on popular government *as sometimes conceived*."[50] The Court need not respond to the ill-considered will of the populace—to that superficial layer of public opinion which is liable to hysteria or hastiness, and which perpetually invites "endeavors by politicians to force the hands of the people."[51] Writing during the immediate aftermath of the Court-Packing struggle, Corwin observed: judicial review

> undoubtedly means, usually at least, some slowing down of the process of government, for it is intended to support a rather complex set of values, some of which may at times oppose minority rights against majority decisions. Also, it is a device—like the common law itself—for conserving the old in the context of the new, and for *inserting in the democratic process* one further, final step in the discussion, clarification, rationalization of public opinion.[52]

Abdication of its self-acquired guardianship of economic privilege left the Court free "to give voice to the conscience of the country,"[53] and thereby to enter—indeed, to perfect—the American political dialogue.

The over-all picture is that of a man deeply committed to democracy; to national democracy; to reasoned democracy. More than any other factor, this commitment explains the implacability of Corwin's early scholarship on judicial supremacy under the pretended enforcement of Due Process, and of his later attack on judicial assumption of responsibilities that properly and solely belonged to the national electorate. Corwin's entire scholarly career developed into a search for resolution of the "basic inconsistency between popular government and judicial supremacy"—a search which finally led to the restoration of judicial review to its historic conception as complement rather than contradiction of political democracy.

[50] See *Constitutional Revolution, Ltd.*, pp. 110–12.

[51] "The Power of the Supreme Court over Legislation," 57 *Chicago Legal News* (Feb. 5, 1925), 228, 231.

[52] *Court Over Constitution*, pp. 208–09.

[53] *Constitutional Revolution, Ltd.*, p. 111.

★ I ★

The Progress of Constitutional Theory Between the Declaration of Independence and the Meeting of the Philadelphia Convention*

. . . the problem of providing adequate safeguards for private rights and adequate powers for a national government were one and the same problem . . .

For Americans hardly less than for Frenchmen the period of the Constitution was "an age of rationalism," whereby is intended not a blind ignoring of the lessons of experience, but confidence in the ability of reason, working in the light of experience, to divert the unreflective course of events into beneficial channels; and in no respect was man more the master of his destiny than in that of statecraft. Surely if any man of the time may be regarded as representative of the sober, unimaginative intelligence of America, it was Washington, in whose "Circular Letter addressed to the Governors," of June 8, 1783, occurs the following passage:

The foundation of our empire was not laid in the gloomy age of ignorance and superstition; but at an epocha when the rights of mankind were better understood and more clearly defined, than at

* *The American Historical Review* (April, 1925), 511.

any other period. The researches of the human mind after *social happiness* have been carried to a great extent; the treasures of knowledge acquired by the labors of philosophers, sages, and legislators, through a long succession of years, are laid open for our use, and their collected wisdom may be happily applied in the establishment of our forms of government. . . . At this auspicious period, the United States came into existence as a nation; and, if their citizens should not be completely free and happy, the fault will be entirely their own.[1]

The same sense of command over the resources of political wisdom appears again and again in the debates of the Convention, in the pages of the *Federalist,* and in writings of contemporaries.[2]

Nor does the economic interpretation of history . . . detract greatly from the significance of such facts. No one denies that the concern felt by the Fathers for the rights of property and contract contributed immensely to impart to American constitutional law its strong bias in favor of these rights from the outset, but the concession only serves to throw certain still unanswered questions into a higher relief. For, what warrant had these men for translating any of their interests as *rights;* and why did they adopt the precise means which they did to advance their interests or secure their rights—in other words, why did they choose the precise system set up by the Constitution to do the work which they put upon it? . . .

I.

A colloquy which occurred between Madison and Sherman of Connecticut in the early days of the Philadelphia Convention as to its purposes affords an excellent preface to the more particular intention of this paper. "The objects of the Union," Sherman had declared, "were few," defense, domestic good order, treaties, the

[1] *Writings,* ed. Ford, X. 254, 256.

[2] See Farrand, *Records of the Federal Convention,* I. 83–84, 134–135, 137, 139, 151–152, 161, 254, 285 ff., 304 ff., 317, 356, 398 ff., 426 ff., 437–438, 444–449, 451, etc. The lessons of the past, its successes and failures, are cited for the most part. The term "political science" is used by Mercer, *ibid.,* II. 284, while "the science of politics" is Hamilton's expression in *Federalist,* no. 9 (ed. Lodge). This, he says, "has undergone great improvement." The entire passage is worth perusal in this connection. See also Madison in *Federalist,* nos. 14 and 47, and Adams's preface to his *Defence* (*Works,* IV. 283–298).

regulation of foreign commerce, revenue. Though a conspicuous omission from this enumeration is of any mention of commerce among the states and its regulation, it was not this omission which drew Madison's fire:

> He differed from the member from Connecticut in thinking the objects mentioned to be all the principal ones that required a National Government. Those were certainly important and necessary objects; but he combined with them the necessity, of providing more effectually for the security of private rights, and the steady dispensation of Justice. Interferences with these were evils which had more perhaps than any thing else, produced this convention. Was it to be supposed that republican liberty could long exist under the abuses of it practiced in some of the States?[3]

These views were heartily chorused by other members: the faulty organization of government within the states, threatening as it did, not alone the Union, but republican government itself, furnished the Convention with a problem of transcendent, even world-wide importance.[4]

In short, the task before the Convention arose by no means exclusively from the inadequacies of the Articles of Confederation for "the exigencies of the Union"; of at least equal urgency were the questions which were thrust upon its attention by the shortcomings of the state governments for their purposes. Indeed, from the point of view of this particular study the latter phase of the Convention's task is, if anything, the more significant one, both because it brings us into contact at the outset with the most persistent problem of American constitutional law—that which has arisen from the existence of a multiplicity of local legislatures with indefinite powers; and also because it was to the solution of this phase of its problem that the Convention brought its "political science" most immediately to bear.

The singular juxtaposition in the Revolutionary state constitutions of legislative supremacy and the doctrine of natural rights need not detain us here.[5] In the words of a contemporary critic of

[3] Farrand, I. 133–134.

[4] *Ibid.*, I. 48, 255, 424, 525, 533, II. 285.

[5] See W. C. Webster, "State Constitutions of the American Revolution," in *Annals of the American Academy of Political and Social Science*. May, 1897.

those constitutions: Although their authors "understood perfectly the principles of liberty," yet most of them "were ignorant of the forms and combinations of power in republics."[6] Madison's protest, on the other hand, against "interferences with the steady dispensation of justice" had reference to something more subtle—to what, in fact, was far less a structural than a functional defect in these early instruments of government. That the majority of the Revolutionary constitutions recorded recognition of the principle of the separation of powers is, of course, well known.[7] What is not so generally understood is that the recognition was verbal merely, for the reason that the material terms in which it was couched still remained undefined; and that this was true in particular of "legislative power" in relation to "judicial power."

Turn . . . to the operation of the principle of the separation of powers in a typical instance in 1787. The New Hampshire constitution of 1784 contained the declaration that "in the government of this State, the three essential powers thereof, to wit, the legislative, executive and judicial, ought to be kept as separate and independent of each other as the nature of a free government will admit or as is consistent with the chain of connection that binds the whole fabric of the constitution in one indissoluble bond of union or amity." Notwithstanding which the laws of New Hampshire for the years 1784–1792 are replete with entries showing that throughout this period the state legislature freely vacated judicial proceedings, suspended judicial actions, annulled or modified judgments, cancelled executions, reopened controversies, authorized appeals, granted exemptions from the standing law, expounded the law for pending cases, and even determined the merits of disputes.[8] Nor do such practices seem to have been more aggravated in New

[6] Niles, *Principles and Acts of the Revolution,* p. 234; from an address by Dr. Benjamin Rush delivered at Philadelphia on July 4, 1787, before members of the Convention and others. The address testifies throughout to the importance of the governmental situation in the states as a problem before the Convention.

[7] See *Federalist,* no. 47.

[8] See *Laws of New Hampshire,* ed. Batchellor, V. *passim.* Some of the less usual items are those on pp. 21, 66, 89, 90–91, 110–111, 125–126, 130–131, 167–168, 243, 320–321, 334–335, 363, 395–396, 400–401, 404–406, 411–412, 417–418, 455–456, 485, 499, 522. The volume is crowded with acts "restoring" a defeated or defaulting party "to his law," "any usage, custom, or law to the contrary notwithstanding."

Hampshire than in several other states. Certainly they were widespread, and they were evidently possible in any of the states under the views then obtaining of "legislative power."[9]

Neither is the explanation of such views far to seek. Coke's fusion of what we should to-day distinguish as "legislative" and "judicial" powers in the case of the "High Court of Parliament" represented the teaching of the highest of all legal authorities before Blackstone appeared on the scene.[10] What is equally important, the Cokian doctrine corresponded exactly to the contemporary necessities of many of the colonies in the earlier days of their existence.[11] Thus, owing to the dearth not only of courts and lawyers, but even of a recognized code of law, bodies like the Massachusetts General Court had thrust upon them at first a far greater bulk of judicial and administrative work, in to-day's sense of these terms, than of lawmaking proper, while conversely such judges as existed in these early days performed administrative as well as judicial functions, very much as had been the case with the earliest itinerant judges in England. By the middle of the eighteenth century, it is true, a distinct improvement had taken place in these regards. Regularly organized systems of courts now existed in all the colonies. A bar trained in the common law was rapidly arising. Royal governors sometimes disallowed enactments interfering with the usual course of justice in the ordinary courts, on grounds anticipatory of modern doctrine.[12]

Then, however, came the outbreak of the Revolution, and with it a reversion to more primitive practices and ideas, traceable in the first instance to the collapse of the royal judicial establishment, but later to the desire to take a short course with enemies of the new régime, against whom, first and last, every state in the Union appears to have enacted bills of pains and penalties of greater or less severity.[13] Furthermore, it should be observed that, owing to a popular prejudice, certain of the states—notably New York and

[9] See the references I have collected in my *Doctrine of Judicial Review*, pp. 69–71; also Baldwin, *The American Judiciary,* ch. II.

[10] McIlwain, *The High Court of Parliament and its Supremacy,* ch. III.

[11] Baldwin, *op. cit.,* ch. I.

[12] See, *e.g., Messages from the Governors* (of New York), ed. Lincoln, I. 55.

[13] A good summary of legislative persecution of the Loyalists appears in Van Tyne, *American Revolution,* pp. 255 ff.

Massachusetts—at first withheld equity powers from their courts altogether, while several others granted them but sparingly.[14] The result was fairly to compel the legislature to intervene in many instances with "special legislation," disallowing fraudulent transactions, curing defective titles, authorizing urgent sales of property, and the like. Between legislation of this species and outright interferences with the remedial law itself there was often little to distinguish.

That, therefore, the vague doctrine of the separation of powers should at first have been interpreted and applied in the light of this history is not astonishing. This, as we have seen, left legislative power without definition on its side toward judicial power, except as the power of the supreme organ of the state, which meant, however, the withholding from judicial power of that which, to the modern way of thinking, is its highest attribute—to wit, power of deciding with finality. . . .

II.

[The] structural and functional shortcomings of the early state constitutions played directly into the hands of both popular and doctrinal tendencies which distinctly menaced what Madison called "the security of private rights." Throughout the Revolution the Blackstonian doctrine of "legislative omnipotence" was in the ascendant. Marshall read Blackstone and so did Iredell—to what effect later developments were to make clear.[15] And even more radical doctrine was abroad. One Benjamin Hichborn's assertion, in a speech delivered in Boston in 1777, that civil liberty was "not a government by laws," but "a power existing in the people at large" "to alter or annihilate both the mode and essence of any former government" "for any cause or for no cause at all, but their own sovereign pleasure"[16] voiced an extension to the right of revolution hitherto unheard outside the pages of Rousseau; and even so good a republican as John Adams was disturbed at manifestations

[14] *Two Centuries' Growth of American Law,* pp. 129–133.

[15] Iredell's perusal of Blackstone produced an entire change in his theory of the basis of judicial review. Compare McRee, *Life and Correspondence of James Iredell,* II. 172–173; and *Calder* v. *Bull,* 3 Dallas 386, 398.

[16] Niles, *Principles and Acts of the Revolution,* p. 47.

Two years later came the early volumes of John Adams's *Defence of the Constitutions,* in answer to M. Turgot's criticism that the American constitutions represented "an unreasonable imitation of the usages of England." In reality the work was much less a "defence" than an exhortation to constitutional reform in other states along the lines which Massachusetts had already taken under Adams's own guidance. A new and significant note, however, appears in this work. In his earlier writings Adams had assumed with Montesquieu that the great source of danger to liberty lay in the selfishness and ambition of the governors themselves. But with the lesson of the paper-money agitation before him, he now gives warning of the danger to which republics, when they have become populous and overcrowded and the inevitable doom of poverty has appeared in their midst, are peculiarly exposed from the rise of parties. "Misarrangements now made," he writes, "will have great, extensive, and distant consequences; and we are now employed, how little soever we may think of it, in making establishments which will affect the happiness of a hundred millions of inhabitants at a time, in a period not every distant."[27]

Copies of the *Defence* reached the United States early in 1787, and were circulated among the members of the Philadelphia Convention, reviving and freshening belief in "political science" and particularly in the teachings of Montesquieu. Yet in one respect at least the idea of reform for which Adams's work stood and that which the Convention represented were poles apart. For while the former still illustrated the opinion that constitutional reform was a purely local problem, the Convention represented the triumph of the idea that reform to be effective must be national in scope and must embrace the entire American constitutional system in a single coherent programme. . . .

III.

. . . The executive veto, which was the practical nub of all Adams' preachments, was brought about, to be sure, through specific provision being made for it in the written constitution, and to so good purpose that it is to be found to-day in nearly every constitution in the country.[28] The other suggested remedy of critics

[27] *Works,* IV. 273 ff. The quotation is from p. 587.

[28] F. J. Stimson, *Federal and State Constitutions,* sect. 304.

of "the legislative vortex," on the contrary, was introduced solely by the processes of interpretation and without the slightest textual alteration being made in the constitutions involved. This was judicial review. . . .

As a practice judicial review made its initial appearance in independent America in 1780, in the case of *Holmes* v. *Walton*,[29] in which the supreme court of New Jersey refused to carry out an act of the legislature providing for the trial of a designated class of offenders by a jury of six, whereas, the court held, the state constitution contemplated the common-law jury of twelve. Although the opinion of the court apparently was never published, the force of the example may have been considerable. From this time on the notion crops up sporadically in other jurisdictions, at intervals of about two years, in a series of dicta and rulings which—thanks in no small part to popular misapprehension as to their precise bearing—brought the idea before the Philadelphia Convention:[30] And meantime the main premises of the *doctrine* of judicial review—the principles whereby it came to be annexed to the written constitution—had been worked out.

First and last, many and various arguments have been offered to prove that judicial review is implied in the very nature of a written constitution, some of them manifestly insufficient for the purpose; though that is not to say that they may not have assisted in securing general acceptance of the institution. "Superstitions believed are, in their effect, truths"; and it has accordingly happened more than once that the actual influence of an idea has been out of all proportion to its logical or scientific merits. These more or less spurious proofs of judicial review, however, we here pass by without further consideration, in order to come at once to what, on both historical and logical grounds, may be termed the true doctrine of judicial review. This embraces three propositions: First, that the Constitution is supreme; second, that it is law in the sense of a rule enforceable by courts; and third, that judicial interpretations of the standing law are final, at least for the cases in the decision of which they are pronounced. Let us consider the two latter propositions somewhat further.

[29] Austin Scott, "*Holmes* v. *Walton*, the New Jersey Precedent," in *The American Historical Review*, IV. 456 ff.

[30] See generally my *Doctrine of Judicial Review*, pp. 71–75, and references there given.

The claim of the Constitution to be considered *law* may rest on either one of two grounds, depending on whether "law" be regarded as an unfolding of the divine order of things or as an expression of human will—as an act of knowledge (or revelation) or an act of power.[31] Considered from the former point of view—which is that of Locke and other exponents of the law of nature—the claim of the Constitution to be obeyed is due simply to its content, to the principles which it incorporates because of their intrinsic sanctity; considered from the latter point of view—that of Hobbes and the "positive school of jurisprudence"—its claim to obedience is due to its source in a sovereign will—that of the people. Actually both views have been taken at different times, but that judicial review originally owed more to the former than to the latter conception seems fairly clear.

Of all the so-called "precedents" for judicial review antecedent to the Convention of 1787, the one which called forth the most elaborate argument on theoretical grounds and which produced the most evident impression on the membership of the Convention, was the Rhode Island case of *Trevett* v. *Weeden*,[32] which was decided early in 1786. The feature of the case which is of immediate pertinence is the argument which it evoked against the act on the part of the attorney for defendant, James Varnum. In developing the theory of a law superior to legislative enactments, Varnum appealed indifferently to the Rhode Island charter, "general principles," "invariable custom," "Magna Carta," "fundamental law," "the law of nature," "the law of God"; asserting with reference to the last, that "all men, judges included," were bound by it "in preference to any human laws." In short, Varnum, going directly back to the Cokian tradition, built his argument for judicial review on the loose connotation of the word "law" still obtaining in the eighteenth century, especially among American readers of Coke and Locke—to say nothing of the host of writers on the Law of Nations. Nor is the conduciveness of such an argument to judicial review open to conjecture. In the first place, it kept alive, even after the fires of revolution had cooled, the notion that the claim of law to obedience

[31] Holland, *Elements of Jurisprudence,* thirteenth ed., pp. 19–21, 32–34, 41–45.

[32] See note 30 above; also Varnum's contemporary pamphlet on the case. The case was the first and last case of judicial review of the sort under the old charter.

consists in its intrinsic excellence rather than its origin. Again, it made rational the notion of a hierarchy of laws in which the will of merely human legislators might on occasion be required to assume a subordinate place. Lastly, by the same token, it made rational the notion of judges pitting knowledge against sheer legislative self-assertion.

Contrariwise, the Blackstonian concept of legislative sovereignty was calculated to frustrate judicial review not only by attributing to the legislature an uncontrollable authority, but also by pressing forward the so-called "positive" conception of law and the differentiation of legal from moral obligation which this impels. Fortunately, in the notion of popular sovereignty the means of checkmating the notion of legislative sovereignty was available. For, once it became possible to attribute to the people at large a lawmaking, rather than a merely constituent, capacity, the Constitution exchanged its primary character as a statement of sacrosanct principles for that of the expressed will of the highest lawmaking power on earth.[33]

But to produce judicial review, the notion of the Constitution as law must be accompanied by the principle of the finality of judicial constructions of the law, which obviously rests upon a definition of the respective rôles of "legislative" and "judicial" power in relation to the standing law. In other words, judicial review raised from the other side of the line the same problem as did "legislative interferences with the dispensation of justice"; and, in fact, it can be shown that the solution of the two problems proceeded in many jurisdictions *pari passu*.[34] The whole subject is one which demands rather ample consideration.

Although the functional differentiation of the three powers of government, first hinted in Aristotle's *Politics*,[35] necessarily preceded their organic distribution to some extent, it is not essential for

[33] Compare in this connection Luther Martin's "Genuine Information," in Farrand's *Records*, III. 230, with Hamilton's argument for judicial review in *Federalist*, no. 78, and Marshall's opinion in *Marbury* v. *Madison*, 1 Cranch 129. The former regards political authority as a *cessio* from the people to the government which "never devolves back to them" except in events amounting to a dissolution of government. The latter regard it as a revocable *translatio* to agents by a principal who is by no means bound to act through agents.

[34] See my "Basic Doctrine of American Constitutional Law," in *Michigan Law Review*, XII. 256, 260.

[35] Bk. IV., ch. 14.

our purposes to trace either process further back than to Coke's repeated insistence in his *Institutes* that "the King hath wholly left matters of Judicature according to his laws to his Judges."[36] In these words, it is not too much to say, the royal prerogative, which had long lain fallow in this respect, was thrust forever from the province of the courts. One of these same courts, on the other hand, was "the High Court of Parliament;" and Coke nowhere suggests that "the power of judicature" which he attributes to Parliament is to be distinguished from the power which Parliament ordinarily exercised in "proceeding by bill."[37] Far different is the case of Locke. His declaration that "the legislative or supreme authority cannot assume to itself a power to rule by extemporary arbitrary decrees, but is bound to dispense justice and decide the rights of the subject by promulgated standing laws and known authorized judges" represents progress towards a "material" as against a merely "formal" definition of legislative power, both in the total exclusion which it effects of the legislative body from the business of judging and also in the ideal which it lays down of statute law.[38] Noteworthy, too, from the same point of view is Montesquieu's characterization of the judges as "but the mouthpieces of the law," accompanied, as it is, by the assertion that the mergence of "the judiciary power" with "the legislative" would render the judge "a legislator" vested with arbitrary power over the life and liberty of the subject.[39]

As usual, Blackstone's contribution is somewhat more difficult to assess. He adopts without qualification the views just quoted from Locke and Montesquieu, and he urges that "all laws should be made to commence *in futuro*." Yet the very illustration he furnishes of his definition of "municipal law" as "a rule . . . permanent, uniform, and universal" violates this precept radically, since it shows that in his estimation the *ex post facto* operation of a rule, however undesirable in itself, does not affect its title to be regarded as "law." Nor, in fact, does it occur to him, in assigning to Parliament power to "expound" the law, to distinguish those instances in which the exercise of this power would mark an intrusion upon judicial freedom of decision, while his sweeping attribution to Parliament of jurisdiction over "all mischiefs and grievances, operations and

[36] *Institutes*, IV. 70, 71; 12 *Reports* 63.
[37] *Institutes*, IV. 23, 26, 36.
[38] *Second Treatise on Civil Government*, ch. XI., sect. 136.
[39] *Spirit of Laws* (trans. Pritchard), bk. XI., ch. 6.

remedies that transcend the ordinary course of the laws"—a matter evidently to be judged of by Parliament itself—lands us again in the Cokian bog from which we set out.[40]

The differentiation of legislative and judicial power, upon which judicial review pivots, appears to have been immediately due, not to any definition of legislative *power,* but to a definition of judicial *duty* in relation to the standing law and especially to the law of decided cases. In the opening sentence of Bacon's Essay on Judicature one reads: "Judges ought to remember that their office is '*jus dicere*' and not '*jus dare*'; to interpret law, and not to make or give law"—words which have been reiterated many times as embodying the doctrine of *stare decisis.*[41] Coke employs different language, but his thought is not essentially different: "judges discern by law what is just;" the law is "the golden metwand whereby all men's causes are justly and evenly measured." He also notes the artificiality of the law's "reason and judgment," and pays full tribute to the burden of study and experience "before that a man can attain to the cognizance of it."[42] Judicial duty is thus matched with judicial aptitude—the judges are the experts of the law—or, in the words of Blackstone, its "living oracles," sworn to determine, not according to their own private judgment, "but according to the known laws and customs of the land; not delegated to pronounce a new law, but to maintain and expound the old one."[43]

In brief, it is the duty of judges to conserve the law, not to change it, a task for which their learning pre-eminently fits them. Yet a mystery remains to clear up; for how came this *duty* of subordination to the law to be transmuted into a claim of exclusive *power* in relation to it—the power of interpreting it with final force and effect? By the doctrine of the separation of powers, the outstanding prerogatives of each department are no doubt its peculiar possession; but still that does not explain why in the final apportionment of territory between the legislative and judicial departments in the United States, the function of law-interpretation fell to the latter. The fact is that we here confront *the* act of creation—or perhaps it would be better to say, act of prestidigitation—attending the elabo-

[40] *Commentaries,* I. 44, 46, 58, 160–161, 267, 269.

[41] Broom, *Maxims* (fifth American ed.), p. 105 and citations; pp. 140–141 of the original edition.

[42] See note 36, *supra.*

[43] *Commentaries,* I. 69–71.

ration of the doctrine of judicial review; and what is more, we know the authors of it—or some of them.

In his argument in the case of *Trevett* v. *Weeden,* Varnum put the question: "Have the judges a power to repeal, to amend, to alter, or to make new laws?" and then proceeded to answer it thus: "God forbid! In that case they would be legislators. . . . But the judiciary have the sole power of judging of laws . . . and can not admit any act of the legislatures as law against the Constitution." And to the same effect is the defense which James Iredell penned of the North Carolina supreme court's decision in *Bayard* v. *Singleton,*[44] while Davie, his associate in the case, was in attendance upon the Convention at Philadelphia.

> The duty of [the judicial] department I conceive in all cases is to decide according to the laws of the State. It will not be denied, I suppose, that the constitution is a law of the State, as well as an act of Assembly, with this difference only, that it is the *fundamental* law, and unalterable by the legislature, which derives all its power from it. . . . The judges, therefore, must take care at their peril, that every act of Assembly they presume to enforce is warranted by the constitution, since if it is not, they act without lawful authority.

Nor is this a power which may be exercised by ministerial officers, "for if the power of judging rests with the courts their decision is final."[45]

Here are all the premises of the doctrine of judicial review either explicitly stated or clearly implied: the superiority of the Constitution to statute law—the case of the common law had still to be dealt with; its quality as law knowable by judges in their official capacity and applicable by them to cases; the exclusion of "legislative power" from the ancient field of parliamentary power in law-interpretation, except in circumstances in which the law is subject to legislative amendment. The classical version of the doctrine of judicial review in *Federalist,* number 78, improves upon the statement of these premises but adds nothing essential to them.

IV.

We turn now to that phase of the problem which confronted the Philadelphia Convention in consequence of the insufficiencies of the

[44] 1 Martin 42.

[45] McRee, *Life and Correspondence of Iredell,* II. 145–149.

government established by the Articles of Confederation. And at the outset let it be remarked that with all their defects, and serious as these were, the Articles none the less performed two services of great moment: they kept the idea of union vital during the period when the feeling of national unity was at its lowest ebb; and they accorded formal recognition that the great powers of war and foreign relations were intrinsically national in character. Those two most dramatic and interesting functions belonged to the general government from the first and became the central magnet to which other powers necessarily gravitated.

The essential defect of the Articles . . . as has been so often pointed out,[46] consisted in the fact that the government established by them operated not upon the individual citizens of the United States but upon the states in their corporate capacity—that, in brief, it was not a government at all, but rather the central agency of an alliance. As a consequence, on the one hand, even the powers theoretically belonging to the Congress of the Confederation were practically unenforceable; while, on the other hand, the theoretical scope of its authority was unduly narrow. Inasmuch as taxes are collectible from individuals, Congress could not levy them; inasmuch as commerce is an affair of individuals, Congress could not regulate it; and its treaties had not at first the force of laws, since to have given them that operation would again have been to impinge upon individuals directly and not through the mediation of the state legislatures. Furthermore, the powers withheld from Congress remained with the states—which is to say, *with their legislatures.* The evil thence resulting was thus a double one. Not only was a common policy impracticable in fields where it was most evidently necessary, but also the local legislatures had it in their power to embroil both the country as a whole with foreign nations and its constituent parts with each other. So the weakness of the Confederation played directly into the hands of the chief defect of government within the states themselves—an excessive concentration of power in the hands of the legislative department.

The endeavors which were made to render the Articles of Confederation a workable instrument of government proceeded, naturally, along the two lines of amendment and construction. In theory the Articles were amendable; but owing to the requirement that

[46] See especially *Federalist,* no. 15.

amendments had to be ratified by all the states, in practice they were not so. Recourse, therefore, had early to be had to the other method, and eventually with fruitful results. . . .

The question . . . upon which the permanently fruitful efforts of constitutional construction were at this time brought to bear was that of treaty enforcement; and while the story is not a new one its full significance seems not to have been altogether appreciated. The starting-point is furnished by the complaints which the British government began lodging with Congress very shortly after the making of the peace treaty that the state legislatures were putting impediments in the way of British creditors and were renewing confiscations of Loyalist property contrary to Articles IV. and VI., respectively, of the treaty.[47]

Now it should be observed that the immediate beneficiaries of these articles were certain classes of *private persons,* whose claims, moreover, were such as would ordinarily have to be asserted against other individuals *in court.* If, therefore, it could only be assured that the state courts would accord such claims proper recognition and enforcement, the obligation of the United States as a government, under the treaty, would be performed and the complaints of the other party to the treaty must thereupon cease. But how could this be assured? The answer was suggested by the current vague connotation of the word "law" and the current endeavor to find in "judicial power" a check upon legislative power in the states.

Nor can there be any doubt as to who first formulated this solution. It was Alexander Hamilton in his argument before a municipal court in New York City in the case of *Rutgers* v. *Waddington* in 1784, practically contemporaneously with the British protests above referred to.[48] The case involved a recent enactment of the state legislature creating a right of action for trespass against Tory occupants of premises in favor of owners who had fled the city during the British possession. In his capacity as Waddington's attorney, Hamilton assailed the act as contrary to principles of the law of nations, to the treaty of peace, which he asserted implied an amnesty,

[47] MacDonald, *Documentary Source Book,* pp. 207–208.

[48] See H. B. Dawson's pamphlet on the case; also Coxe's and Haines's well-known volumes. Hamilton had the year previous been a member of a committee of Congress which had the subject of violations of the treaty of peace under consideration. For the report of this committee, see *Journals of the American Congress* (Washington, 1823), IV. 224–225.

and the Articles of Confederation, and as, therefore, void. Only the manuscript notes of his argument are extant, but these sufficiently indicate its bearing for our purpose:

Congress have made a treaty. A breach of that would be a breach of their constitutional authority. . . . as well a County may alter the laws of the State as the State those of the Confederation. . . . While Confed. exists its cons. Autho. paramount. But how are Judges to decide & Ans. Cons. giving Jud. Power only in prize causes; in all others Judges of each State must of necessity be judges of United States. And the law of each State must adopt the laws of Congress. Though in relation to its own Citizens local laws might govern, yet in relation to foreigners those of United States must prevail. It must be conceded Leg. of one State cannot repeal law of United States. All must be construed to Stand together.[49]

There is a striking parallel between the cases of *Rutgers* v. *Waddington* and *Trevett* v. *Weeden,* and especially between the subsequent fate of Hamilton's argument in the one and Varnum's in the other. In each case the court concerned decided adversely to the party relying upon the statute before it, but did so on grounds which avoided its committing itself on the issue of judicial review. In each case, nevertheless, the exponents of Blackstonian absolutism raised loud protests in behalf of the threatened legislative authority, with the result of spreading the impression that the judges had met the issue squarely. Yet since what the judges had said hardly bore out this impression, interested attention was naturally directed in turn to the franker and more extensive claims of counsel; and while Varnum was spreading his argument broadcast as a pamphlet, Hamilton was reiterating his views in his "Letters from Phocion."[50]

Of the various repercussions from Hamilton's argument in *Rutgers* v. *Waddington* the most important is the report which John Jay—a fellow New Yorker—rendered to Congress as secretary for foreign affairs, in October, 1786, on the subject of state violations of treaties. The salient passage of this document reads as follows:

Your secretary considers the thirteen independent sovereign states as having, by express delegation of power, formed and vested in

[49] Allan McLane Hamilton, *Intimate Life of Alexander Hamilton,* pp. 457, 460–461. "Our sovereignty began by a Federal act," he asserts (p. 459).

[50] See *Works,* Constitutional ed., IV. 238–240.

Congress a perfect though limited sovereignty for the general and national purposes specified in the confederation. In this sovereignty they cannot severally participate (except by their delegates) or have concurrent jurisdiction. . . . When therefore a treaty is constitutionally made, ratified and published by Congress, it immediately becomes binding on the whole nation, and superadded to the laws of the land, without the intervention, consent or fiat of state legislatures.

It was therefore, Jay argued, the duty of the state judiciaries in cases between private individuals "respecting the meaning of a treaty," to give it full enforcement in harmony with "the rules and maxims established by the laws of nations for the interpretation of treaties." He accordingly recommended that Congress formally deny the right of the state legislatures to enact laws construing "a national treaty" or impeding its operation "in any manner," that it avow its opinion that all acts on the statute books repugnant to the treaty of peace should be at once repealed, and that it urge the repeal to be in general terms which would leave it with the local judiciaries to decide all cases arising under the treaty according to the intent thereof "anything in the said acts . . . to the contrary notwithstanding."[51]

The following March Congress adopted the resolutions which Jay had proposed, without a dissenting vote, and in April, within a month of the date set for the assembling of the Philadelphia Convention, transmitted them to the state legislatures, by the majority of which they were promptly complied with[52] . . .

From all this to Article VI. of the Constitution is manifestly only a step, though an important one. The supremacy which Jay's plan assured the national treaties is in Article VI. but part and parcel of national supremacy in all its phases; but this broader supremacy is still guaranteed by being brought to bear upon individuals, in contrast to states, through the intervention in the first instance often of the state courts. Thus the solution provided of the question of treaty enforcement, whereby the cause of national supremacy was linked with that of judicial review, clearly foreshadowed the ultimate character of the national government as a government acting upon individuals in the main rather than upon the states. Logically, national

[51] *Secret Journals of Congress* (Boston, 1821), IV. 185–287.

[52] Jefferson's letter of May 29, 1792, to the British minister Hammond, gives all the facts. *Writings,* Memorial ed., XVI. 183–277.

power operative through courts is a deduction from a government over individuals; chronologically, the order of ideas was the reverse.

V.

The theory that the Articles of Confederation were for some purposes law, directly cognizable by courts, entirely transformed the character of the Confederation so far forth, and must sooner or later have suggested the idea of its entire transformation into a real government. Nor was judicial review the only possible source of such a suggestion. As Madison points out in the *Federalist,* "in cases of capture; of piracy; of the post-office; of coins, weights, and measures; of trade with the Indians; of claims under grants of land by different States; and, above all, in the case of trials by courts-martial in the army and navy," the government of the Confederation acted immediately on individuals from the first.[53] Again, proposals which were laid at various times before the states for conferring a customs revenue on Congress, though none was ever finally ratified, served to bring the same idea before the people as also did the proposals which never reached the states from Congress to endow the latter with "the sole and exclusive" power over foreign and interstate trade. . . .

But the great essential precursor to the success of all such proposals was the consolidation of a sufficient interest transcending state lines, and this was slow in forming. It was eventually brought about in three ways: first, through the abuse by the states of their powers over commerce; secondly, through the rise of the question—in which Washington was especially interested—of opening up communications with the West; thirdly, on account of the sharp fear which was aroused among property owners everywhere by the Shays Rebellion. The last was the really decisive factor. The call for a constitutional convention which had emanated from Annapolis in the autumn of 1786 was heeded by only three states, Virginia, New Jersey, Pennsylvania, and was ignored by Congress; but the call which Congress itself issued in the following February under the stimulus imparted by the uprising in Massachusetts was responded to by nine states in due course—New Hampshire being the last on account of the late date of the assembling of its legislature.[54]

[53] *Federalist,* no. 40.

[54] See the credentials, Elliot's *Debates,* second ed., I. 159 ff.

Testimony from private sources is to the same effect; it shows how the Massachusetts uprising completed the work of the paper-money craze in convincing men that constitutional reform had ceased to be a merely local problem.[55]

In this connection a paper prepared by Madison in April, 1787 and entitled "Vices of the Political System of the United States,"[56] becomes of great interest both for its content and because of the leading part later taken by its author in the work of the Convention. The title itself is significant: "the Political System of the United States" is *one,* and therefore the problem of its reform in all its branches is a single problem; and the argument itself bears out this prognosis. The defects of the Confederation are first considered: the failure of the states to comply with the requisitions of Congress, their encroachments on the central authority, their violations of the treaties of the United States and the Law of Nations, their trespasses on the rights of each other, their want of concert in matters of common interest, the lack of a coercive power in the government of the Confederation, the lack of a popular ratification of the Articles—all these are noted. Then in the midst of this catalogue appears a hitherto unheard-of specification: "want of guaranty to the States of their constitutions and laws against internal violence" —an obvious deduction from the Shays Rebellion.

It is, however, for the legislative evils which he finds within the states individually that Madison reserves his strongest words of condemnation. "As far as laws are necessary," he writes, "to mark with precision the duties of those who are to obey them, and to take from those who are to administer them a discretion which might be abused, their number is the price of liberty. As far as laws exceed this limit, they are a nuisance; a nuisance of the most pestilent kind." Yet "try the Codes of the several States by this test, and what a luxuriancy of legislation do they present. The short period of independency has filled as many pages as the century which preceded it." Nor was this multiplicity of laws the greatest evil—worse was their mutability, a clear mark "of vicious legislation"; and worst of all their injustice, which brought "into question the fundamental principle of republican Government, that the majority who rule in such governments are the safest Guardians both of public Good and private rights."

[55] Beveridge, *Life of John Marshall,* vol. I., ch. 8.
[56] *Writings,* ed. Hunt, II. 361 ff.

Indeed Madison proceeded to argue, in effect, that majority rule was more or less of a superstition. No doubt the evils just recounted were traceable in part to the individual selfishness of the representatives of the people; but their chief cause lay in a much more stubborn fact—the natural arrangement of society.

All civilized societies are divided into different interests and factions, as they happen to be creditors or debtors—rich or poor—husbandmen, merchants or manufacturers—members of different religious sects—followers of different political leaders—inhabitants of different districts—owners of different kinds of property, etc., etc. In republican Government the majority however composed, ultimately give the law. Whenever therefore an apparent interest or common passion unites a majority what is to restrain them from unjust violations of the rights and interests of the minority, or of individuals?

Merely moral or persuasive remedies Madison found to be useless when addressed to political selfishness—which itself never lacks a moral excuse—nor does he once refer to the teachings of Montesquieu, for the reason, it may be surmised, that the model constitution of the Union by this test had broken down at the very moment of crisis. One device, nevertheless, remained untried: the enlargement of the geographical sphere of government. For the advantage of a large republic over a small one, Madison insisted, was this: owing, on the one hand, to the greater variety of interests scattered through it, and, on the other, to the natural barrier of distance, a dangerous coalescence of factions became much more difficult. "As a limited monarchy tempers the evils of an absolute one; so an extensive Republic meliorates the administration of a small Republic."

And how precisely was this remedy to be applied in the case of the United States? In the paper before us, Madison seems to imply the belief that the states ought to surrender all their powers to the national government, but his letters make it plain that this was not his programme. Rather, the powers of the central government should be greatly enlarged, and it should be converted into a real government, operative upon individuals and vested with all the coercive powers of government; then this enlarged and strengthened government, which on account of the territorial extent of its constituency would with difficulty fall a prey to faction, should be set as a check upon the exercise by the state governments of the considerable powers which must still remain with them. "The national government" must "have a negative in all cases whatsoever on the legislative acts of the states," he wrote, like that of the King in colonial days. This was "the least possible abridgment of the State sovereignties." "The happy effect" of such an arrangement would be "its control on the internal vicissitudes of State policy and the aggressions of interested majorities on the rights of minorities and individuals." Thus was the Balance of Power, which Montesquieu had borrowed from the stock teachings of the eighteenth-century diplomacy, to transform it into a maxim of free constitutions, projected into the midway field of federal government.

Every constitutional system gives rise, in relation to the interests of the people whom it is designed to serve, to certain characteristic and persistent problems. The most persistent problem of the American constitutional system arises from the fact that to a multitude of state legislatures are assigned many of the most important powers of government over the individual. Originally, indeed, the bias in favor of local autonomy so overweighted the American constitutional system in that direction that it broke down entirely, both within the states, where the basic rights of property and contract were seriously infringed, and throughout the nation at large, because from the central government essential powers had been withheld.

In the solution of the problems thence resulting, four important constructive ideas were successively brought forward in the years immediately preceding the Philadelphia Convention, all of them reflecting the doctrine of the separation of powers or the attendant notion of a check and balance in government. The abuses resulting from the hitherto undifferentiated character of "legislative power" were met by the idea that it was something intrinsically distinct from "judicial power," and that therefore it was exceeded when it interfered with the dispensation of justice through the ordinary courts. Then building upon this result, the finality of judicial determinations was represented as extending to the interpretation of the standing law, a proposition which, when brought into association with the notion of a higher law, yielded the initial form of the doctrine of judicial review. Meantime, the idea was being advanced that the Articles of Confederation were, in relation to acts of the local legislatures, just such a higher law, thus suggesting a sanction for the acts of the Confederation which in principle entirely transformed its character. Finally, from Madison, who from the first interested himself in every phase of the rising movement for constitutional reform both in his own state and the country at large, came the idea that the problem of providing adequate safeguards for private rights and adequate powers for national government was one and the same problem, inasmuch as a strengthened national government could be made a make-weight against the swollen prerogatives of the state legislatures. It remained for the Constitutional Convention however, while it accepted Madison's main idea, to apply it through the agency of judicial review. Nor can it be doubted that this determination was assisted by a growing comprehension in the Convention of the *doctrine* of judicial review.

★ II ★

The Basic Doctrine of American Constitutional Law*

Without the Doctrine of Vested Rights it is inconceivable that there would have been any Constitutional Law.

The two leading doctrines of American Constitutional Law before the Civil War, affecting state legislative power, were the Doctrine of Vested Rights and the Doctrine of the Police Power. The two doctrines are in a way complementary concepts, inasmuch as they represent the reaction upon each other of the earlier conflicting theories of natural rights and legislative sovereignty. But the older doctrine is the doctrine of vested rights, which may be said to have flourished before the rise of the Jacksonian Democracy. Furthermore, if Constitutional Law be regarded from the point of view of its main purpose, namely, that of setting metes and bounds to legislative power, it is the more fundamental doctrine.

Judicial review, we are told repeatedly, rests only upon the written constitution. We shall find ample reason presently to impugn the accuracy of this assertion, particularly for that most important formative period when the tree of Constitutional Law was receiving its initial bent. But letting it for the moment pass unchallenged, the question still remains, what is a constitution for—does it exist to grant power or to organize it? The former of these views is undoubtedly the older one, not only of the national Constitution, but

* *Michigan Law Review,* XII (February, 1914).

of the state constitutions as well. For the written constitution, wherever found, was at first regarded as a species of social compact, entered into by sovereign individuals in a state of nature. From this point of view, however, governmental authority, wherever centered, is a trust which, save for the grant of it effected by the written constitution, were non-existent, and private rights, since they precede the constitution, gain nothing of authoritativeness from being enumerated in it, though possibly something of security. These rights are not, in other words, fundamental because they find mention in the written instrument; they find mention there because fundamental. Suppose then the enumeration of such rights to have been but partial and incomplete, does that fact derogate from the rights not so enumerated? Article IX of the Amendments to the United States Constitution answers this question. The written constitution is, in short, but a nucleus or core of a much wider region of private rights, which, though not reduced to black and white, are as fully entitled to the protection of government as if defined in the minutest detail.

And by the other view of the written constitution, whether the so-called "natural rights" were enumerated or not was also a matter of indifference, but for precisely the opposite reason. By this view too the constitution was in a certain sense a grant of power, since government always rests upon the consent of the governed. The power granted, however, was not simply this or that item of specifically designated power but the sum total of that unrestrained sovereignty which in the state of nature was each man's dower. By the very act of calling government into existence, or more accurately, the legislative branch of government, this vast donation of power was conferred upon it, and irretrievably too, save for the right of revolution. Thus, whereas by the first view a constitution is wrapped about, so to say, by an ocean of rights, by this view it is enclosed in an enveloping principle of sovereign power. It thus follows first, that the mere co-existence of three departments within a written constitution leaves the legislature absolute, and secondly, that a mere enumeration of rights in the written constitution leaves them subject to legislative definition. Only by pretty specific provision of the written constitution is the legislative power, by this view, to be held in leash, even with judicial review a recognized institution, and the maxim that all doubts are to be resolved in its favor is to be taken for all that it seems to mean.

But let us consider the effect of these two theories of the nature of the constitution upon the question of the scope of judicial review more directly. The two theories were brought into juxtaposition in the classic case of *Calder* v. *Bull*,[1] which was decided by the Supreme Court in 1798. In that case an act of the Connecticut legislature setting aside a decree of a probate court and granting a new hearing for the benefit of those claiming under a will was denounced by the heirs at law as *ex post facto* and so void under Art. I, §10 of the United States Constitution. The court rejected this view, holding partly upon the authority of Blackstone, partly upon the *usus loquendi* of the state constitutions, and partly on that of the United States Constitution, that the prohibition in question did not extend to all "retrospective" legislation, but only to enactments making what were innocent acts when they were done criminal or aggravating the legal character and penalty of past acts. The prohibition was intended, said Justice Chase, "to secure the *person* of the subject from injury or *punishment*, in consequence of such a *law*." It was not intended to secure the citizen in his *"personal rights,"* *i.e.*, "his *private rights*, of either *property* or *contracts*."

Whether this construction of the *ex post facto* clause of Art. I, § 10 met the intentions of the framers of the Constitution is an open question.[2] But it is certain that it did not entirely satisfy the court that made it. Said Justice Paterson: "I had an ardent desire to have extended the provision in the Constitution to retrospective laws in general. There is neither policy nor safety in such laws." Justice Chase's condemnation was hardly less sweeping. He admitted that there were "cases in which laws may justly and for the benefit of the community, and also of individuals, relate to a time antecedent to their commencement, as statutes of oblivion, or of pardon," but statutes taking away or impairing "*rights vested*, agreeably to existing laws," were also "retrospective," "generally unjust," and "oppressive." Nor was it at all his intention to throw open the doors to such legislation. True the *ex post facto* clause bore a narrow technical meaning, but other clauses of the same section were of broader application: the clause prohibiting states from making laws impairing the obligation of contracts and that prohibiting them from

[1] 3 Dall. 386 (1798).

[2] See Farrand, *Records of the Federal Convention*, II, 368, 375, 378, 448, 571, 596, 610, 617, 656; III, 165. See also note by Johnson, J., in 2 Pet. 681 (1829).

making anything but gold or silver a legal tender. Furthermore there were certain fundamental principles of the social compact and republican government.

"I cannot subscribe," wrote Justice Chase in a passage which must be regarded as furnishing American Constitutional Law with its leavening principle, "to the *omnipotence* of a *state legislature,* or that it is *absolute* and *without* control, although its authority should not be *expressly* restrained by the *constitution or fundamental law* of the state. The people of the United States erected their constitutions . . . to establish justice, to promote the general welfare, to secure the blessing of liberty, and to protect persons and property from violence. The purposes for which men enter into society will determine the nature and terms of the social compact; and as they are the foundation of the legislative power, they will decide the proper objects of it. The *nature* and *ends* of *legislative* power will limit the *exercise* of it. . . . There are acts which the federal or state legislatures cannot do without exceeding their authority. There are certain vital principles in our free republican governments which will determine and overrule an apparent and flagrant abuse of legislative power. . . . An *Act* of the legislature (for I cannot call it a *law*) contrary to the great principles of the social compact cannot be considered a rightful exercise of legislative authority. . . . A law that punishes an innocent action . . .; a law that destroys, or impairs the lawful private contracts of citizens; a law that makes a man a judge in his own cause; or a law that takes *property* from A and gives it to B: it is against all reason and justice for a people to entrust a legislature with *such* powers; and therefore it cannot be presumed that they have done it. The *genius,* the *nature,* and the *spirit* of our state governments amount to a prohibition of such acts of legislation; and the *general principles of law and reason* forbid them." To hold otherwise were a "political heresy" "altogether inadmissible."

This appeal from the strict letter of the Constitution to general principles Chase's associate Iredell, on the other hand, flatly pronounced invalid. True, "some speculative jurists" had held "that a legislative act against the natural justice must, in itself, be void," but the correct view was that if "a government composed of legislative, executive and judicial departments were established by a constitution which imposed no limits on the legislative power . . . whatever the legislative power chose to enact would be lawfully enacted, and the judicial power could never interpose to pronounce it void. . . . Sir William Blackstone, having put the strong case of an act of Parliament which should explicitly authorize a man to try his own cause, explicitly adds that even in that case "there is no court that has the power to defeat the intent of the legislature" when couched in unmistakable terms.[3] Besides, "the ideas of natural justice are regulated by no fixed standard: the ablest and purest men have differed upon the subject; and all that the court could properly say in such an event, would be that the legislature (possessed of an equal right of opinion) had passed an act which, in the opinion of the judges, was inconsistent with the abstract principles of justice."

Now which of these two views of the range of judicial power under the constitution has finally prevailed? In appearance, Iredell's has, but in substance, as I have already hinted, it is Chase's theory that has triumphed. The evidence for both these propositions is to be found in Cooley's *Constitutional Limitations*.[4] Dealing with the subject "of the circumstances under which a legislative enactment may be declared unconstitutional," Cooley writes: "If the courts are not at liberty to declare statutes void because of their apparent injustice or impolicy, neither can they do so because they appear to the minds of the judges to violate fundamental principles of republican government, *unless it shall be found that those principles are placed beyond the legislative encroachment by the Constitution.* . . . Nor are the courts at liberty to declare an act void, because in their opinion it is opposed to a *spirit* supposed to pervade the Constitution, *but not expressed in words.*"

. . .

And thus far the victory seems to rest with Iredell's view,—but it is in appearance only, as we immediately discover. For whatever terms he may use at times, it is as far as possible from Cooley's intention to admit in any real sense the principle of legislative sovereignty. Thus he proceeds: *"It does not follow however, that in every case the courts, before they can set aside a law as invalid, must be able to find in the constitution some specific inhibition which has been disregarded, or some express command which has*

[3] 1 *Comm.* 91.
[4] Cooley, *Constitutional Limitations* (ed. 1) 169–173; (ed. 7) 237–242.

been disobeyed. Prohibitions are only important when they are in the nature of exceptions to a general grant of powers; and if the authority to do an act has not been granted by the sovereign to its representative, it cannot be necessary to prohibit its being done." But he has just said that a state constitution exists to limit the *otherwise plenary* power of the legislature. How explain this apparent contradiction? An explanation has already been supplied by a quotation from the New York decision of *Sill* v. *Corning*.[5] The object of the constitution, runs the passage quoted, "is not to grant legislative power, but to confine and restrain it. Without constitutional limitations, the power to make laws would be absolute. These limitations are created and imposed by the express words, *or, arise by necessary implication. The leading feature of the constitution is the separation and distinction of the powers of the government. It takes care to separate the executive, legislative and judicial powers and to define their limits."* In a word the power which is conferred upon the legislature is the *legislative* power and no other. This single phrase tells the tale. It is no longer good form, because it is no longer necessary, for a court to invoke natural rights and the social compact in a constitutional decision. But the same result is achieved by construing the very term by which "legislative power" is conferred upon the legislature. . . . Cooley . . . reposes the main structure of Constitutional Law upon the simple fact of the coexistence of the three departments in the same constitution. Natural rights, expelled from the front door of the constitution are readmitted through the doctrine of the separation of powers. And what does this fact signify for judicial review? The answer is self-evident. Once it was recognized that to define "legislative power" finally and authoritatively lay with the courts, the power of judicial review became limited only by the discretion of the judges and the operation of the doctrine of *stare decisis*. The history of judicial review is, in other words, the history of constitutional limitations.

Preliminary, however, to entering upon this story, it is necessary for us to turn back a little way to supply a phase of the topic just under discussion. The date of the decision in *Sill* v. *Corning* was 1857 and Cooley's great work did not appear until 1868. Such recognition moreover as is accorded the principle of legislative sovereignty in

[5] 15 N. Y. 297, 303 (1857). See also *Weister* v. *Hade*, 52 Pa. St. 474, 477 (1866).

these places, slight and banal as upon investigation it is seen to be, was due to developments lying this side the formative period of American Constitutional Law, in fact to developments that brought that period to a close. Despite therefore his tone of disparagement for the views of "speculative jurists," if we are to judge of views from their comparative success in establishing themselves in practice, it was Iredell himself who was "speculative." The fact of the matter is that Iredell's tenet that courts were not to appeal to natural rights and the social compact as furnishing a basis for constitutional decisions was disregarded by all the leading judges and advocates of the early period of our constitutional history. Marshall, it is true, had imbibed from Blackstone's pages much the same point of view as had Iredell. But on the crucial occasion of his decision in *Fletcher* v. *Peck,*[6] he freely appealed to "the nature of society and government" as setting "limits to the legislative power," and putting the significant query, "How far the power of giving the law may involve every other power," proceeded to answer it in a way that he could not possibly have done had he not, for the once, at least, abandoned Blackstone. The record of others has not even this degree of ambiguity. Justices Wilson, Paterson, Story and Johnson, Chancellors Kent and Walworth, Chief-Justices Grimke, Parsons, Parker, Hosmer, Ruffin and Buchanan all appealed to natural rights and the social compact as limiting legislative powers. They and other judges based decisions on this ground. The same doctrine was urged by the greatest lawyers of the period, without reproach. How dominant indeed were Justice Chase's "speculative" views with both bench and bar throughout the period when the foundation precedents of constitutional interpretation were being established is shown well by what occurred in connection with the case of *Wilkinson* v. *Leland,*[7] decided by the Supreme Court of the United States in 1829, at the very close of this epoch. The attorney of defendants in error was Daniel Webster. "If," said he, "at this period, there is not a general restraint on legislatures, in favor of private rights, there is an end to private property. Though there may be no prohibition in the constitution, the legislature is restrained from acts subverting the great principles of republican liberty and of the social compact." To this contention his opponent William

[6] 6 Cranch 87 (1810).
[7] 2 Pet. 627, 646–7, 652, 657 (1829).

Wirt, responded thus: "Who is the sovereign? Is it not the legislature of the state and are not its acts effectual, *unless they come in contact with the great principles of the social compact?"* The act of the Rhode Island legislature under review was upheld, but said Justice Story speaking for the court: "That government can scarcely be deemed to be free where the rights of property are left solely dependent upon the will of a legislative body without any restraint. The fundamental maxims of a free government seem to require that the rights of personal liberty and private property should be held sacred." Forty-five years later, Justice Miller, speaking for an all but unanimous bench in *Loan Association* v. *Topeka,*[8] makes the same doctrine the basis of a decision overturning a state enactment, while Iredell's view receives reiteration in the lone dissent of Justice Clifford.

But now was it the intention of these men to leave it with the courts to draw the line between legislative power and *all* rights which might be designated "natural rights"? We speedily discover that it was not, and in so doing discover at last Iredell's vindication. *A priori,* it is difficult to see how our judges, having set out to be defenders of "natural rights," were in a position to decline to defend, and therefore to define, all such rights whether mentioned in the constitution or not. The difficulty is disposed of, however, the moment we recollect that our judges envisaged their problem not as moral philosophers but as lawyers, and especially as students of the *Common Law.* "Natural rights," in short, were to be defined in light of Common Law precedents.

But there was also a second consideration limiting and easing the task of the judges. In his chapter on "The Absolute Rights of Individuals" Blackstone had written thus: "These may be reduced to three principal or primary articles . . . I. The right of personal security" consisting "in a person's legal and uninterrupted enjoyment of his life, his limbs, his body, his health, and his reputation. . . . II. . . . the personal liberty of individuals . . ." consisting "in the power of locomotion, of changing situation, or moving one's person to whatsoever place one's own inclination may direct, without imprisonment or restraint, *unless by due course of law.* . . . III. . . . The absolute right, inherent in every Englishman . . . of property: which consists in the free use, enjoyment and disposal of

[8] 20 Wall. 655 (1874).

all his acquisitions, without any control or diminution, *save only by the laws of the land*."[9] As we have already seen Blackstone regarded Parliament's power as legally unlimited. His subordination of the "Absolute Rights of Individuals" in each case to the law signifies therefore their plenary control by the legislature and so for our purpose must be ignored. What *is* to our purpose is the definition given in the above quotation of the rights pronounced "absolute." For these are the rights precisely which, with judicial review based upon the social compact and directed to keeping legislative power within its inherent limitations, the courts were called upon to protect against legislative attack.

But were all these rights in fact exposed to legislative attack? The right of *personal security* certainly was not. On the contrary from the very beginning we find the courts characterizing the legislative power as calculated to safeguard that right by assuring the prevalence of the maxim of the Common Law: "*Sic utere tuo ut alienum non laedas.*" Again it was little likely that the right of *personal liberty* would be infringed under a republican form of government. This was a right that all were capable of enjoying equally merely by virtue of their being persons. Furthermore, the rights of accused persons were safeguarded in both the federal Constitution and, for the most part, the state constitutions by elaborate and detailed specification; and the decision in *Calder* v. *Bull* had not weakened these safeguards. The right meant to be safeguarded by the appeal to the social compact and natural rights was therefore the Property Right. This was the right which, the old *Dialogue of Doctor and Student* informs us, was protected by the "law of reason," by which term those "learned in the law of England" were wont to designate the "law of nature."[10] More than that, it was the right precisely which, in the estimation of the fathers, representative institutions had left insecure.

We are now prepared to consider the underlying doctrine of American Constitutional Law, a doctrine without which indeed it is inconceivable that there would have been any Constitutional Law. This is the Doctrine of Vested Rights, which—to state it in its most rigorous form—setting out with the assumption that the prop-

[9] 1 Black, *Comm.* 129–137.

[10] C. H. McIlwain, *The High Court of Parliament and its Supremacy*, 105–6.

erty right is fundamental, treats any law impairing *vested rights,* whatever its intention, as a bill of pains and penalties, and so, void.

The fundamental character of the property right was asserted repeatedly on the floor of the Convention of 1787.[10a] It is therefore no accident that the same doctrine was first brought within the purview of Constitutional Law by a member of that Convention, namely, Justice Paterson in his charge to the jury in *Van Horne's Lessee* v. *Dorrance,*[11] the date of which is 1795. "The right of acquiring and possessing property and *having it protected* is one of the natural, inherent and unalienable rights of man. Men have a sense of property: property is necessary to their subsistence, and correspondent to their natural wants and desires; its security was one of the objects that induced them to unite in society. . . . The preservation of property, then, is a primary object of the social compact and by the late constitution of Pennsylvania was made a fundamental law. . . . The legislature therefore had no authority to make an act divesting one citizen of his freehold and vesting it in another, without a just compensation. It is inconsistent with the principles of reason, justice, and moral rectitude; it is incompatible with the comfort, peace and happiness of mankind; it is contrary to the principles of social alliance, in every free government; and lastly, it is contrary both to the letter and spirit of the constitution." On the basis of this reasoning an act of 1789 is pronounced "void, . . . a dead letter and of no more virtue or avail than if it never had been made."

A full decade earlier, however than *Van Horne's Lessee* v. *Dorrance,* the doctrine of vested rights is simply assumed by the Supreme Court of Connecticut in the *Symbury* case.[12] Again in 1789 in the case of *Ham* v. *McClaws and wife,*[13] the Supreme Court of South Carolina had invoked similar principles to give to a particular statute such construction as would "be consistent with justice and the dictates of natural reason, though contrary to the strict letter of the law." Three years later, the same court pronounced invalid an act of the assembly passed in 1712, transferring a freehold from the heir at law to another individual.

[10a] Farrand, *loc. cit.* I, 424, 533–4, 541–2, II, 123. cf. *ib.* I, 605. See also *Federalist* No. 10.

[11] 2 Dall. 304, 310 (1795).

[12] Kirby 444 (1785).

[13] 1 Bay 93 (1789).

. . . It is a striking fact that in at least half of the original fourteen states, to include Vermont in the reckoning, the doctrine of judicial review was first recognized in connection with cases involving also an acceptance of the doctrine of vested rights.[14] We are able therefore to comprehend the significance of a remark by Justice Chase in 1800 to the effect that the court ought to accord different treatment to laws passed by the states during the Revolution and those passed since the Constitution of the United States had gone into effect, since "few of the revolutionary acts would stand the rigorous tests now applied."[15]

But the acceptance of this doctrine by the courts one after the other is but the beginning of the story. We must see how the progress of the doctrine was aided by the obscuration on the part of the courts of essential distinctions, or even their deliberate obliteration; how the doctrine attracted to its support other congenial principles; how it vitalized certain clauses of the written constitution; how in short it gradually operated to give legal reality to the notion of governmental power as *limited power*.

Of the distinctions above referred to the one whose disappearance we should first note is that between "retrospective laws," in the strict sense of laws designed "to take effect from a time anterior to their passage," and laws "which though operating only from their passage affect vested rights and past transactions." The distinction is recognized by Story in *Society* v. *Wheeler,*[16] but only to be thrust aside. "Upon principle," he declares, "every statute which takes away or impairs vested rights acquired under existing laws or creates a new obligation, imposes a new duty, or attaches a new disability in respect to transactions or considerations already past, must be deemed retrospective." In support of his argument he cites *Calder* v. *Bull,* and warrantably. The distinction in fact was not so much obscured as entirely ignored from the first. Of more vital necessity, however, to the doctrine of vested rights, was the elimination of the distinction underlying the decision in *Calder* v. *Bull* between legis-

[14] Besides the cases just mentioned, see the case described by Jeremiah Mason in his *Memories*, pp. 26–7, in which the New Hampshire court pronounced an Act unconstitutional, in 1784. The same case is referred to by Wm. Plumer's *Life of Wm. Plumer,* p. 59. See also *Proprietors etc.* v. *Laboree,* 2 Greenl. (Me.) 275, 294 (1823); *Emerick* v. *Harris,* 1 Binn. (Pa.) 416 (1808); *Whittington* v. *Polk,* 1 Harr. & J. (Md.) 236 (1802).

[15] *Cooper* v. *Telfair,* 4 Dall. 14, 19 (1800).

[16] 2 Gall. C. C. 105, 139 (1814), Fed. Cas. 13, 156.

lative enactments designed to punish individuals for their past acts and enactments which in giving effect to the legislature's view of public policy incidentally affected private rights detrimentally. Doubtless, this result was facilitated by the oft-expressed reluctance of the courts to enter into the question of the motives of the legislature, *i.e.,* of its members. And this question and that of the intention underlying the legislature's acts, though two quite different matters, it was easy to confuse. Hence it became doctrine in many quarters that the validity of statutes must depend upon external tests, particularly upon their actual operation upon private rights. The matter is one that will receive further attention later on.

But if the obliteration of one distinction is thus sufficiently explained, that of another is by the same line of reasoning made the more difficult of palliation. This is the very obvious distinction between *special* acts and *general* acts. The mischief of what has been called "prerogative legislation," that is, legislation modifying the position of named parties before the law, was one of the most potent causes of the general disrepute into which state legislatures had fallen before 1787.[17] For such measures, furthermore, rarely or never could the justification be pleaded of an imperative public interest. When accordingly such measures bore heavily upon the vested rights of particular, selected persons it was not strange that the courts should have treated them as equivalent to bills of pains and penalties. But the case of general statutes is obviously different. To enact these is of the very essence of legislative power. Their generality indeed furnishes the standard of legislation from which special acts are condemned. It is true that such measures will often bear more particularly upon some members of the community than others, but this fact is perhaps but the obverse of the necessity for their enactment. Notwithstanding these considerations the courts, building upon the Common Law maxim that statutes ought not in doubtful cases be given a retrospective operation, laid down from the first the doctrine as one of constitutional obligation, that in no case was a statute to receive an interpretation which brought it into conflict with vested rights.[18] So far as a statute did not impair vested rights, it was good, but so far as it did, it was a bill of pains and penalties and void, not under Art. I, § 10 of the United States Constitution,

[17] See, e.g., *Federalist* No. 48 (Lodge's Ed.).

[18] Cf. *Elliott* v. *Lyell,* 3 Call 268, 286 (1802) and *Turpin* v. *Locket,* 6 Call 113 (1804). See also *Dash* v. *Van Kleeck,* 7 Johns. (N. Y.) 477, 498 (1811).

—for the actual precedent of *Calder* v. *Bull* still held, despite protests from eminent judges,—but under the general principles of Constitutional Law held to underlie all constitutions.

. . .

But of all principles brought to the support of the doctrine of vested rights, the one destined to prove, at least before the Civil War, of most varied and widest serviceability was the principle of the separation of powers. I have already touched upon the matter a few pages back. At this point I wish to review briefly some historical phases of the subject. Our starting point is the case of *Cooper* v. *Telfair,*[19] decided by the Supreme Court of the United States in 1800 on appeal from the United States Circuit Court for the District of Georgia. The measure under review was the act of the Georgia legislature of May 4, 1782, inflicting penalties on, and confiscating the estates of, certain persons declared guilty of treason. In opposition to the statute it was urged especially that it transgressed Art. I of the Georgia Constitution of 1777, which provided that "the legislative, executive and judiciary departments shall be separate and distinct, so that neither exercise the powers properly belonging to the other." The act was nevertheless upheld as valid. Said Justice Cushing: "The right to confiscate and banish, in the case of an offending citizen, must belong to every government. It is not within the judicial power, as created and regulated by the constitution of Georgia: and it naturally, as well as tacitly, belongs to the legislature." Said Justice Paterson: "The legislative power of Georgia, though it is in some respects restricted and qualified, *is not defined* by the constitution of the state." To the same effect were the words of Justice Chase: "The general principles contained in the constitution are not to be regarded as rules to fetter and control, but as *matter merely declaratory and directory.*"

At first, in other words, the doctrine of the separation of powers, even when formulated in the written constitution, was not deemed precise enough to admit of its being applied by courts as a constitutional limitation. The other point of view, however, was not long in making its appearance. In *Ogden* v. *Blackledge,*[20] which was certified to the Supreme Court from the United States Circuit Court for

[19] 4 Dall. 14 (1800).

[20] Cranch 272 (1804); see also *Ogden* v. *Witherspoon,* 2 Haywood 227, 3 N.C. 404 (1802).

the District of North Carolina in 1804, the question to be determined was whether the state statute of limitations of 1715 had been repealed in 1789, the North Carolina legislature having declared in 1799 that it had not been. Said attorneys for plaintiff: "To declare what the law is, or has been, is a judicial power; to declare what it shall be, is legislative. One of the fundamental principles of all our governments is that the legislative power shall be separated from the judicial." "The Court," runs the report, "stopped counsel, observing that it was unnecessary to argue that point." Without recurring to the constitutional question, the court held that "under all the circumstances stated," the act in question had been repealed in 1789. Fifteen years later, the New Hampshire Supreme Court, in the leading case of *Merrill* v. *Sherburne,*[21] brought the principle of the separation of powers squarely to the support of the doctrine of vested rights. There was henceforth no apology or evasion on the part of judges in the manipulation of this principle.

As we have already seen, the doctrine of vested rights takes its origin from a certain theory of the nature and purpose of government. But political theory is not Constitutional Law, though often the source of it. The doctrine of vested rights, however, is Constitutional Law; indeed in one disguise and another it is a great part of it. Its protean faculty of appearing ever in new forms and formulations is, however, to be of later concern. What we need to do now is to see it at work in the forms which it assumed from the first, shaping the great uncontroverted powers of the American state, the power of taxation, the power of eminent domain, and what is today designated "the police power."

Mention has been made of the conservative New York doctrine. The founder of this doctrine and so to no small extent the founder of American Constitutional Law was the great Chancellor Kent, whose *Commentaries* were and remain not only a marvel of legal learning but also of literary expression, and altogether one of the greatest intellectual achievements to the credit of any American.

. . .

Kent sets out by disparaging the idea of "a state of man prior to the existence of any notion of separate property." "No such state," he contends, "was intended for man in the benevolent dispensations

[21] 1 N. H. 199, 204 (1819).

of Providence. . . . Man was fitted and intended by the author of his being for society and government and for the acquisition and enjoyment of property. It is, to speak correctly, the law of his nature: and by obedience to this law, he brings all his faculties into exercise and is enabled to display the various and exalted powers of the human mind." . . . "The legislature," therefore, "has no right to limit the extent of the acquisition of property. . . . A state of equality as to property is impossible to be maintained, for it is against the laws of our own nature; and if it could be reduced to practice, it would place the human race in a state of tasteless enjoyment and stupid inactivity, which would degrade the mind and destroy the happiness of social life." And by the same token, "civil government is not entitled, in ordinary cases, . . . to regulate the uses of property in the hands of the owners by sumptuary laws or any other visionary schemes of frugality and equality." . . . But the matter of especial importance at this stage is to find out how this point of view manifested itself when brought into contact with those prerogatives which Kent freely accorded government.

As to taxation, Kent's theory is obviously the *quid pro quo* theory and this has remained the theory of American courts from that day to this. From it follows the maxim that taxation must be "equal in proportion to the value of property."[22]

With reference to the power of eminent domain, Kent but reiterates in his *Commentaries* the views which as Chancellor he had earlier developed in the leading case of *Gardner* v. *Newburgh*,[23] to which therefore we turn directly. In this case, which was decided in 1816, the statute under review was one authorizing the trustees of the village of Newburgh to supply its inhabitants with water by means of conduits. As stated by the Chancellor, the statute made "adequate provision for the party injured by the laying of the conduits through his land" and also "to the owners of the spring or springs from whence the water" was to be taken. But no compensation was provided the plaintiff Gardner, "through whose land the water issuing from the spring" had been accustomed to flow. At this date there was no provision in the New York constitution with reference to the power of eminent domain. Nevertheless upon the authority of Grotius, Puffendorf, Bynkershoeck and Blackstone,

[22] 2 Kent, *Comm.* 332.
[23] 2 Johns. Ch. 162, 166–7 (1816).

Kent developed the following propositions: 1st, that the legislature might "take private property for necessary or useful *public* [sic] purposes"; 2ndly, that such taking, however, did not involve the absolute "stripping of the subject of his property," but, in the language of Blackstone, "the giving him a full indemnification," since "the public is now considered as an individual treating with an individual for an exchange"; 3rdly, that such indemnification was due not merely those whose property was actually appropriated by the state but also those whose property should be injured in consequence of the use made by the state of the property appropriated; 4thly, that the legislature itself was not the final judge of what sum was "a full indemnification" of owners whose property was taken or injured. . . .

The third power of government touching property rights Kent describes in the following terms: "But though property be thus protected, it is still to be understood, that the law-giver has a right to prescribe the mode and manner of using it so far as may be necessary to prevent the abuse of the right to the injury or annoyance of others or of the public. The government may by general regulations interdict such uses of property as would create nuisances and become dangerous to the lives and health or peace or comfort of the citizens. . . ."

But is the power thus described unlimited, that is, limited only by the discretion of the lawgiver? In the first place, be it noted, the power in question is described as a power of *regulation,* which, at least so it came eventually to be urged, is distinguishable from a power of *prohibition.* True, Kent himself admits that there are uses of property which constitute *nuisances* in certain cases, and he says in another place, that there are "cases of urgent necessity" in which property may be destroyed, as for instance when houses are razed to prevent the spread of a conflagration.[24] But it is apparent from his citations that he regards such cases as already provided for in Common Law precedent, that he has no intention of recognizing in the legislature a power to define cases of nuisance and urgency, unrestrained by precedent. Again his doctrine of consequential damages must not be forgotten in this connection. For if it was incumbent upon the state to render compensation for damages resulting from its use of the power of eminent domain, why

[24] 2 Kent, *Comm.* 338–9 and notes.

should it not also be the state's duty to pay private owners for damages resultant from the use of its police powers? Lastly, it is entirely apparent that Kent had not the least idea in the world of abandoning the doctrine which had received his repeated sanction, that a legislative enactment must never be so interpreted as to impair vested rights.[25] . . .

Vested rights are rights vested in specific individuals in accordance with the law in what the law recognizes as *property*. But what for the purposes of the doctrine of vested rights, did the law recognize as property? What, in other words, was the objective of the rights which this doctrine treated as vestable?

In his *Essay on Property,* composed in 1792, Madison had written thus: "This term in its particular application means 'that dominion which one man claims and exercises over the external things of the world, in exclusion of every other individual.' But in its larger and juster meaning, it embraces everything to which a man may attach a value and have a right; and which leaves to *every one else the like advantage*. In the former sense, a man's land, or merchandise, or money is called his property. In the latter sense, a man has property in his opinions and a free communication of them. He has a property of peculiar value in his religious opinions, and in the profession and practice dictated by them. He has property very dear to him in the safety and liberty of his person. He has an equal property in the free use of his faculties and free choice of the objects on which to employ them. In a word, as a man is said to have a right to his property, he may be equally said to have a property in his rights. . . . If there be a government then which prides itself on maintaining the inviolability of property, which provides that none shall be taken directly even for public use without indemnification to the owner, and yet directly violates the property which individuals have in their opinions, their religion, their person, and their faculties, nay more which indirectly violates their property in their actual possessions, in the labor that acquires their daily subsistence, and in the hallowed remnant of time which ought to relieve their fatigues and soothe their cares, the inference will have been anticipated that such a government is not a pattern for the United States. If the United States mean to obtain or deserve the full

[25] *Dash* v. *Van Kleeck,* 7 Cow. 349 (1827) and *Coates et al.* v. *Mayor etc.,* 7 Cow. 585 (1827).

praise due to wise and just governments they will equally respect the rights of property and the property in rights."[26]

These words are important as showing the elasticity attaching to the term "property," as used by American statesmen, from the beginning. Such latitudinarian views, however, found little or no support from the Common Law, and had in consequence before the Civil War little influence upon judges. So far as the courts liberalized the legal notion of the property right it was chiefly by analyzing it into its constituent elements, the right of use, the right of sale, the right of control, and so on, which were sometimes recognized as property rights even when inhering in another than the legal owner.[27] But the objective of these rights remained for the most part, tangible property, property which could be taken by the power of eminent domain, hence especially real property.[28] . . . Certainly no one would have thought of suggesting before the Civil War that the right to engage in trade, the right to contract, the right—to employ Madison's phrase—of the individual "in the use of his faculties," were "vested rights." To this fact Madison's own antithesis between "rights to property" and "property in rights" is indirect testimony, but most direct evidence is by no means lacking. . . . Two cases especially to the point are a Massachusetts case of 1835, *Hewitt* v. *Charier*,[29] and an Ohio case of 1831, *Jordan* v. *Overseers of Dayton*.[30] In these cases the statutes drawn into question confined the practice of medicine to members of certain medical societies and to persons qualified in other stipulated ways. In the Massachusetts case the protestant, who had continued in practice in defiance of the statute, based his case, not upon the ground that would seem most available today, that the statute operated to deprive him of his livelihood and chosen profession, but upon art. 6 of the Massachusetts Declaration of Rights, which forbids, in essence, special privileges to favored individuals. The court overruled the

[26] Madison, *Writings* (Hunt ed.) VI, 101 ff.

[27] See some New York cases: *Holmes* v. *Holmes*, 4 Barb. 295 (1848); *White* v. *White*, 5 Barb. 474 (1849); *Perkins* v. *Cottrell*, 15 Barb. 446 (1851); *Westervelt* v. *Gregg*, 12 N. Y. 202 (1854).

[28] See McLean, J., in *West River Bridge Co.* v. *Dix*, 6 How. 507 (1848) at 536–7.

[29] 16 Pick. 353 (1835).

[30] 4 Ohio 295 (1831). Some other citations of like import may be added: *Furman* v. *Knapp*, 19 Johns (N. Y.) 248 (1821); *People* v. *Jenkins*, 1 Hill (N. Y.) 469 (1841); *Com.* v. *Ober*, 12 Cush. (Mass.) 493 (1853).

argument. Said Chief Justice Shaw: "Taking the whole article together, we think it manifest that it was especially pointed to the prevention of hereditary rank." But even in applying it according to its literal meaning, "it is necessary to consider whether it was the *intent or one of the leading and substantive purposes of the legislature* to confer an exclusive privilege on any man or class of men," or whether "this is indirect and incidental, . . . not one of the purposes of the act," and therefore not "a violation of this article of the Bill of Rights." His conclusion was that the act under review was not "a violation of any principle of the constitution."

In the Ohio case, the argument of plaintiff in error was even more far-fetched, being based upon a patent which he held from the national government for certain drugs and concoctions. Said the court in response: "The sole purpose of a patent is to enable the patentee to prevent others from using the products of his labor except with his consent. But his own right of using is not enlarged or affected. There remains in him . . . the power to manage his property or give direction to his labors at his pleasure, subject only to the paramount claims of society, which require that his enjoyment may be . . . regulated by laws which render it subservient to the general welfare." . . .[31]

Our conclusion then from these and similar cases must be that the doctrine of vested rights was interposed to shield only the property right, in the strict sense of the term, from legislative attack. When that broader range of rights which is today connoted by the terms "liberty" and "property" of the Fourteenth Amendment were in discussion other phraseology was employed, as for example the term "privileges and immunities" of Art. IV, § 2, of the Constitution. In his famous decision in *Corfield* v. *Coryell*,[32] rendered in 1823, Justice Washington defined this phrase to signify, as to "citizens in the several states," "those privileges and immunities which are in their nature, *fundamental,* which belong of right to the

[31] See also *Portland Bank* v. *Athorp,* 12 Mass. 252 (1815); *Commonwealth* v. *Blackington,* 24 Pick. 352 (1837); *Commonwealth* v. *Worcester,* 3 Pick. 462 (1826); *Nightingale*'s Case, 11 Pick. 168 (1831); *Vandine*'s Case, 6 Pick. 187 (1828). The point of view of Marshall, C. J., in *Ogden* v. *Saunders* is the same. The obligation of contracts which arose from moral law, was protected by Art I, Sec. 10 of the Constitution, but the right to contract was subject absolutely to legislative control. 12 Wheat. 213, 346–49.

[32] 4 Wash. C.C. 371, 380–1 (1823), Fed. Cas. 3230.

citizens of all free governments; and which have, at all times, been enjoyed by the citizens of the several states which compose this union." "What these fundamental principles are," he continued, "it would perhaps be more tedious than difficult to enumerate. They may, however, be all comprehended under the following heads; protection by the government: the enjoyment of life and liberty, with the right to acquire and possess property of every kind, and to pursue and obtain happiness and safety; subject nevertheless to such restraints as the government may justly prescribe for the good of the whole."

But now of all the rights included in this comprehensive schedule, one only, and that in but a limited sense, was protected by the doctrine of vested rights, the right namely of one who had *already* acquired some title of control over some particular piece of property, in the physical sense, to continue in that control. All other rights, however fundamental, were subject to limitation by the legislature, whose discretion as that of a representative body in a democratic country, was little likely to transgress the few, rather specific, provisions of the written constitution.

To conclude:—The doctrine of vested rights represents the first great achievement of the courts after the establishment of judicial review. In fact, in not a few instances, judicial review and the doctrine of vested rights appeared synchronously and the former was subordinate, in the sense of being auxiliary, to the latter. But always, before the Fourteenth Amendment, judicial review, save as a method of national control upon the states, would have been ineffective and lifeless enough, but for the *raison d' etre* supplied it by the doctrine of vested rights, in one guise or other.[33] Furthermore, the doctrine represented the essential spirit and point of view of the founders of American Constitutional Law, who saw before them the same problem that had confronted the Convention of 1787, namely, the problem of harmonizing majority rule with minority rights, or more specifically, republican institutions with the security of prop-

[33] For the most important guise which the doctrine assumed in state courts, particularly the New York courts, see the writer's article on "The Doctrine of Due Process of Law before the Civil War" in 24 *Harv. L. Rev.* 366, 460. The most important guise which the doctrine developed in the federal courts is to be seen in their interpretation of Art. I, § 10. See *Fletcher* v. *Peck*. 6 Cranch 87 (1810), and *Trustees of Dartmouth College* v. *Woodward*, 4 Wheat. 518 (1819).

erty, contracts, and commerce. In the solution of this problem the best minds of the period were enlisted, Wilson, Marshall, Kent, Story, and a galaxy of lesser lights. But their solution, grounded though it was upon theory that underlay the whole American constitutional system, would yet hardly have survived them had it not met the needs and aspirations of a nation whose democracy was always tempered by the individualism of the free, prosperous, Western World. That distrust of legislative majorities in which Constitutional Limitations were conceived, from being the obsession of a superior class, became, with advancing prosperity, the prepossession of a nation, and the doctrine of vested rights was secure.[34]

[34] See the discussion of the relation of government to the Property Right, in the Mass. Convention of 1820, Journal (Boston, 1853), pp. 247, 254, 275–6, 278, 280, 284–6, 304 ffg. The speakers are Webster, Story, John Adams, et al. Webster's "Oration on the Completion of Bunker Hill Monument" is a splendid statement of the theory that a democracy in which men are equal will inevitably want to protect private rights against governmental excesses. *Writings and Speeches* (National Ed., 1903) I, 259 ff'g. On Mar. 21, 1864 Lincoln addressed a committee from the Workingmen's Association of N. Y. He closed with the following words: "Property is the fruit of labor; property is desirable; is a positive good in the world. That some should become rich shows that others may become rich, and hence is just encouragement to industry and enterprise. Let not him who is houseless pull down the house of another, but let him work diligently and build one for himself, thus by example assuring that his own shall be safe from violence when built." *Complete Works* (Ed. of 1905) 54. See also V, 330, 361.

★ III ★

Due Process of Law Before the Civil War*

The Legislatures were pressing upon the Courtroom from one side and private interests from the other . . .

The phrase "due process of law" comes from Chapter 3 of 28 Edw. III, which reads as follows:

No man of what state or condition he be, shall be put out of his lands or tenements, nor taken, nor imprisoned, nor disinherited, nor put to death, without he be brought to answer by due process of law.

This statute in turn harks back to the famous Chapter 39 of Magna Carta, which the Massachusetts Constitution of 1780 paraphrases thus:

No subject shall be arrested, imprisoned, despoiled, or deprived of his property, immunities, or privileges, put out of the protection of the law, exiled, or deprived of his life, liberty, or estate, but by the judgment of his peers or the law of the land.[1]

The important phrase in this passage for our purposes is of course "by the law of the land," which is made by Sir Edward Coke in his Institutes synonymous with the later phrase, "by due process of law," and that in turn to signify "by due process of the common

* 24 *Harvard Law Review* (March, 1911) 366 and (April, 1911) p. 460.
[1] *Declaration of Rights,* Art. XII.

law," that is, "by the indictment or presentment of good and lawful men . . . or by writ original of the common law."[2] It must not be thought, however, that in writing thus Coke is recording the facts of history. Rather, to quote a recent authority upon Magna Carta, he was but "following his vicious method of assuming the existence in Magna Carta of a warrant for every legal principle established in his own day," a method which has enabled him to mislead utterly "several generations of commentators."[3] Among those thus misled are the three great commentators on American constitutional law, Kent, Story, and Cooley,—willing dupes no doubt, yet dupes none the less.[4] . . .

"Law of the Land" and "Due Process of Law" . . . derive their great contemporary importance not from their character as restrictions upon the power of the legislature in the enactment of procedure merely, but from their character as restrictions upon the power of legislation in general. Not everything that is passed in the form of law is "law of the land," say the courts, not only with reference to enactments which have nothing to do with the subject of procedure, but even with reference to enactments sanctioned by methods of enforcement admittedly unexceptionable. . . . How has this come about? The essential fact is quite plain, namely, a feeling on the part of judges that to leave the legislature free to pass arbitrary or harsh laws, so long as all the formalities be observed in enforcing such laws, were to yield the substance while contending for the shadow. But such a feeling is of course not in itself constitutional law: the question is, therefore, how did it become such? . . .

I.

The accession of Taney to the Chief Justiceship of the Supreme Court marks an epoch in the history of American constitutional law, though perhaps somewhat less distinctly than is often supposed. Marshall's guiding notion with respect to the national Constitution was, that it was intended to provide a realm of national rights subject to national control, a point of view from which state legislation limiting individual action became impertinence. Had the politi-

[2] *Inst.* II, 50–1.

[3] McKechnie, *Magna Carta,* 447; *ibid.*, generally on "Chapter 39."

[4] 2 Kent, *Comm.*, 2 ed., 13; Story, *Comm.*, 4 ed., sec. 1789; Cooley, *Const. Lim.*, 2 ed., 351 *et seq.*

cal branches of the national government been of Marshall's way of thinking all along, and willing, therefore, to assert the necessary degree of national control, perhaps this theory would have worked out very well even at that period. With the election of Jackson, however, the doctrine of States' Rights and strict construction laid a paralyzing hand upon the sources of national power. On the other hand, at the very same moment, what with the revival of revolution abroad and the rise of transcendentalism at home, and last, but not least, the phenomenal success of the Erie Canal, the demand went forth for a large governmental programme: for the public construction of canals and railroads, for free schools, for laws regulating the professions, for anti-liquor legislation, for universal suffrage and for the abolition of slavery. I say "governmental programme," but what government? Necessarily the state governments, which must, therefore, be furnished with the adequate constitutional theory to carry it forward. It is true that the panic of 1837 struck off the first item of this programme, but, save in a way presently indicated, it does not seem to have affected permanently the development of constitutional theory. Taney became Chief Justice in 1836, bringing with him to the Supreme Bench the fixed intention of clothing the states, so far as a faithful adherence to precedent would allow, with the sovereign and complete right to enact useful legislation for their respective populations. In his great *Charles River Bridge*[5] decision, accordingly, Taney laid down the maxim that in a public grant nothing passes by implication, a doctrine which, as Story showed conclusively in his dissent, would have made the decision in [Marshall's] *Dartmouth College* case originally impossible, and which did in point of fact, in the decades following, pave the way for the great but necessary curtailment of the efficacy of that decision.[6] Again, in the *License* Cases,[7] Taney reveals his point of view by refusing to extend to the field of interstate commerce the principle of Marshall's decision in *Brown* v. *Maryland*[8] with reference to Congress' power over foreign commerce, namely,

[5] 11 Pet. (U. S.) 420 (1837).

[6] See particularly *West River Bridge Co.* v. *Dix.* 6 How. (U. S.) 507; *Beer Co.* v. *Massachusetts,* 97 U. S. 25; *Fertilizing Co.* v. *Hyde Park, ibid.* 659; *Stone* v. *Mississippi,* 101 U. S. 814, and *Butchers Union Co.* v. *Crescent City Co.,* 111 U. S. 746; also see *Murray* v. *Charleston,* 96 U. S. 432.

[7] 5 How. (U. S.) 504 (1846).

[8] 12 Wheat. (U. S.) 419 (1827).

that that power is exclusive, and this Taney did in the very face of Marshall's dictum to the contrary. Finally, in this and in other opinions and decisions Taney diluted Marshall's doctrine of the paramountcy of national power within the sphere of its competence with the doctrine of the reserved sovereignty of the states, whereby he meant not merely that the states have left to them certain powers in consequence of their not being granted to the national government, which is all that the Tenth Amendment says, but that the states had an area of power which was positively reserved to them and which therefore no legitimate exercise of federal power could ever invade.[9]

But what was happening on the Supreme Bench was the index of what was happening also in the state judiciaries, where popular sovereignty and states' rights united to force a recognition of the plenitude of legislative power. One illustration was the case of *Mobile* v. *Yuille*,[10] in which the question was the power of the legislature to authorize a municipality to regulate the weight and price of bread. The attorney for defendant in error was the reporter of *Ex parte Dorsey*,[10a] who, upon the basis particularly of Justice Ormond's opinion in that [earlier] case, now "strenuously contended" "that no such power exists because [as he contends] it would interfere with the right of a citizen to pursue his lawful trade or calling in the mode his judgment might dictate," and also because such by-laws, being in restraint of trade, are void under the common law. But, rejoined Ormond, J., sweeping aside defendant's interpretation of *Ex parte Dorsey*, "in this case the power is expressly given by the statute to do the act complained of," wherefore what the common law ordains is not in point. For the rest,

> the legislature having full power to pass such laws as is [sic] deemed necessary for the public good, their acts cannot be impeached on the ground that they are unwise or not in accordance with just and enlightened views of political economy, as understood at the present day . . . arguments against their policy must be addressed to the legislative departments of government.

Mobile v. *Yuille*, however, is a comparatively late case, and more than a decade earlier, some years even before Taney had become

[9] See particularly the Chief Justice's opinions in *Groves* v. *Slaughter*, 15 Pet. (U. S.) 449, and *Pollard* v. *Hagan's Lessee*, 3 How. (U. S.) 212.

[10] 3 Ala. 137 (1841). See also *State* v. *Maxey*, 1 McMul. (S. C.) 501 (1837).

[10a] 7 Porter (Ala.) 293.

Chief Justice, a similar doctrine was struggling for recognition in the New York courts, whose dilemma, comprising as it did the tradition of judicial review created by Kent on the one hand, and the victorious principles of Jacksonian Democracy on the other, if it was rather painful, was also of the greatest possible importance in connection with the history of due process of law.[11] . . . [T]he situation that confronted the New York courts was this: the power of eminent domain is rather the most invidious branch of governmental authority, even when exercised by the state directly. Within a very few years, however, hundreds and hundreds of private corporations organized for the business of transportation had been endowed by the state with this power. Kent's doctrine of consequential damages and the resultant blending, at their outer edges, of the police power and that of eminent domain, had already gone by the board in 1827 in the cases of *Vanderbilt* v. *Adams*[12] and *Stuyvesant* v. *New York*.[13] Kent's other doctrine, that the power of eminent domain is exercisable for a public purpose only, that is to say, for what the courts may regard as a public purpose, was also in grave danger of extinction, being first rested, by Chancellor Walworth, upon the untenable basis of the Obligation of Contracts clause of the federal Constitution[14] and then transferred again to its original position upon the doctrine of "natural rights" and the "spirit of the constitution."[15] But the doctrine of natural rights no longer sufficed either. What, then, was to be done? In *Taylor* v. *Porter*[16] an act

[11] For an excellent illustration of the difficulty created by the dilemma referred to, read Justice Nelson's opinion in *People* v. *Morris*, 13 Wend. (N. Y.) 329 (1835).

[12] 7 Cowen (N. Y.) 349.

[13] *Ibid.* 585. For the derivation of the doctrine of these cases from the common law, see 12 Mass. 220 (1815) and 1 Pick. (Mass.) 417 (1823), decisions which Kent pronounces "erroneous." 2 *Comm.* 339, note c. See also in condemnation of the same doctrine, Story, J., in his dissent in the Charles River Bridge Case, 11 Pet. (U. S.) 638, 641. See also *Baker* v. *Boston,* 12 Pick. (Mass.) 184 (1831), in which the doctrine of 7 Cow. (N. Y.) 349 and 585 is applied.

[14] *Beekman* v. *Saratoga,* etc. R. R., 3 Paige (N. Y.) 45 (1831).

[15] Albany Street Matter, 11 Wend. (N. Y.) 149 (1834); *Bloodgood* v. *Mohawk,* etc. R. R., 18 Wend. (N. Y.) 1 (1837).

[16] Hill (N. Y.) 140; preceded, in 1839, by the *Matter of John and Cherry Sts.,* 19 Wend. (N. Y.) 676. Besides the fact that the line of argument is more clearly cut in *Taylor* v. *Porter,* citation also makes it the more important case by far. Cf. *Harvey* v. *Thomas,* 10 Watts (Pa.) 63, and the *Pacopson Rd. Case,* 16 Pa. St. 15 (1851).

authorizing a private road under the eminent domain power was under review. The act was overturned; and Bronson, J., speaking for the majority of the court, annexed the doctrine of natural rights and of limitations inherent to legislative power to the written constitution by casting around that doctrine the phrase "law of the land" and the phrase "due process of law," which had also since 1821 been a part of the New York constitution.

Justice Bronson's line of argument is most instructive. Setting out with the proposition that the people alone are absolutely sovereign, he follows it up with the assertion that the legislature can exercise only such powers as have been delegated it, which is evidently either a restatement of the doctrine of limitations inherent to legislative power or an assertion that a state constitution, like the federal Constitution, is a grant of powers. Quotations from Story's opinion in *Wilkinson* v. *Leland*[17] make it evident that it is the former, as does also the invocation of the social compact at this point. But it is a phrase of the written constitution that Bronson, J., is in particular search of. . . . "[L]aw of the land" is asserted to mean that before a man can be deprived of his property "it must be ascertained judicially that he has forfeited his privileges, or that someone else has a superior title to the property he possesses." But if there is doubt as to the meaning of the phrase "law of the land," at least there can be none as to that of "due process of law" of the same article of the constitution; for this means nothing "less than a proceeding or suit instituted and conducted according to prescribed forms and solemnities for ascertaining guilt or determining the title to property." One exception to this definition is indeed furnished by the case of an exercise of the power of eminent domain, when due process of law means due compensation. The eminent domain power, however, can be exercised only for a public purpose. But who is to ascertain whether a given purpose is a public one or not? Justice Bronson's evident assumption—and it is only assumption—is that it is the courts, as preliminary to their task of determining whether due process of law has been observed. Nelson, J., dissented; at the same time, however, he accepted the general principle of the decision, but confessed that he was uncertain as to what grounds it rested upon.

Taylor v. *Porter* . . . was followed in 1849 by *White* v. *White*,[18]

[17] 2 Pet. (U. S.) 657 (1829).

[18] 5 Barb. (N. Y.) 474.

in which a general statute was pronounced void. . . . The statute in question removed the disability of married women under the common law in the control of their property. As an exercise of legislative power it was closely analogous to the statutes enacted early in our national history abolishing the right of primogeniture, statutes which, as we have seen, received enforcement even against rights of succession vested at the time of their passage. But the virus of natural law had spread since those days. In the first case, *Holmes* v. *Holmes*,[19] in which the Married Women's Act is challenged successfully, the decision was put upon the Obligation of Contract clause of the federal Constitution. But Mason, J., who decided *White* v. *White*, was very justifiably skeptical of the reasoning by which this result was attained. He accordingly decided to avail himself of the Due Process of Law clause and the doctrine of natural rights. . . . Eventually this decision also was superseded by decisions upholding the Married Women's Act but confining its operation to property acquired subsequently to the passage of the act. The cases in question were those of *Perkins* v. *Cottrell*[20] and *Westervelt* v. *Gregg*,[21] in the former of which the decision was based upon the doctrine of vested rights, the Obligation of Contracts clause of the federal Constitution, and the "spirit of the constitution which declares" that no person shall be deprived of life, liberty or property without due process of law; and in the latter, explicitly upon the Due Process of Law clause: "such an act as the legislature may, in the uncontrolled exercise of its power, see fit to pass, is in no sense," said the court, "the due process of law designated by the constitution." Similar acts were similarly construed in other states, but generally upon the ground that their prospective operation had been plainly intended by the legislature itself.[22]

[19] 4 Barb. (N. Y.) 295.

[20] 15 Barb. (N. Y.) 446 (1851).

[21] 12 N. Y. 209 (1854). See also the case of *Powers* v. *Bergen*, 6 N. Y. 358, in which use is made of the Law of the Land clause of the Constitution to overturn a special act of legislation.

[22] Cf. 24 Ala. 386 (1854); 43 Ill. 52 (1857); 28 N.J.L. 219 (1860); 20 Oh. St. 128; with 34 Me. 148 (1852), and 8 Fla. 107 (1858); in the latter two cases the doctrine of vested rights plays its part.

II.

And thus by adopting the . . . doctrine of "law of the land" . . . the New York courts, in 1843, rescued from disuse the doctrine of public purpose in connection with the power of eminent domain, and ten years later succeeded in drawing the teeth of the Married Women's Property Act. The real tussle with the reforming tendencies of the period was, however, yet to come. During the decade 1846 to 1856 no fewer than sixteen states passed anti-liquor laws of a more or less drastic character. Never since the doctrine of vested rights had been formulated had such reprehensible legislation, from the standpoint of that doctrine, been enrolled upon the statute books. How was it to be withstood? Some of the earlier of these laws took the form of local option measures, and to meet these a new dogma of constitutional law, drawn originally from John Locke's Second Treatise on Civil Government, was invented, namely, the doctrine that the legislature cannot delegate its power,—an utterly absurd doctrine, at least in this application of it, and one which was in singular contradiction both with legislative practice anterior to 1846, and with judicial decision.[23] Furthermore, as was immediately shown, it was generally an utterly futile doctrine; for the easy retort of the reforming legislatures was state-wide prohibition.

[23] The courts to whose fertility of mind is due this doctrine were those of Delaware and Pennsylvania. See *Rice* v. *Foster,* 4 Harr. (Del.) 479 (1847), and *Parker* v. *Commonwealth,* 6 Pa. St. 507 (1847). The doctrine is refuted in *People* v. *Reynolds,* 10 Gilman (Ill.) (1848), and in *Bull et al.* v. *Read,* 13 Gratt. (Va.) 78 (1855). Also in *Johnson* v. *Rich,* 9 Barb. (N. Y.) 680 (1848), with which however cf. *Barto* v. *Himrod,* 8 N. Y. 483. For the contradictory position of the Delaware and Pennsylvania courts cf. *Rice* v. *Foster* with 3 Harr. (Del.) 335 and 4 Harr. (Del.) 82; and *Parker* v. *Commonwealth* with 8 Barr (Pa.) 391 and 10 Barr (Pa.) 214. The Pennsylvania court subsequently abandoned the dogma, in connection with local option legislation, in Locke's Appeal, 72 Pa. St. 491. For a very early Pennsylvania case in which the doctrine was offered to the court but ignored, see 2 Yeates (Pa.) 493 (1799); a later Massachusetts case in which the same idea was brought forward but specifically repelled by the court, is that of *Wales* v. *Belcher,* 3 Pick. (Mass.) 508 (1827). The immediate responsibility for this absurdity must fall to Gibson, C. J., in which connection see 5 W. & S. (Pa.) 281 (1843). The passage from Locke's work is sec. 141. On the history of the referendum, see E. P. Oberholtzer, *Referendum in America.*

Such a law was enacted by the New York legislature in 1855. It forbade all owners of intoxicating liquors to sell them under any conditions save for medicinal purposes and forbade them further to store such liquors when not designed for sale in any place but a dwelling house, made the violation of these prohibitions a misdemeanor, and denounced the offending liquors as nuisances and ordained their destruction by summary process. In the great case of *Wynehamer* v. *State of New York,*[24] which comprises a new starting point in the history of due process of law, this act was overturned, the essential ground of the decision being that the harsh operation of the statute upon liquors in existence at the time of its going into effect comprised an act of destruction not within the power of government to perform, *"even by the forms which belong to due process of law."*[25] The significance of this statement of the matter is this: in every previous case of due process of law the court had had its opportunity in treating a civil enactment as, in certain applications, a bill of pains and penalties. In *Wynehamer* v. *State of New York,* however, the court was confronted with a frankly penal statute which provided a procedure, for the most part unexceptionable, for its enforcement. That statute was none the less overturned under the Due Process of Law clause, which was thereby plainly made to prohibit, regardless of the matter of procedure, a certain kind and degree of exertion of legislative power altogether. The result is obvious, even if somewhat startling, and it serves to bring into strong light once more the dependence of the derived notion of due process of law upon extra-constitutional principles; for it is nothing less than the elimination of the very phrase under construction from the constitutional clause in which it occurs. The main proposition of the decision in the Wynehamer case is that the legislature cannot destroy by any method whatever what by previous law was property. But why not? To all intents and purposes the answer of the court is simply that "no person shall be deprived of life, liberty or property."

But how can the elimination of the phrase "due process of law" from the constitutional clause be regarded as furnishing a new starting point in the history of the development of that clause?

[24] 13 N. Y. 378 (1856).

[25] A. S. Johnson, J., 420: "The legislature cannot make the mere existence of the rights secured the occasion of depriving a person of them even by the forms which belong to 'due process of law.' "

The answer is that from now on the attention of the courts is drawn to the other words of the clause; more particularly to the words "liberty" and "property" and the word "deprive." Indeed the attention is seen to shift to these terms on this very occasion, in the case of the dissenting opinion of T. A. Johnson, J., who bases his argument against the decision partly upon his construction of the word "deprived" and partly upon a reductio ad absurdum involving the term "liberty." The word "deprive," he contends, is used in the constitutional clause,

> in its ordinary and popular sense, and relates simply to divesting of, forfeiting, alienating, taking away property. It applies to property in the same sense that it does to life and liberty and no other. . . . When a person is deprived of his property by due process of law the thing itself . . . with the legal title is taken away. . . . The act itself does indeed . . . directly provide for depriving the owner of his property by forfeiture and destruction, but that is where it is kept for an unlawful purpose and after trial and judgment. That provision has no bearing upon the question under consideration. When property is taken from the owner and destroyed, he is deprived of it by virtue of the act, not before. It might be urged with precisely the same pertinency and force, that a statute which prohibits certain vicious actions and declares them criminal deprives persons of their liberty and is therefore in derogation of the constitution.

Undoubtedly Johnson, J., reveals a grave danger attending the decision he is criticizing. For the moment the danger was not practically serious on account of the conservative view taken by the court of "property," which is defined by implication as the valuable use of the thing possessed. But let "property" come to mean—as indeed it does in this very case with one or two of the judges—any particular item of such right, for example, the right of sale; let "liberty" be made to signify the rights which one enjoys in the community under the standing law, and the decision in this case, together with the distinction between regulation and destruction upon which it is based, becomes immediately untenable and a new solution of the eternal issue between legislative sovereignty and private rights at once imperative. But what line is this solution to take? Must outright choice be made between, on the one hand, allowing the legislature to destroy or even to regulate at discretion or, on the other hand, absolutely tying the hands of the legislature? . . . Or is there a midway course? By construing the word "deprive," Johnson J., pointed the way, though no doubt unintentionally, to such a midway course and so provided an escape from the difficulty which it was his purpose merely to expose.

But at another point also is the Wynehamer decision a starting point. As we have just seen, the decision rests upon an alleged disstinction between regulation and destruction: but are regulation and destruction two such different things, or is the latter often merely consequential upon the former? Common sense inclines to the latter view. Yet admit this view and what becomes of Marshall's famous maxim, that "questions of power do not depend upon the degree to which it is exercised"? In this connection a remark of Comstock, J., becomes of greatest significance in view of modern developments. "We," he contends, "must be allowed to know what is known by all persons of common intelligence, that intoxicating liquors are produced for sale and consumption as a beverage. . . ." Here is the first assertion of that doctrine of "judicial cognizance" which lies at the very basis of the modern flexible idea of "due process of law."[26] Questions of power do to-day emphatically depend upon the degree to which it is exercised, and this because the courts are able to take cognizance of facts which make different degrees of power harmonious with the "due process of law" requirement in different cases.

The last feature of the Wynehamer decision that I desire to call attention to is the fact that by it the New York Court of Appeals finally dismisses the doctrine of natural rights from the firing line as a defender of property. The ungracious task falls to Comstock, J., whose opinion heads the others, and he performs it with great considerateness. He says:

It has been urged upon us that the power of the legislature is restricted not only by the express provisions of the written constitution but by limitations implied from the nature and form of our government; that aside from all special restrictions the right to enact such laws is not among the delegated powers of the legislature, and

[26] See the *Lochner* case, 198 U. S. 45 (1905); also *In re Jacobs,* 98 N. Y. 98 (1885). Cf. *Powell* v. *Pennsylvania,* 127 U. S. 678 (1887).

that the act in question is void as against the fundamental principles of liberty and against common reason and natural rights.

Moreover, he admits that "high authority has been cited" for these views, and himself quotes at length from Justice Chase's opinion in *Calder* v. *Bull*. . . . He then proceeds to furnish us with his own point of view in the following words:

I entertain no doubt that, aside from the special limitations of the constitution, the legislature cannot exercise powers which are in their nature essentially judicial or executive. These are by the constitution distributed to the other departments of the government. It is only 'legislative power' which is vested in the Senate and Assembly. But where the constitution is silent and there is no clear usurpation of the powers distributed to the other departments, I think there would be great difficulty and great danger in attempting to define the limits of this power. Chief Justice Marshall said [*Fletcher* v. *Peck*]: 'how far the power of giving the law may involve every other power in cases where the constitution is silent never has been and perhaps never can be definitely stated.' That very eminent judge felt the difficulty; but the danger was less apparent then than it is now when theories, alleged to be founded in natural reason and inalienable rights, but subversive of the just and necessary powers of government attract the belief of considerable classes of men, and when too much reverence for government and law is certainly among the least of the perils to which our institutions are exposed. I am reluctant to enter upon this field of inquiry, satisfied as I am that no rule can be laid down in terms which may not contain the germs of great mischief to society, by giving to private opinion and speculation a license to oppose themselves to the just and legitimate powers of government. Nor is it necessary to push our inquiries in the direction indicated. There is no process of reasoning by which it can be demonstrated that the 'act for the prevention of intemperance, pauperism and crime,' is void upon principles and theories outside the constitution, which will not also and by an easier deduction, bring it in direct conflict with the constitution itself.

This surely is a remarkable passage betwixt the Scylla and Charybdis of tweedle-dee and tweedle-dum. What it all comes to is this: Comstock, J., dismayed by the abolitionists' quoting the same scripture to their purpose, refuses to annex the doctrine of natural rights to the written constitution, save only as a protection of property rights, that is to say, of vested rights; and generally speaking, this is always the significance of the doctrine of due process of law.

III.

But now let us inquire how the doctrine of the Wynehamer decision accorded with the general constitutional law of the period. Within a year or two either side of the New York case similar cases involving similar questions arose in an even dozen states, and in all these states, save one, laws very closely analogous to the New York statute, or indeed sometimes more drastic in their provisions than that statute, were sustained. With reference to these cases two facts of foremost importance immediately present themselves. The first is that in only one case, and that occurring subsequently to the New York decision, is any argument against the body of the statutes under review based upon the Due Process of Law, or Law of the Land clauses of the constitution involved. The second is that the decisions, save in two or three instances, are based upon views of the police power which leave the definition of that power essentially to legislative discretion. Both these facts demand illustration from the cases themselves.

In *State* v. *Noyes,*[27] a New Hampshire case, a municipal ordinance pronouncing bowling alleys a nuisance and discontinuing those in existence was under review. The constitutional question raised is precisely the same as that raised by the provision of the New York statute which pronounced existing stocks of liquors nuisances. The attorney for Noyes urged that the question of what is a nuisance is a question of law and therefore for the courts. But, said the court, we have the law before us.

> The legislature do not exceed their legitimate authority when they make a change of laws and constitute that an offense which was not such before. . . . There may be an apparent unfitness sometimes in such legislation, but its validity has never been questioned.

In all the other cases the statutes involved were anti-liquor enactments, the arguments against which were based either—though but timidly on account of the attitude of the United States Supreme

[27] 10 Foster (N. H.) 279 (1855). See also *ibid.* 286, also 289.

Court—on the Commerce clause of the federal Constitution or on the doctrine of natural rights. The latter argument was used in *Beebe* v. *State,*[28] an Indiana case, and the statute was overturned, Perkins, J., holding in a remarkable opinion that the right to manufacture, the right to sell, and the right to drink, spirituous liquors were inalienable rights. This decision, however, accompanied as it was by a well-argued dissent, marked the exception to the rule. In *Lincoln* v. *Smith,*[29] a Vermont case, a similar line of argument was taken by attorneys but was decisively rejected by the court. "Every member of society," runs the first article of the Vermont Bill of Rights, "hath a right to be protected in the enjoyment of life, liberty and property." But said the court in comment, "We do not well see how it can be claimed that the act in question is a violation" of this article, "unless it be assumed that the law is invalid, which is the very thing in question." Natural rights, the court continues, are subject to the civil law, and quotes Blackstone to the effect that certain rights are "absolute and inherent" and "without any control or limitation save only by the laws of the land." But the statute under review is law of the land unless invalid. The court proceeds to point out,

The right to life, liberty, and property are all placed in the same connection; and certainly the two former are as sacred as the latter; although they have not seemed at all times to have called out the same legal acumen in their behalf as the latter.

Of similar purport is the decision of the Supreme Court of Illinois in *Goddard* v. *Jacksonville.*[30] Natural rights are surrendered or modified upon entering into the social compact. This surrender and modification, such as are indispensable to good government and the wellbeing of society, are comprehended under the police power of the government. "The framers of Magna Carta and of the constitutions of the United States and of the states never intended to modify, abridge, or destroy the police powers of government. They only prohibited its exercise by ex post facto laws and regulated the mode of trial for offenses." Finally, the court argues, the police power must be recognized as a developing power, a power which

[28] 6 Ind. 501 (1855).
[29] 27 Vt. 328 (1854).
[30] 15 Ill. 589 (1854).

unfolds with the increasing complexity of society and the advance of social needs. These decisions belong to the years 1854 and 1855. That of *State* v. *Gallagher,*[31] however, in which the Michigan Supreme Court defines legislative power even more broadly if possible, was rendered in 1856 and some weeks after the Wynehamer decision. The attorneys for Gallagher based their argument both upon the doctrine of natural rights and the derived doctrine, that the legislature has only "legislative power," of which it is therefore for the court to prescribe the limits. The court rejects both arguments. The opinion runs:

The whole sovereignty of the people is conferred upon the different departments of government; what the judiciary and executive have not would seem from necessity to have been granted to the other; and that other must possess all the powers of a sovereign state except such as are withheld by the state constitution and such as are conceded to the general government. In that grant there are many powers that are not strictly legislative and which are essential to administrative government. If this department is limited as a law-making power, what is the limitation upon the exercise of those powers strictly administrative? . . . It must be conceded there is none.

But let us consider more particularly the attitude revealed by the courts in these decisions toward due process of law. A good illustrative case anterior to the Wynehamer decision is the Massachusetts case of *Fisher* v. *McGirr.*[32] Said Shaw, C. J., in his decision:

We have no doubt that it is competent for the legislature to declare the possession of certain articles of property, either absolutely or when held in particular places and under particular circumstances, to be unlawful because they would be injurious, dangerous, and noxious; and by due process of law, by proceedings in rem, to provide both for the abatement of the nuisance and the punishment of the offender, by the seizure and confiscation of the property, by the removal, sale or destruction of the noxious article.

Still more in point, however is the language of the opinions in *State* v. *Paul*[33] and *State* v. *Keeran,*[34] which the Rhode Island Supreme

[31] 4 Gibbs (Mich.) 244 (1856). See also 3 Gibbs (Mich.) 330 (1854).
[32] 1 Gray (Mass.) 1 (1854).
[33] 5 R. I. 185 (1858).
[34] *Ibid.* 497. See also 3 R. I. 64 (1854); also *ibid.* 289.

Court decided with the Wynehamer decision before it and indeed with particular animadversion to that decision. With reference to attorney's argument based upon the derived view of the Law of the Land clause, the court said:

It is obvious that the objection confounds the power of the assembly to create and define an offense with the rights of the accused to trial by jury and due process of law . . . before he can be convicted of it.

Later the court enters protest against—

the loose habit of taking constitutional clauses, which from their history and obvious purpose have a well defined meaning, away from all their natural connections, and by drawing remote inferences from them, of pressing them into the service of any constitutional objection which the ingenuity or fancy of the objector may contrive or suggest,—

a practice which has gone far, it thinks, to bring constitutional questions into "jest and ridicule." But surely, it continues,

if any clause in the constitution has a definite meaning which should exclude all vagaries which render courts the tyrants of the constitution, this clause [law of the land] . . . can claim to have [it] both from its history and long received interpretation.

It is urged that it limits the legislature in regulating the vendability of property.

Pushed to its necessary conclusions the argument goes to the extent, that once make out that anything real or personal is property, as everything in a general sense is, and legislation as to its use and vendability . . . must stop at the precise point at which it stood when the thing first came within the protection of this clause of the constitution.

A better reasoned or more conclusive refutation of the derived doctrine of due process of law, both from the standpoint of logic and history, could not well be asked for.

Thus the Wynehamer decision found no place in the constitutional law that was generally recognized throughout the United States in the year 1856. Neither had it been foreshadowed by decisions in similar cases in other States, nor was it subsequently accepted in such cases. Also it met locally an immense amount of hostile criticism, both lay and professional. Altogether it must be considered an adversity, for the time being, to the derived doctrine of due process of law. All that was needed apparently to dispose of that doctrine at once and for all time was another such Pyrrhic victory: nor was such event long impending.

Just as the Court of Appeals of New York had persuaded itself that it must intervene to save the proprietors of spirituous liquors from the too harsh hand of legislative wrath, so also the Supreme Court of the United States had convinced itself that "the peace and harmony of the country" was to be preserved only by its "settling by judicial decision" the question of slavery in the territories adversely to the power of the National Legislature. It came about, therefore, that exactly a twelvemonth after the Wynehamer decision, Taney, C. J., read his famous opinion in *Scott v. Sandford,*[35] pronouncing the Missouri Compromise to have been void under the Due Process of Law clause of the Fifth Amendment of the United States Constitution. His language is as follows:

> An act of Congress which deprives a citizen of the United States of his liberty or property merely because he came himself or brought his property into a particular territory of the United States and who had committed no offense against the laws could hardly be dignified with the name of due process of law.

The extraordinary character of this pronouncement is shown by two circumstances: first, the fact that counsel at the bar did not allude in the remotest way to any such restriction upon Congressional power; and secondly, by the fact that at this point the Chief Justice carries with him only two of his associates, Grier and Wayne, both of whom present but short opinions accepting perfunctorily the Chief Justice's line of argument. Daniel, Campbell, and Catron, JJ., also held the Missouri Compromise to have been unconstitutional but upon far different grounds, Catron availing himself of the doctrine of the equality of the states, and Campbell and Daniel—and particularly the former—of Calhoun's doctrine of state sovereignty and the correlative doctrine that Congress is but

[35] 19 How. (U. S.) 393 (1857).

the agent of the states in the exercise of its delegated powers. Furthermore, at no other point is Justice Curtis' dissent more convincing than in his refutation of this use of the term "due process of law." Already two years earlier Curtis, J., speaking for the court in *Murray* v. *Hoboken Land and Improvement Co.*,[36] had ruled that legal process is not necessarily due process, and that the due process required by the Fifth Amendment means the processes of the common and statute law as these stood at the time of the adoption of the Constitution, that Congress in providing procedure for the enforcement of its acts must provide the procedure that is due. But no question of procedure was at issue in connection with the Missouri Compromise. How then could the Fifth Amendment be invoked? If the Missouri Compromise did indeed comprise one of a class of legislative enactments proscribed by the Fifth Amendment, what then, inquired Curtis, J., was to be said of the Ordinance of 1787, which Virginia and other states had ratified notwithstanding the presence of similar clauses within their constitutions? What again was to be said upon that hypothesis of the act of Virginia herself passed in 1778, which prohibited the further importation of slaves? What was to be said of numerous litigations in which this and analogous law had been upheld and enforced by the Courts of Maryland and Virginia against their own citizens who had purchased slaves abroad, and that without anyone's thinking to question the validity of such laws upon the ground that they were not law of the land or due process of law?[37] What was to be said of the Act of Congress of 1808 prohibiting the slave trade, and the assumption

[36] 18 How. (U. S.) 272 (1855). See also Justice Curtis' opinion in *Greene* v. *Briggs*, 1 Curt. (U. S.) 311. See also Johnson, J., in *Bank of Columbia* v. *Okely*, 4 Wheat. (U. S.) 235 (1819): The words "law of the land" (of the Maryland constitution) "were intended to secure the individual from the arbitrary exercise of the powers of government, unrestrained by the established principles of private rights and distributive justice." The purport of this vague dictum has been much abused by late writers and judges: see, for example, Cooley, *Const. Lim.* 355, where it is praised as a "terse" and "accurate" statement. *Bank of Columbia* v. *Okely* involved only questions of procedure, and procedure is all that Johnson, J., had in mind, as is shown by his remark shortly afterward: "the forms of administering justice and the duties and powers of courts . . . must ever be subject to legislative will." 4 Wheat. (U. S.) 245.

[37] Citing 5 Call (Va.) 425; 1 Leigh (Va.) 172; and 5 Harr. & J. (Md.) 107. See *Murray* v. *McCarty*, 2 Munf. (Va.) 393 (1811), applying and enforcing the act of 1792, similar in purport to that of 1778.

of the Constitution that Congress would have that power without its being specifically bestowed, but simply as an item of its power to regulate commerce? What, again, was to be said of the Embargo Act, if the scope of Congressional authority to legislate within the limits of powers granted it was restricted by the Fifth Amendment; and what, finally, was to be said of a recent decision of the Supreme Court itself upholding in principle at least the claim of power represented by the Embargo Act?[38] Such were some of the questions which Curtis, J., put, to which obviously the Chief Justice's easy assumption of the point to be proved afforded no answer at all.

IV.

With Chief Justice Taney's decision in the *Dred Scott* case the story of Due Process of Law anterior to the Fourteenth Amendment comes practically to a close. Proceeding to gather up our results, we discover at once that the most conspicuous fact about our constitutional law as it stood on the eve of the Civil War was the practical approximation of the police power of the states to the sovereignty of the state legislatures within their respective constitutions, the purpose of which constitutions was universally held to be not to grant power but to organize and limit powers which were otherwise plenary.[39] But while this was the general rule, due in part to the temporary eclipse of the judiciary and in part to the dominance of the notion of States Rights, yet there survived a number of restrictive principles, now in a state of suspended animation, so to speak, but easily susceptible of resuscitation. And one of these was the doctrine of "due process of law," whose title to continued vitality may be put upon the following grounds: First, the availability imparted to the Due Process of Law clause by the decision in *Murray* v. *Hoboken Land and Improvement Co.*, as a constitutional buffer in connection with summary and administrative proceedings, a function hitherto subserved almost entirely by the Trial by Jury clause; secondly, the steady extension, even among courts the most attached to the doctrine of legislative sovereignty, of the notion of "law of the land" and "due process of law" as equivalent to "general law" and as

[38] *United States* v. *Marigold,* 9 How. (U. S.) 560.

[39] See particularly Redfield, C. J., in *Thorpe* v. *Rutland,* etc. *R. R. Co.,* 27 Vt. 140 (1854).

therefore inhibiting "special legislation";[40] thirdly, the equivalence established in *Taylor* v. *Porter* between "due process of law" and "due compensation" in questions of eminent domain; fourthly, the growing practice, for example, on the part of critics of the *Dred Scott* decision, to shift construction from the phrase "due process of law," to the terms "liberty" and "property" of the constitutional clause;[41] fifthly, the tendency of these terms, as shown in Ormond, J.'s opinion in the *Dorsey* case and in Hubbard, J.'s opinion in the *Wynehamer* case, to take on a progressively broader signification;[42] sixthly, the fact that the Massachusetts Supreme Court, owing to the formula by which power is vested by the Massachusetts constitution in the legislature to pass "all manner of wholesome and reasonable" laws, had never ceased to describe the police power, even when according it the broadest possible field of operation, as a power of "reasonable" legislation;[43] seventhly, the fact that the courts of New York had never surrendered the notion of legislative power as inherently limited;[44] eighthly, the fact that no court had *eo nomine* cast overboard the doctrine of vested rights;[45] ninthly, the fact that all courts generally described the police power, though without any apparent intention as yet of making such description a judicially enforceable limitation, in terms of its historical applications;[46] tenthly, and lastly, the fact that similarly the police power was often grounded upon the common-law maxim *sic utere tuo ut alienum non laedas*,[47] a definition which like the historical definition bore with it the possible implication that the police power was a peculiar kind of power, exercisable constitutionally only for peculiar ends.

[40] See particularly Coulter, J., in *Ervine's* Appeal, 16 Pa. St. 263 (1851); and Christiancy, J., in *Sears* v. *Cottrell,* 5 Mich. 251 (1858).

[41] See the Republican Platform of 1860, paragraph 8.

[42] See a remark of the court in *Board of Excise* v. *Barrie,* 34 N. Y. 657 (1866), on "inconsiderate dicta" in the Wynehamer decision.

[43] See Massachusetts Constitution, Pt. II, Ch. I, Art. IV; Shaw, C. J., in *Commonwealth* v. *Alger,* 7 Cush. (Mass.) 53 (1851); *State* v. *Gurney,* 37 Me. 156 (1853).

[44] See particularly *Sill* v. *Corning,* 15 N. Y. 297 (1857), and *People* v. *Draper, ibid.* 532.

[45] See, for example, Miller, J., in *Bartemeyer* v. *Iowa,* 18 Wall. (U. S.) 129 (1874).

[46] See *Lincoln* v. *Smith, Goddard* v. *Jacksonville,* supra.

[47] *Thorpe* v. *Rutland,* etc. *R. R. Co., Commonwealth* v. *Alger,* supra, following 2 Kent, *Comm.* 340.

But now in this enumeration we have included many, if not all, of the essential elements of the modern flexible doctrine of due process of law. True, the proper admixture of these elements had not as yet in 1860 been suggested, but that it would be in the course of time, with the legislatures pressing upon the courts from one side and private interests from the other, who could doubt?

★ IV ★

The Supreme Court and the Fourteenth Amendment*

The institutional character of the law rests, partly upon the conception of precedent as binding, but much more largely—and it may be added, much more securely—upon the fact that views of policy themselves tend to become institutional in social and political theories.

It was formerly the wont of legal writers to regard court decisions in much the same way as the mathematician regards the x of an algebraic equation: given the facts of the case and the existing law, the outcome was inevitable. This unhistorical standpoint has now been largely abandoned. Not only is it admitted that judges in finding the law act not as automata, as mere adding machines, but creatively, but also that the considerations which determine their decisions, far from resting exclusively upon a narrowly syllogistic basis, often repose very immediately upon concrete and vital notions of what is desirable and useful. "The very considerations," says Holmes in his *Common Law,* "which judges most rarely mention and always with an apology, are the secret root from which the law draws all the juices of life. I mean, of course, considerations of what is expedient to the community concerned. Every important principle which is developed by litigation is in fact and at bottom the result of more or less definitely understood views of public

* 7 *Michigan Law Review* (June, 1909), 643.

policy; most generally, to be sure, under our practice and traditions, the unconscious result of instinctive preferences and inarticulate convictions, but none the less, traceable to views of public policy in the last analysis."

Holmes has in mind of course the common law, but his argument is equally to the point in the study of our American constitutional law. A great and growing part of this law is, like the common law, judge made. It is true that constitutional limitations are generally referred to some clause or other of the written Constitution. But this after all is a circumstance of which too much may be made very easily. Given a sufficient hardihood of purpose at the rack of exegesis, and any document, no matter what its fortitude, will eventually give forth the meaning required of it. Nor does this necessarily mean that the law is a nose of wax, to be moulded according to the caprice of the hour. What it does mean is that the institutional character of the law rests, partly upon the conception of precedent as binding, but much more largely—and it may be added, much more securely—upon the fact that views of policy themselves tend to become institutional in social and political theories.

The police power we may define for our purposes as that power of government under the control of which private rights fall. From the time of the decision in *Barron* v. *Baltimore* (7 Pet. 243), in which the Supreme Court of the United States, after some vacillation, finally decided that the first eight amendments to the Constitution bind only the Federal Government, down to the adoption of the Fourteenth Amendment in 1867, it was generally admitted that this ample realm of governmental competence belonged to the States, limited only by Congressional regulation of interstate and foreign commerce, and by the necessity of not impairing the obligation of contracts. The Fourteenth Amendment however is directed explicitly to the States. "No *State* shall make or enforce any law which shall abridge the privileges or immunities of citizens of the United States; nor shall any *State* deprive any person of life, liberty, or property without due process of law; nor deny to any person within its jurisdiction the equal protection of the laws." Such is the language of the first section of the Fourteenth Amendment. There can be no kind of doubt that its authors designed that, at the very least, it should make the first eight amendments binding upon the States as well as the Federal Government and that it should be susceptible of enforcement both by the Federal Courts and by Congress. But now to give such scope to the Fourteenth Amendment obviously meant to bid farewell to the old time federal balance which before the war had seemed the very essence of our constitutional system. It meant, in the language of contemporary protest "the institution of a solid sovereignty instead of a government of limited power," "the transfer of municipal control of the State governments over their internal affairs into the hands of Congress," the subordination of the "State judiciaries to Federal supervision and control," the annihilation of the "independence and sovereignty of the State Courts in the administration of State laws"—in short, "a deep and revolutionary change in the organic law and genesis of the government." But as often happens, the large issue thus raised was obscured by numerous lesser ones. Popular attention was riveted upon the second, third and fourth sections of the Fourteenth Amendment, and thus what was potentially a revolution in our constitutional system was effected entirely incidentally.[1]

Nor did this vast change seem likely to remain long a mere possibility. The Fourteenth Amendment authorizes Congress to enforce its provisions by appropriate legislation. In pursuance of what it deemed to be the authority thus bestowed, Congress in May, 1870, passed the so-called Enforcement Act, which enacted severe penalties not only against state officers and agents, but also against any *person* within the States who should under the color of any statute, ordinance, regulation, or custom deprive any other person of his civil rights and civil equality. This act was followed a year later by the Ku Klux Act which was of the same general purport but more stringent in its provisions and somewhat wider in its pretensions. Finally in 1875 Congress passed the Civil Rights Act which decreed the "equal enjoyment of the accommodations . . . of inns, public conveyances . . . theatres, and other places of public amusement . . . to citizens of every race and color regardless of any previous condition of servitude," and imposed penalties upon all persons violating these provisions. The theory of these enactments comprises three points: 1. that the rights to which citizens of the United States are entitled by the Fourteenth Amendment comprehend all the rights which the ordinary person enjoys in his community; 2nd, that a denial of the equal protection of the law may

[1] See Flack, *Adoption of the Fourteenth Amendment,* Chs. II and III.

be effected as much by acts of omission on the part of a State and its functionaries as by acts of commission; and that therefore, 3rdly, the power of Congress to enforce the provisions of the Fourteenth Amendment extends not merely to remedial measures in rectification or disallowance of adverse State legislation, but also to affirmative legislation, designed to supply the inadequacies of State legislation and directly impinging upon private individuals as well as upon official representatives of the State. It is true that the intention of all this legislation was to secure an equality of black and white races before the law, but it was enacted under color of sanction by the first section of the Fourteenth Amendment, the provisions of which are not specifically limited to such an end. To allow Congress's competence in this one case was, therefore, it could be contended, to allow it in all and to allow it in all was to make actual the revolution which the Fourteenth Amendment had been held to menace.

So far so good, but at this point it became evident that one element of the situation had yet to be dealt with, viz: the power of the Supreme Court of the United States to pass upon the constitutionality of both State enactments and of Congressional enactments, and with the Supreme Court the Federal Theory was still dominant. In the following pages, therefore, I shall show how the Supreme Court, out of devotion to this theory, at first proceeded to eliminate the Fourteenth Amendment from the law of the land. This, however, will comprise but the preliminary part of my task. For the questions raised by the outcome of the war were presently in a manner disposed of and a new set of problems—those namely arising from the growth of capital and the development of corporate industry,—confronted government and particularly the State legislatures, which are still—thanks to the Supreme Court itself—the repositories of the police power. These now began to exercise this power more aggressively than ever before, with the natural result of arousing that jealousy of governmental control in which our constitutional system was initially conceived and which had, years before the Fourteenth Amendment had been thought of, found enduring expression, not only in our political theory, but also to a great degree in the constitutional jurisprudence of the States themselves, in the days when constitutional limitations fell largely to the device and enforcement of the local judiciaries. To this viewpoint the Supreme Court of the United States was the spiritual heir. Dismissing, therefore, its earlier concern for the federal equilibrium, this tribunal began a reinterpretation of the Fourteenth Amendment in the light of the principles of Lockian individualism and of Spencerian *Laissez Faire,* which traverses the results it had previously reached at every point. To demonstrate this, then, is my task. In its discharge I shall naturally interest myself principally in those cases which have arisen under the Fourteenth Amendment in connection with State legislation affecting property and business.

Two decisions of the Supreme Court are of prime importance as illustrating the point of view from which the Fourteenth Amendment was first interpreted: the decision in the *Slaughter House* cases, (16 Wall. 36) and the decision in *Munn* v. *Illinois* (94 U. S. 113). In the *Slaughter House* cases, which were decided in 1873, the issue was the validity under the Fourteenth Amendment of defendant's charter, which, in the supposed interest of the public health, granted defendant a certain degree of control over its competitors in the business of slaughtering cattle, and certain exclusive and, so it was alleged, monopolistic privileges. Complainants in error contended that inasmuch as they were engaged in a lawful pursuit, it was their privilege as citizens of the United States to continue in that pursuit unhampered by the legislation in question. The Court, however, considered the invitation to interfere equivalent to an invitation to set up a new and comprehensive system of national jurisdiction, within which should be brought the sum total of the rights of citizenship and of the powers of government to deal with those rights; and it declined to commit itself to so "revolutionary" a course. A straight line was drawn between citizenship of the United States and the citizenship of a State; and only the rights of the former, relatively few in number and already secured by the Constitution against adverse State action, even before the adoption of the Fourteenth Amendment, were held to be beneath the protecting ægis of the Court. The opposing view, said Justice Miller, speaking for the Court, "would constitute this Court a perpetual censor upon all legislation of the States, on the civil rights of their own citizens with authority to nullify such as it did not approve as consistent with those rights as they existed at the time of the adoption of this amendment." And the effect of doing this would be "to fetter and degrade the State governments by subjecting them to the control of Congress in the exercise of powers heretofore universally conceded to them of the most ordinary and fundamental character" and thus to change radically "the whole theory of the relations of the State and Federal Governments." "We are convinced that no such results were intended by the Congress which proposed these amendments, nor by the legislatures of the States which ratified them."

But the argument was also offered that the legislation under review deprived complainants of their property "without due process of law" and that it denied them the "equal protection of the laws." Significantly enough, these arguments were not much pressed, although the Court thought it necessary to animadvert upon them briefly. The prohibition of a deprivation of property without due process of law, it said, "has been in the Constitution since the adoption of the Fifth Amendment, as a restraint upon the Federal power. It is also to be found in some form of expression in the Constitutions of nearly all the States, as a restraint upon the power of the States . . . We are not without judicial interpretation therefore both State and National of the meaning of this clause. And it is sufficient to say that under no construction of that provision that we have ever seen, or any that we deem admissible, can the restraint imposed by the State of Louisiana upon the exercise of their trade by the butchers of Louisiana be held to be a deprivation of property within the meaning of that provision." The other objection he dismissed even more curtly: "We doubt very much whether any action of a State not directed by way of discrimination against the negroes as a class or on account of their race will ever be held to come within the purview of this provision."

The task of the Court in the *Slaughter House* decision was to draw the line between its own power under the Fourteenth Amendment and the police power of the States. Still more immediately was this its task in *Munn* v. *Illinois,* the most important of the *Granger* cases, in which the validity of State enactments designed to establish a uniform rate for the transportation and warehousing of grain and other classified products was challenged on the ground again of their alleged conflict with the Fourteenth Amendment. The opponents of this legislation urged in *Munn* v. *Illinois,* that on two accounts it effected a "deprivation of property without due process of law": first because it attempted to transfer to the public an interest in a private business, and secondly, because the owner of property is entitled to reasonable compensation for its use and "what is reasonable is a judicial and not a legislative question."

The Court, speaking through Chief Justice Waite, overruled both contentions. Business, it said, is subject to the police power, and a well recognized item of that power is the right to regulate the charges of businesses "affected with a public interest." It is true that the Court does not at first sight seem to accept the enactment under review as evidence conclusive of the public character of complainant's business, but appears to canvass the subject anew on its own initiative. The purport of this inquiry is, however, quite different from what it has often been entirely misconceived to be. A careful examination of the language of the Court will show that this inquiry is entered upon not with the design of insinuating that the Court might, if it chose, overrule the legislative determination as to the public character of a particular pursuit, but in order to ascertain whether the field which the legislature in this instance had assumed to occupy was one which a legislature might ever enter legitimately. There is, the Court finds, a category of businesses "affected with a public interest," and secondly, a line of precedents demonstrating the right of the legislature to regulate the charges of such businesses. "For us," it says, "the question is one of power, not of expediency. If *no* state of circumstances *could* exist to justify such a statute, then we may declare this one void, because in excess of the legislative power of the State. *But if it could, we must presume it did.* Of the propriety of legislative interference within the scope of legislative power the legislature is exclusive judge."

The allocation of the power in question to the police power made easy the answering of a second objection to the enactment under review, viz: that the question of what is a reasonable compensation for the use of property is a judicial and not a legislative one. Said the Court: "The practice has been otherwise. In countries where the Common Law prevails it has been customary from time immemorial for the legislature to declare what shall be a reasonable compensation under such circumstances, or perhaps more properly speaking, to fix a maximum beyond which any charge made would be unreasonable. . . . In fact, the Common Law rule which requires the charge to be reasonable is itself a regulation as to price. . . . But mere Common Law regulation of trade or business may be changed by statute. A person has no property, no vested interest, in any rule of the Common Law. That is only one of the forms of municipal law and is no more sacred than the other. Rights of property which have been created by the Common Law cannot be taken away without due process, but the law itself, as a rule of conduct, may be changed at the will or even at the whim of the legislature, unless prevented by constitutional limitation. Indeed the great office of statutes is to remedy the defects in the Common Law as they are developed, and to adapt it to the changes of time and circumstances. . . . We know that this power [of rate regulation] may be abused, but this is no argument against its existence. For protection against abuses by legislatures the people must resort to the polls, not to the Courts."

Both in the decision in *Munn* v. *Illinois* and in the *Slaughter House* decision the Supreme Court is dominated by the view that the States ought to be left to enjoy the same scope of police power which was theirs before the Civil War, unrestricted by the Fourteenth Amendment or the Federal Judiciary in the interpretation of that amendment except in so far as they might attempt to discriminate against persons on account of race or previous condition of servitude. Let us summarize the leading principles stated in these decisions which plainly flow from this view: 1—The phrase "privileges and immunities of citizens of the United States" comes to signify those privileges and immunities which are secured to citizens of the United States by the United States Constitution independently of this phrase, which therefore becomes entirely gratuitous and unnecessary. 2—The phrase "equal protection of the laws" is construed to prohibit only legislation directed against racial classes. 3—The phrase "due process of law" is scarcely allowed any efficacy at all as a limitation upon legislative power, at the mercy of which the Common Law lies as completely as statute law. These principles receive moreover not merely reiteration but enlargement in adherent decisions, some of which, since we shall have occasion to refer to them later on, we may briefly mention at this point. In the *Bradwell* case (16 Wall. 130) the Court upheld the exclusion of women from practice of the law in the courts of Illinois. In the *Bartemeyer* case (18 Wall. 129) it was similarly held that the right to manufacture and sell intoxicants is not a privilege of United States citizenship. In a number of cases it was held that the legislature cannot divest itself of its power of police, and that all rights, including those of contract, are subject to that power. (E.g. 101 U. S. 814 and 109 U. S. 527.) In *Barbier* v. *Connelly* (113 U. S. 27) the Court upheld a municipal ordinance regulating the hours of labor in a laundry, which, it was charged, was "class legislation." Said Justice Field, speaking for the Court,: "Special burdens are often necessary for general benefits"; nor do they "furnish just ground of complaint if they operate alike upon all persons and property under the same circumstances and conditions, . . . and it would be a most extraordinary usurpation of the authority of a municipality if a federal tribunal should undertake to supervise such regulations." On the other hand, in *Yick Wo* v. *Hopkins* (118 U. S. 356) the Court reiterated its intention not to allow legislative discriminations on account of race. But the phrase "equal protection of the laws," which is construed in these cases, was apt to be invoked rather less often by those seeking the downfall of State legislation than the phrase "due process of law." Says Justice Miller in *Davidson* v. *New Orleans* (96 U. S. 97): The phrase "due process of law" remains to this day "without that satisfactory precision of definition which judicial decisions have given to nearly all the other guarantees of personal rights found in the Constitutions of the several States and of the United States." What is the result? Though as a restraint upon the States the phrase in question has been a part of the Constitution only a few years, yet "the docket of this court is crowded with cases in which we are asked to hold that State courts and State legislatures have deprived their own citizens of life, liberty and property without due process of law." "There is here abundant evidence," he continues, "that there exists some strange misconception of the scope of this provision as found in the Fourteenth Amendment. In fact it would seem . . . that the clause under consideration is looked upon as a means of bringing to the test of the decision of this court the abstract opinion of every unsuccessful litigant in a State court of the justice of the decision against him and of the merits of the legislation on which such decisions may be founded." In this same case of *Davidson* v. *New Orleans* complainant was urging that in cases of eminent domain "due process of law" meant "just compensation." The Court, however, arguing strictly from the *usus loquendi* of the Fifth Amendment in which "just compensation" and "due process" appear as distinct phrases, overruled the contention. This was in 1877. Somewhat earlier than this in the *United States* v. *Cruikshank* (92 U. S. 542) the Court repelled the argument that the Fourteenth Amendment makes the first eight amendments binding upon the States, and somewhat later in *Hurtado* v. *Cali-*

fornia (110 U. S. 516), upon the basis of Webster's definition of "due process of law" in his argument in the *Dartmouth College* case, showed itself indisposed to interfere with the right of a State to elaborate its own judicial processes. Rather broader was the issue raised in *Powell* v. *Pennsylvania* (127 U. S. 678), in which an anti-oleomargarine law was attacked upon the ground that it did not further the public health or public morals and was therefore not within the scope of the police power. The Court refused to make a hypothetical definition of the police power a judicially enforceable limitation upon that power. "Whether" said Justice Harlan, "the manufacture of oleomargarine . . . involves such danger to the public health as to require . . . the entire suppression of business . . . are questions of fact and public policy which belong to the legislative department to determine. And as it does not appear upon the face of the statute or from any facts which the Court may take cognizance of that it infringes rights secured by the fundamental law, the legislative determination of those questions is conclusive upon the courts. It is not a part of their functions to conduct investigations of facts entering in questions of public policy merely and to sustain or frustrate the legislative will, embodied in statutes, as they happen to approve or disapprove their determination of such questions. The legislature of Pennsylvania, upon the fullest investigation, we must conclusively presume, . . . has determined that the prohibition of the sale [of oleomargarine, etc.] . . . will promote the public health and prevent fraud in the sale of such articles."

Thus again and again is the point of view from which the Fourteenth Amendment was at first construed by the Supreme Court brought to light. But we have dwelt too long already upon this phase of the subject. Today, as we know, this point of view has been abandoned. What we have to do now, therefore, is to inquire how this change has come about. The truth is that the Court was committed by the traditions at its back even from the outset to a theory of the relation of government to private rights which was gradually discovered, with the developing self-assertion of State legislatures, to be utterly incompatible with the intention of leaving to those bodies the range of power that had been theirs before the Civil War. Is the legislature or is the United States Supreme Court the final guardian of individual rights?—This was, in all the cases above reviewed, the ultimate questions before the Court. In the decisions rendered in these cases the victory rested with the cause of legislative autocracy, but this victory was not uncontested and much less was it final. With each decision upholding the power of the legislature in the particular case at issue, there usually went forth one or more dissenting opinions, wherein was bespoken for a minority of the Court its allegiance to the idea of judicial supervision. How have these dissents become finally incorporated in the law of the land? This really is the question before us.

To Justice Field, vehement and dogmatic exegete, fell the task of developing primarily the canons of an individualistic interpretation of the Fourteenth Amendment. To Justice Miller's identification, in his *Slaughter House* decision, of "the privileges and immunities of citizens of the United States" with the relatively few and meager rights that arise because of the existence of the United States as a government, Field responded by identifying the rights of citizens of the United States with "the natural rights of man." "The question presented," says he, "is . . . nothing less than the question whether the recent amendments to the Federal Constitution protect the citizens of the United States against the deprivation of their common rights by State legislation." His own answer to this question is as follows: "That amendment was intended to give practical effect to the declaration of 1776 of inalienable rights, which are the gift of the Creator, which the law does not confer, but only recognizes." Unless the amendment referred "to the natural and inalienable rights which belong to all citizens," its inhibitions were needless. Though concurring in the *Bartemeyer* decision, Justice Field nevertheless found an opportunity to reiterate these views and to elaborate upon them. The Fourteenth Amendment was not, as the majority insisted in the *Slaughter House* case, primarily "intended to confer citizenship upon the negro race. It had a much broader purpose; it was intended to justify legislation, extending the protection of the national government over the common rights of all citizens of the United States. . . . It therefore recognized, if it did not create, a national citizenship and made all persons citizens . . . and declared that their privileges and immunities, which embraced the fundamental rights belonging to the citizens of all free governments, should not be abridged by any State." Field refused, however, to admit that this view took from the States their power of police; but it did take from them "the power to parcel out to favorite citizens the ordinary trades . . . of life. . . . It was supposed that there were no privileges or immunities of citizens more sacred than those which are involved in the right to the pursuit of happiness which is usually classed with life and liberty; and that in the pursuit of happiness, since that amendment became part of the fundamental law, every one was free to follow any lawful employment without other restraints than such as equally affect all other persons."

The view embodied in this final sentence Field himself subsequently rejected in *Barbier* v. *Connelly,* in which he upheld the propriety of so-called class legislation. It will be interesting therefore to observe the Court at a still later period blinking the view set forth in this decision, which is precedent, in order to draw for support upon his dicta just quoted, which are not precedents. But this is a later story. Meantime we find Field renewing his protest in *Munn* v. *Illinois,* declaring that that decision left "all property and all business . . . at the mercy of the majority of the legislature." It will be remembered that the Court's chief task in *Munn* v. *Illinois* was to ascertain what constituted a deprivation of "life, liberty and property without due process of law." Naturally, therefore, it is to this task that Field also addresses himself in his dissenting opinion. Life, he contends, signifies not merely animal existence but "whatever God has given" for its growth and enjoyment; liberty means freedom of pursuit; property connotes the use and income of property as well as its title and possession. These terms, however, have no efficacy independently of the term "due process of law" and this term Justice Field defines only by implication. Thus he complains that the police power is too often spoken of as if it were an irresponsible element of government, whereas, he insists, it is limited to the prevention of injury and quotes the maxim of the Common Law; *Sic utere tuo ut alienum non laedas,* as its controlling principle. It assuredly does not comprise the right, he declares, to regulate compensation unless a business is affected with the public interest. But who is to decide these questions—the question of *when* an injury exists and the other question of *when* a business is affected with the public interest? Again Justice Field fails of explicitness, but the unavoidable inference from all that he says is that, while primarily these are questions of policy calling for legislative determination, yet ultimately they are questions to be determined by the Court, to whose determination that of the legislature must of course succumb in case of conflict.

Justice Field then is the pioneer and prophet of our modern constitutional law, but this is so not because his natural law creed was his own peculiar possession, but on the contrary because, though none of them was so ready to proclaim the faith that was in him both in season and out, it was shared none the less by almost all of his associates on the Supreme Bench. Thus in the *Slaughter House* case Justice Field spoke not only for himself but also for at least two other associates, and in *Munn* v. *Illinois* for one other associate. Then, in the *Bartemeyer* case the tone of the decision itself which the Court was glad to make turn upon a technical point, was strongly indicative of the conflict going on in *gremio judicis* between the Court's sense of duty to private rights and the allegiance it had pledged to the menaced dignity of the States. But the most impressive example of the strength of theoretic individualism upon the Supreme Bench at this time is furnished by the decision in the *Loan Association* v. *Topeka* (20 Wall. 655), in which an all but unanimous Court, speaking moreover through the author of the *Slaughter House* decision, adopted the notion, that a tax must be for a public purpose, as a limitation upon the State's power of taxation. It is not the outcome of the Court's reasoning, however, to which I desire to call particular attention—for the principle above stated is simply one of several dubious restrictions upon legislative authority that the courts have from time to time created out of hand; it is the reasoning itself that is the important consideration. "It must be conceded," says Justice Miller, "that there are . . . rights in every free government beyond the control of the State. A government which recognized no such rights, which held the lives, the liberty, and the property of its citizens subject at all times to the absolute disposition and unlimited control of even the most democratic repository of power is after all but a despotism. . . . The theory of our governments, State and National, is opposed to the deposit of unlimited power anywhere. . . . There are limitations on such power which grow out of the essential nature of all free governments, implied reservations of individual rights without which the social compact could not exist." From this view Justice Clifford alone dissented, contending that, "except where the Constitution has imposed limits upon the legislative power the rule of law appears to be that the power of the legislature must be considered as practically absolute, whether the law operates according to natural justice or not in any particular case" and this "for the reason that the Courts are not the guardians of the rights of the people of the State save where those rights are secured by some constitutional provision which comes within judicial cognizance," otherwise the courts would become "sovereign over both the Constitution and the people and convert the government into a judicial despotism." Despite the obvious weight of this protest it passed unheeded. The champions of the view that the social compact and natural rights imposed judicially ascertainable and enforceable limitations upon legislative power stood eight strong against Justice Clifford's sole advocacy of legislative independence within the limits set by the written constitution.

But now it may well be asked, why did not the Court, since it was willing to do so at this time, enforce its views of natural rights in the other cases we have reviewed? Two duties, more or less in conflict, confronted the Court, it is true; but if it could be loyal to both, as it was apparently persuaded it could, on the one occasion, why not on the other occasions as well? The answer is to be sought in the question of jurisdiction as it was raised before the Court on these several occasions. The *Loan Association* case was one of those cases that fall within federal jurisdiction not because of the nature of the issue involved but because of the character of the parties to the suit: thus the Court's jurisdiction was unmistakable and could by no means be represented as an act of aggression against the prerogative of the State legislature. The Court accordingly felt perfectly free, as Justice Miller afterwards explained in *Davidson* v. *New Orleans,* to enforce "general principles of constitutional law" in that case. Quite otherwise was it in the *Slaughter House* cases and the other kindred litigation. If the Court was to assume jurisdiction in those cases—and whether it should or not was the entire issue—it must do so under the Fourteenth Amendment, and under an interpretation of that amendment moreover which would, in Justice Miller's language, not only constitute the federal judiciary "a perpetual censor upon all legislation of the States" but would also enable Congress "to degrade and fetter" the State governments in the exercise of "their most ordinary powers." It was not unnatural that the Court should be reluctant to take a step the consequences of which might turn out to be so revolutionary.

But again the question that we are discussing obtrudes itself upon our inquiring minds in a new form. We know that eventually the Court's reluctance was overcome: How was this brought about?

Three circumstances may be adduced in partial satisfaction of this inquiry:

First. The first circumstance to which I allude is the pressure upon the Court of which Justice Miller speaks in *Davidson* v. *New Orleans,* to adopt a definition of "due process of law" which would cancel the effect of the narrow construction given to the phrase "privileges and immunities of citizens of the United States." This pressure was the more formidable in that, notwithstanding Justice Miller's assertion in the *Slaughter House* decision, the definition that the attorneys were contending for was well warranted by certain results that had been arrived at by the State courts before the Civil War. It must moreover always be borne in mind that, as Judge Baldwin puts it, it is counsel rather than judges that make the law, the latter interposing only to winnow counsel's results. The insistence of counsel upon a broad view of "due process of law" was bound eventually to bear fruit.

Second. In an earlier paragraph I referred to a series of congressional enactments between the years 1870 and 1875 by which the independence and indeed the continuance of the legislative authority of the States seemed seriously menaced. In 1883, however, the last of these enactments was erased from the statute book, by the concluding one (109 U. S. 3) of a line of decisions by which they were, one after the other, brought under the ban of unconstitutionality. In these decisions the Court held that the Fourteenth Amendment prohibited only discriminatory action on the part of the State itself or its functionaries. From this it followed that Congress's power under the fifth section of the amendment was merely remedial: in other words, was of the same scope essentially as that of the Court itself to set aside discriminatory State legislation. But what was this except to condemn constitutional action by Congress as gratuitous meddling? The Civil Rights Act eliminated and the equality of the two great political parties once more restored in the national government, the Court had little further reason to apprehend the substitution of congressional legislation for State legislation.

Third. Meantime, in 1883, in the *Butchers Union Company* v. *Crescent City Company* (111 U. S. 746), the opportunity was afforded the dissenting minority in the *Slaughter House* cases to appear as a concurring minority and to give their views thereby something of the guise of court doctrine. The question at issue before the Court in this case was the right of the legislature of Louisiana to limit the grant of privileges upheld in the earlier litigation. The majority of the Court again rested its case upon the latitudinarian view of legislative power. The minority, on the other hand, preferred to look upon the legislation under review as vindicating the private rights that were, to their way of thinking, transgressed by the original charter of the Crescent City Company. Again it is Justice Field who heads the minority, renewing his allegiance "to those inherent rights which lie at the foundation of all action" and to "that new evangel of liberty to the people," the Declaration of Independence. It is, however, Justice Bradley's opinion that subsequent use has made most important. Summarizing his views under three captions, he holds, first, "that liberty of pursuit . . . is one of the privileges of a citizen of the United States," and again enters a protest against the *Slaughter House* decision. Still he is willing to abandon this contention; for, secondly, if the law creating the monopoly "does not abridge the privileges and immunities of a citizen of the United States . . . it certainly does deprive him—to a certain extent—of his liberty. . . . And, if a man's right to his calling is property, as many maintain, then those who had already adopted the prohibited pursuits in New Orleans were deprived, by the law in question, of their property, as well as their liberty without due process of law." And thirdly, "Still more apparent in the violation by this monopoly of the last clause of the section, 'no State shall deny to any person equal protection of the laws.' "

As we shall discover presently, one of the central canons of present day interpretation of the Fourteenth Amendment is the concept of "class legislation." When a particular class of the community is selected by the legislature for additional privileges or duties, the Court's approval of the legislation whereby this selection is effected is necessary to meet the requirements of "due process of law" and "equal protection of the laws." In most of the cases which we shall subesquently review, therefore, these phrases attend upon each other in an interesting and significant fashion. But now it is in Bradley's opinion as given above that this concomitance is first suggested. Likewise in this same opinion, as well as in Field's various opinions recited above, the terms "liberty" and "property" take on the meaning of liberty of pursuit and freedom of contract, which also are today leading ideas with attorneys and with the Court. It is true that Bradley's opinion in the *Bartemeyer* case shows that his views in the *Slaughter House* case were determined by the fact that he regarded the *Crescent City Company* as a monopoly; and it is equally evident that this was still his attitude in the *Crescent City* case. Nevertheless, we have in his utterance given above a form of words, so to say, which is capacious of varied use and of which, it is a fact, that the very greatest use has been made in the elaboration of present day constitutional law. These then are the circumstances which made it easy for the Court to assume a supervisory power over State legislation, in the pretended enforcement of the Fourteenth Amendment. In the first place, the pressure upon the Court to do so by adopting a view of due process of law that would settle the question of jurisdiction in its own favor was constantly increasing. In the second place, after the Civil Rights decision, all danger that Congress would take advantage of a broad construction of the Fourteenth Amendment to assert its own authority aggressively seemed at an end. Finally, the doctrine by which the Court was to assert its jurisdiction was already at hand in a form that bore the guise of an adequate precedent. But even now the Court still held back from occupying at one stroke the whole region of jurisdiction that lay before it. It must proceed step by step. And in this connection the downfall of *Munn* v. *Illinois* is important.[2]

Interesting enough, it was Chief Justice Waite himself who laid the axe to the tree. In the *Railroad Commission* cases (116 U. S. 307), in 1886, the Court again declared the right of the legislature to regulate railroad charges, but in the very body of the opinion is to be found this warning of a veering in the judicial mind: "From what has thus been said it is not to be inferred that this form of limitation or regulation is itself without limit. This power to regulate is not a power to destroy, and limitation is not the equivalent of confiscation. . . . The State cannot . . . do that which in law amounts to a taking of private property for public use without just compensation or without due process of law." The important feature of this utterance is the use of "just compensation" and "due process of law" as equivalent phrases,—a usage involving two assumptions, each of which contradicts flatly the previous pronouncement of the Court. The first of these assumptions is that the power to regulate carrier's charges is an item, not of the State's police power, but of

[2] In tracing the downfall of *Munn* v. *Ill.*, I have made large use of Smalley's *Railroad Rate Control*.

that much more special branch of the State's power, the power of eminent domain. The second assumption is that this power of eminent domain is limited by the Fourteenth Amendment. This assumption is of course to the entire derogation of *Davidson* v. *New Orleans,* as the other is both of historical fact and of *Munn* v. *Illinois.* Nevertheless we find Justice Gray in *Dow* v. *Beidelman* (125 U. S. 680) ratifying Waite's dictum in the *Commission* cases as the "general rule of law." Gray's utterance is also obiter dictum, but it warrants the assertion that the identification of a branch of the police power with the power of eminent domain and the overruling of *Davidson* v. *New Orleans* together comprise the initial step in the overthrow of *Munn* v. *Illinois.*

But only the first step. To his acquiescence in Waite's dictum Justice Gray adds: "Without proof of the sum invested (by complainant in error) . . . the Court has no means, *if it would under any circumstances have the power,* of determining that the rate fixed by the legislature is unreasonable." How is the doubt thus expressed to be reconciled with the reiteration of the general rule of law which it follows so immediately? The answer is to be found in the argument for counsel for complainant in error in the *Dow* case. This argument reveals the fact that the railroads were by no means satisfied with the limitation which Chief Justice Waite had suggested in the *Commission* cases upon the power of rate regulation; for that limitation still left the power of the legislature very ample. The legislature must not impose a confiscatory rate, a rate in other words that might mean positive loss to the carrier; for such loss would amount to a taking of the physical property of the railroad for public use without compensation: this, it seems, is the sum and substance of Chief Justice Waite's thinking in the *Commission* cases. In the *Chicago & Northwestern Railway* v. *Dey,* moreover, we find Judge Brewer, then of the United States Circuit Court, applying Waite's principle as follows: "Counsel for complainant urge that the lowest rates the legislature may establish must be such as will secure to the owners of the railroad property a profit on their investment at least equal to the lowest current rate of interest, say three per cent. Decisions of the Supreme Court seem to forbid such a limit to the power of the legislature in respect to that which they apparently recognize as a right of the owners of the railroad property to some reward; and the right of judicial interference exists only when the schedule of rates established will fail to secure to the owners of the property some compensation or income for their investment. As to the amount of such investment, if some compensation or reward is in fact secured, the legislature is the sole judge." Put more concisely, Judge Brewer's idea seems to be that legislatively imposed rates must not be confiscatory, and to secure that they shall not be, the Courts may interfere, but farther than that they must keep their hands off. But certainly to have secured such an illusory restraint as this upon legislative power was an empty triumph for the railroads, and so they regarded it. Accordingly we find them urging a stricter pinioning of the legislature's hands and devising a new argument, or rather perfecting an old one, upon which to base their contention.

In brief compass this argument is simply that when the reasonableness of legislative rates is questioned, "due process" requires that the Courts shall finally decide the matter; that is, that the question of the reasonableness of legislative rates is a judicial one, under the Fourteenth Amendment's guaranty of "due process of law." This argument had been met directly and resolutely repulsed by Judge Brewer in the *Chicago & Northwestern* case, which occurred in 1886. Justice Gray's dictum in the *Dow* case is perhaps evidence that, three years later, the Supreme Court was also adversely minded, but the year following the Court yielded to the inevitable and adopted the argument of the railroad attorneys, making it the basis of their decision in the decisive case of the *Chicago, St. Paul & Milwaukee Railroad* v. *Minnesota* (134 U. S. 418). Complainant in error asserted its rights under the Fourteenth Amendment to contest the reasonableness of certain rates imposed by the Railroad Commission of defendant State. The law establishing this commission made the rates fixed by it conclusively reasonable. The constitutionality of this law under the Fourteenth Amendment was therefore the question before the Court, and it was held to be unconstitutional. Said Justice Blatchford, delivering the opinion of the Court: "The question of the reasonableness of a rate of charge for transportation by a railroad company, involving as it does *the element of reasonableness both as regards the company and as regards the public,* is eminently a question for judicial investigation, requiring due process of law for its determination. If the company is deprived of the power of charging rates for the use of its property, and such deprivation takes place in the absence of an investigation by judicial machinery, it is deprived of the lawful use of its property and thus, in substance and effect, of the property itself, without due process of law, and in violation of the Constitution of the United States, and in so far as it is thus deprived, while other persons are permitted to receive reasonable profits upon their invested capital, the company is deprived of the equal protection of the laws."

Thus was the doctrine of judicial review of legislative rates brought forth. Its appearance marks a complete volte-face on the part of the Court that fourteen years before pronounced the decision in *Munn* v. *Illinois*. The completeness of the change of view is well indicated in the dissenting opinion delivered by Justice Bradley for himself and Justices Gray and Lamar. "It is urged," says Bradley, "that what is a reasonable rate is a judicial question. On the contrary, it is preeminently a legislative one, involving considerations of policy as well as of remuneration. The legislature has the right and it is its prerogative, if it chooses to exercise it, to declare what is reasonable. This is just where I differ from the majority of the Court. They say in effect, if not in terms, that the final tribunal of arbitrament is the judiciary; I say it is the legislature . . . unless the legislature . . . has made it judicial. . . . By the decision now made we declare in effect, that the judiciary, and not the legislature, is the final arbiter in the regulation of fares and freights of railroads. . . . It is an assumption of authority on the part of the judiciary which it seems to me, with all due deference to the judgment of my brethren, it has no right to make."

Justice Bradley's protest fell on deaf ears. In *Budd* v. *New York*, Justice Blatchford attempted to reconcile his decision in the *Chicago, Milwaukee & St. Paul* case with *Munn* v. *Illinois* by confining the operation of the former to cases where rates had been fixed by commission and denying its application to rates directly imposed by the legislature. This attempt is important as showing the step that still lay between the *Chicago, Milwaukee & St. Paul* decision when it was first pronounced and the doctrine at which the Court was finally to arrive. Otherwise this distinction has long since dropped out of judicial ken, while the decision it was meant to limit has been progressively expanded. We shall, however, have to be brief with the record. "It has always been recognized," says Justice Brewer in *Regan* v. *Farmers' Loan & Trust Co.* (154 U. S. 362, 397), "that if a carrier attempted to charge a shipper an unreasonable sum, the Courts had jurisdiction to inquire into that matter and to award the shipper any amount exacted from him in excess of a reasonable rate. . . . The province of the Courts is not changed, nor the limit of judicial inquiry altered because the legislature instead of the carrier prescribes the rates." This language, besides setting forth in a very illuminating manner the theory which the Courts of this country entertain of their position in the State, marks the final definition of "due process of law" in this species of cases, viz.: law which the Court has pronounced reasonable. The same doctrine finds reiteration in *Smyth* v. *Ames* (169 U. S. 466), but at the same time it is assimilated to the doctrine of Chief Justice Waite's dictum in the *Commission* cases, with the result that the distinction between confiscatory and unreasonable rates, against which the railroad attorneys had waged war from the outset, disappears. "What the company is entitled to ask," says Justice Harlan, "is a fair return upon the value of that which it employs for the public convenience." Finally, in the recent *Consolidated Gas Company* case the Court stipulates six per cent as its idea of a "fair return."

At this point we may dismiss the railroad decisions, our concern with which has been simply to trace the development through them of the doctrine of due process of law. With the results obtained in mind we return to the larger subject of the relation of the police power of the State, as a whole, to the Fourteenth Amendment as interpreted today. The first matter that we have to take note of is this. While the Supreme Court of the United States was engaged in the obliteration of *Munn* v. *Illinois,* the State judiciaries had seized upon Bradley's dissent in the *Crescent City* case and, divesting it of all its original qualifications, had elevated it to the position of an authoritative canon of constitutional law, applying it moreover in a manner against which Bradley himself would have been the first to protest. These decisions we have no space within the limits of this article to review. Instead we shall content ourselves with sketching their ratification by the Supreme Court, under the following topics: 1. Due process of law; 2. Class legislation; 3. Liberty and property; 4. Judicial cognizance; 5. Legal presumption.

1. The constitutional requirement of "due process of law" is recognized as a limitation upon legislative power from the outset of our constitutional history, but in a very definite sense: the legislature must provide "due process" for the *enforcement* of the law. But what is due process in the *enforcement* of the law? One indis-

pensable element, it came to be held, was a hearing: wherefore, it followed that a visitation of pains and penalties or other inconveniences upon selected individuals by direct legislative action, as in bills of attainder or in acts of confiscation, is not allowable. This view of the matter finds expression with some enlargements, in Webster's definition of "due process of law" in his argument in the *Dartmouth College* case, which definition is adopted by the Supreme Court in *Hurtado* v. *California.* Nor is it evident that Justice Bradley thought that he was going beyond this view of the matter when, in the *Crescent City* case, he protested against the monopoly which, he alleged, had been created by legislative enactment, at the expense of particular persons engaged in a business which the law itself viewed as legitimate. Nevertheless the connection between this view of "due process of law" and the present very sweeping view is palpable enough. Suppose, for example, that the legislature, while providing satisfactory machinery for the *enforcement* of a particular statute should by that same statute impose pains and penalties for the performance of an act generally deemed harmless or even beneficial; in such a case the question of the method by which the act was to be enforced would be a very trivial consideration as compared with the requirements visited by the act upon those to whom it was addressed. It is still, I believe, a maxim formally recognized by the courts in constitutional cases, that the possibility that power may be abused is no argument against its existence. In point of fact, however, this maxim has been entirely cast aside. In the matter under review, therefore, the courts, moved by some such consideration as finds illustration in the hypothesis just given, have set up, in the first place, certain purposes which it is assumed the police power ought always to subserve and, in the second place, their own opinions as to the reasonableness of legislation viewed from the standpoint of these purposes, as limitations answering to the constitutional requirement of "due process of law" and therefore as judicially enforceable limitations upon legislative power. "Due process of law," therefore, comes to mean reasonable law, in the Court's opinion. This view is first deduced by the State Courts from Bradley's dissent in the *Crescent City* case. Meantime, the Supreme Court itself was elaborating a kindred doctrine out of Blatchford's opinion in the *Chicago, Milwaukee & St. Paul* case. It was quite ready, therefore, to appreciate and, when the time came, to ratify the more broadly applicable doctrine of the State courts. This it does for the first time in *Mugler* v. *Kansas* (123 U. S. 623). Later cases will be noted below.

2. But the view that the courts today hold of "due process of law" is intimately involved with their view of what is called "class legislation." Most police legislation, as was insinuated in *Barbier* v. *Connelly,* indicates some class in the community for special privileges or special burdens. Such legislation therefore tends to approximate, if the question of its reasonableness be eliminated from the discussion, to that type of legislation in which the legislature, without the intervention of the courts, designates certain persons for unfavorable treatment and which was brought under judicial condemnation long before the Fourteenth Amendment had been framed. This being the case, it is easy to see that that amendment's requirement of "an equal protection of the laws" for all persons greatly assisted the Court in arriving at its final view of "due process of law." Again, however, there was no sudden evolution but a step by step development. In the *Slaughter House* cases this clause was construed to require merely that there should be no legislative discrimination against the negro, but in *Yick Wo* v. *Hopkins,* the Chinese were also brought within its contemplation. The first great step toward the modern view was taken in the county of *Santa Clara* v. *The Southern Pacific Railroad Company* (118 U. S. 394). In this case the issue raised by defendant was the validity of a law under which certain corporations were subjected to a special method of assessment for purposes of taxation. The Court refused, much to Justice Field's disappointment, to pass upon the constitutional question. At the same time, however, it ruled unanimously, and without listening to argument on the point, that a corporation is a "person" in the sense in which that term is used in the final clause of the First Section of the Fourteenth Amendment. Meantime, in *Munn* v. *Illinois,* an idea had cropped up of which the Court was years later to make the greatest possible use; viz.: the application of the historical test of the Common Law in the partial determination of what are reasonable legislative classifications. Thus in *Holden* v. *Hardy* (169 U. S. 366), where the Court assumes its final position, and in later related cases, it comes out that there is an important difference in the mind of the Court between what it calls persons *sui juris,* meaning adult males, and dependent persons, such as women and children. In some of the State decisions in which this distinction is first utilized, the right of the legislature to go further

and distinguish classes of persons *sui juris,* for the purpose of placing special duties upon some or bestowing special privileges upon others is totally denied. The Supreme Court does not go that far, but contents itself with thrusting upon the State the burden of showing the reasonableness of such legislative classifications.

3. The third topic is the phrase "liberty and property" in the constitutional requirement that no state "shall deprive any person of life, liberty or property without due process of law." The evident assumption underlying the attempt in the *Commission* cases to identify "due process of law" with "just compensation" is that property is tangible property, or evidences thereof, and this indeed is the view of the Common Law, where similarly liberty means simply freedom from physical distraint, a violation of which would be remediable by an action in damages for false imprisonment. The whole tendency, however, of the effort succeeding the Civil War to put the negro on a parity with the white race was, in the first place, to enlarge very greatly the significance of both these terms, and, secondly, by investing civil rights with the sancity of property rights, to merge them and thus to confer upon property something of the broad connotation that it bears in the pages of Locke. Justice Field, in his various dissents, accepts these enlarged but decidedly vague notions of liberty and property apparently without qualification. Bradley's tone, on the other hand, even in his monumental *Crescent City* opinion, is noticeably diffident and tentative. Naturally the more confident view won its way, first with the State courts, and then with the Supreme Court. In *Allgeyer* v. *Louisiana* (165 U. S. 578) the Court was confronted with the task of obviating an uncomfortable precedent without incurring the responsibility of overturning it. This it does by adopting Justice Field's definition of liberty and then applying it in a totally illogical fashion to the case under review. In *Holden* v. *Hardy,* Justice Brown seeks for a definition of "due process of law," and finally fastens upon the definition of liberty given in the *Allgeyer* case.

4. Thus far we have been dealing with phrases. The law, however, is not a mere matter of phrases: it has to be applied by the Court to facts. And what sort of facts? In constitutional cases the answer given to this question will depend upon the theory held of the nature of the power of judicial review. Is it, as is often asserted, a power analogous to that of the courts at the Common Law to pass upon the validity of executive commissions, or is it a broader power

and analogous rather to that of equity, to set aside a rule of law which it finds productive of injustice in a particular case? This at bottom is the point in a dispute that arose very early in the judiciary itself. Ostensibly the former of these two views won out, but actually it is the latter that has triumphed, the best proof of which is the doctrine of due process of law which we have been tracing. Accordingly a part of the process by which this doctrine has become established has been a concomitant change of view upon the part of the Court as to the sort of facts of which it could take "judicial cognizance" in deciding constitutional cases. In *Munn* v. *Illinois,* the Court sets about to canvass only facts of law, the only question for determination being the question of legal power. In *Powell* v. *Pennsylvania* the same point of view is adhered to with emphasis. Meantime, however, the State courts, in setting up their views of what is conducive to the public health, etc., as a limitation upon the police power, had adopted a different practice, and in the *Jacobs* case the New York Court of Appeals had taken "judicial cognizance" of the effect of tobacco upon the human system. The ratification of this method by the Supreme Court of the United States takes place in *Mugler* v. *Kansas. Powell* v. *Pennsylvania,* which comes shortly after, is therefore a retreat, but only a temporary one, for the lost ground is recovered and new territory gained in *Holden* v. *Hardy.*

5. The Court, then, in passing upon constitutional cases, judges of both the law and the facts: but even this is not the whole story. For in judging of the law and the facts the Court sets out with certain presumptions in mind whereby it directs its inquiries. No judicial maxim is more venerable than that a legislative enactment must be *presumed* to be valid until it is shown to be the contrary. The inevitable implication, however, from the distinction drawn by the Court, in cases affecting their liberty or property, between persons *sui juris* and dependent persons, is that legislation touching these matters stands upon a diverse footing; that, in short, the presumption shifts from the side of the State to that of private rights, or vice versa, according as the persons affected by the legislation are adult males or not. In *Holden* v. *Hardy* the burden of proof is still held to rest upon the opponents of the legislation under review, despite the principle just stated. In *Lochner* v. *New York* (198 U. S. 45) the burden of proof is shifted.

All this, however, is a very abstract statement of the development of the law. Let me therefore review a decision that furnishes illustration of the various points made above, and of the present state of the law. In *Lochner* v. *The People of the State of New York* the issue was the validity of a statute limiting employment in bakeries to sixty hours a week and to ten hours a day. Complainants in error contended that this statute comprised an unreasonable and arbitrary regulation of an innocuous trade and was therefore not within the police power; and they propounded the following questions, which, they contended, the State must answer satisfactorily, in order to justify such an enactment as the one in question. "Does a danger exist which the enactment is designed to meet? Is it of sufficient magnitude? Does it concern the public? Does the proposed measure tend to remove it? Is the restraint or requirement in proportion to the danger? Is it possible to secure the objects sought without impairing essential rights and principles? Does the choice of a particular measure show that some other interest than safety or health was the actual motive of legislation?" These questions are interesting as showing counsel's estimate of the present state of the law. Judged by the standard set by the court in *Powell* v. *Pennsylvania,* none of them is pertinent. But much water had poured over the judicial mill wheel since that decision. The extremest proposition that the defenders of the statute could adduce with which to ward off this fusilade of questions was the equivocal maxim that "the propriety of the exercise of the police power within constitutional limits is purely a matter of legislative discretion with which the courts cannot interfere," thus leaving it still to be determined, it is obvious, what such constitutional limits are.

Justice Peckham, speaking for a bare majority of the Court, pronounced the statute void as in transgression of the right of contract safeguarded by the Fourteenth Amendment. His statement of the law governing the case is far from clear, and deals very freely in those ambiguous platitudes the constant reiteration of which, without attempt at definition, has from the outset of the development we are tracing, constituted the Court's most formidable weapon in its struggle for jurisdiction. The assertion is ventured that under the Fourteenth Amendment "no State can deprive any person of life, liberty and property without due process of law;" also that the police powers "relate to the safety, health, morals and general welfare of the public;" that "both property and liberty are held on such reasonable conditions as may be imposed by the governing power of the States, in the exercise of those powers, and with such conditions the Fourteenth Amendment was not designed to interfere;" that "the State therefore has the power to prevent the individual from making certain kinds of contracts, and in regard to them the Federal Constitution offers no protection;" that "if the contract be one which the State, in the legitimate exercise of its police powers, has the right to prohibit, it is not prevented from prohibiting it by the Fourteenth Amendment." All of which seems fairly indisputable but gets us no further. The next statement is more illuminating: "When the State," it runs, "by its legislature, in the assumed exercise of its police powers, has passed an act which seriously limits the right to labor or the right to contract in regard to their means of livelihood between persons who are *sui juris*—both employer and employee,—it becomes of great importance to determine which shall prevail—the right of the individual to labor for such time as he may choose, or the right of the State to prevent the individual from laboring, or from entering into any contract to labor, beyond a certain time prescribed by the State." "It must of course be conceded," the opinion continues, "that there is a limit to the valid exercise of the police power by the State. . . . Otherwise the Fourteenth Amendment would have no efficacy in the legislatures, and the legislatures of the States would have unbounded power, and it would be enough to say that any piece of legislation was enacted to conserve the morals, the health, or the safety of the people; such legislation would be valid no matter how absolutely without foundation the claim might be. The claim of the police power would be a mere pretext—become another and elusive name for the supreme sovereignty of the State, to be exercised free from constitutional restraint. . . . In every case that comes before this Court, therefore, where legislation of this character is concerned and where the protection of the Federal Court is sought, the question necessarily arises: Is this a fair, reasonable, and appropriate exercise of the police power of the State, or is it an unreasonable, unnecessary, and arbitrary interference with the right of the individual to his personal liberty?" This does not mean, however, Justice Peckham insists, that the Court is substituting its own judgment for that of the legislature. "If," he asserts, "the act be within the power of the State it is valid, although the judgment of the Court might be totally opposed to the enactment of such a law. But the question would still remain: Is it within the police power of the State? And that question must be answered by the Court." But certainly this is a rather dark saying, since, taken in its literal and grammatical sense, it means that the question of whether it is within the police power of the States may be raised even of an entirely valid statute. Probably, though, Justice Peckham does not mean that, but is contending simply that the validity, which in this connection means reasonableness, of a law is something absolute. But if this be true, why was the statute in this particular litigation overturned by the Supreme Court of the United States by a vote of five to four after having been sustained by the New York Court of Appeals by a vote of four to three?

But to return to the decision itself, we find Justice Peckham animadverting upon the statute under review in this fashion: "In looking through statistics regarding all trades and occupations it may be true that the trade of a baker does not appear to be as healthy as some trades, and is also vastly more healthy than still others. To the common understanding the trade of a baker has never been regarded as an unhealthy one. Very likely physicians would not recognize the exercise of that or of any other trade as a remedy of ill health. . . . It might be safely affirmed that almost all occupations more or less affect the health. . . . But are all on that account at the mercy of legislative majorities? . . . Not only the hours of employees, but the hours of employers could be regulated, and doctors, lawyers, scientists, or professional men, as well as athletes and artisans, could be forbidden to fatigue their brain and body by prolonged hours of exercise lest the fighting strength of the State be impaired." This method of proceeding by the *reductio ad absurdum* is scarcely convincing, since the whole question at issue is whether the statute under consideration is reasonable or unreasonable; and to the query, whether all trades are to be at the mercy of legislative majorities, inquiry may be returned, whether they are to be at the mercy of judicial majorities.

Justice Peckham's mode of arguing nevertheless has its value; for it brings out the fact that this decision rests, immediately, upon considerations of policy with regard to which there is ample room for debate, and, ultimately, upon a highly controversial view of public policy in general. Addressing himself to the former of these topics, Justice Harlan, speaking in dissent for himself and justices White and Day, adduces the *Eighteenth Annual Report by the New York Bureau of Statistics of Labor,* a Professor Hirt's treatise on *The Diseases of the Workers,* and "another writer," who testifies to the chronic suffering of bakers from inflamed lungs and bronchial tubes and sore eyes, and to their lack of resisting power to diseases, and short average life. Thus the reasonableness of the enactment under consideration is at any rate open to discussion, and that fact of itself makes it, under *Holden* v. *Hardy* and kindred precedents, within legislative discretion. "Responsibility," Harlan concludes, "therefore rests upon legislators, not upon the courts. No evils arising from such legislation could be more far reaching than those that might come through our system of government if the judiciary, abandoning the sphere assigned to it by the fundamental law, should enter the domain of legislation, and upon grounds merely of justice or wisdom annul statutes that had received the sanction of the people's representatives. We are reminded by counsel that it is the solemn duty of the courts in cases before them to guard the constitutional rights of a citizen against merely arbitrary power. That is unquestionably true. But it is equally true—indeed the public interests imperatively demand—that legislative enactments should be recognized and enforced by the courts as embodying the will of the people, unless they are plainly and palpably beyond all question in violation of the fundamental law of the Constitution."

Justice Holmes' dissent is still more trenchant, cutting as it does through the momentary question of policy to the deeper, though inarticulate, major premise underlying all preference for or against the political will when it appears arrayed against private rights. "This case," says Holmes, "is decided upon an economic theory which a large part of the country does not entertain. If it were a question whether I agreed with that theory, I should desire to study it further and long before making up my mind. But I do not conceive that to by my duty, because I strongly believe that my agreement or disagreement has nothing to do with the right of a majority to embody their opinions in law. It is settled by various decisions of this Court that State constitutions and State laws may regulate life in many ways which we as legislators might think as injudicious or, if you like, as tyrannical as this and which, equally with this, interfere with the liberty of contract. . . . The Fourteenth Amendment does not enact Mr. Herbert Spencer's *Social Statics*. . . . A constitution was not intended to embody a particular economic theory, whether of paternalism and the organic relation of the citizen to the State or of *laissez faire*. It is made for people of fundamentally differing views, and the accident of our finding certain opinions natural and familiar, or novel and even striking, ought not to conclude our judgment upon the question whether statutes embodying them conflict with the Constitution of the United States. . . . I think that the word 'liberty' in the Fourteenth Amendment is perverted when it is held to prevent the natural outcome of a dominant opinion, unless it can be said that a rational and fair man necessarily would admit that the statute proposed would infringe fundamental principles as they have been understood by the traditions of our people and of our law."

The value of these dissenting opinions is that of most of the other dissenting opinions that we have noted, viz.: that they serve to measure the advance that the law receives in a given direction from the decision dissented from. On the other hand, they are both of them open to criticisms of a rather obvious sort. Thus Justice Harlan was himself the author of *Mugler* v. *Kansas,* and the line connecting that decision with the one in *Lochner* v. *New York* is both direct and logical. Much the same criticism has to be levelled against Justice Holmes' dissent also. For it is to be noted that he accepts in toto the present day view of due process of law. Moreover his "rational and fair man" without a social philosophy of some kind and, equally, his constitution devoid of preconceptions are the veriest fictions. And certainly it was ungracious on Justice Holmes' part to imply a lack of rationality on the part of his majority brethren. The truth is that, the moment the Court, in its interpretation of the Fourteenth Amendment, left behind the definite, historical concept of "due process of law" as having to do with the *enforcement* of law and not its *making,* the moment it abandoned, in its attempt to delimit the police power of the State, its ancient maxim that the possibility that a power may be abused has nothing to do with its existence, that moment it committed itself to a course that was bound to lead, however gradually and easily, beyond the precincts of judicial power, in the sense of the power to ascertain the law, into that of legislative power which determines policies on the basis of facts and desires. Moreover, and this is another point at which Justice Holmes seems to blink the truth, the feeling instigating the first step was the same as that which prompted the last, viz.: a fear of popular majorities, which fear, however, lies at the very basis of the whole system of judicial review, and indeed of our entire constitutional system.

Thus it comes about that Justice Miller's apprehension of a perpetual censorship of State legislation by the Supreme Court has been realized, and Chief Justice Waite's counsel that the remedy for abuses of legislative power is to be sought at the polls and not in the court has been rendered obsolete: and this in brief is the theme I have been pursuing. I desire to add but two remarks. In the first place, this development which we have been tracing is often represented as a centralizing movement in our government, and the cry of "States Rights" has been recently revived in consequence. Is this protest a really relevant one? On the one hand, in support of the view which it represents, the following facts may be adduced: the "Twilight Zone," which also is a creation of the federal judiciary at the expense of State power; the increased use of the injunction by the federal courts in constitutional cases, the enlarged view held by these tribunals today of their power under the Eleventh Amendment (*Ex parte Young,* U. S. Sup. Ct. Reps., 52 L. ed. 714), the recent action of the Supreme Court in sweeping aside the line drawn by the new Virginia constitution between legislative and judicial power in the creation of a Railroad Commission (*Virginia R. R. Commission* cases, 211 U. S. 210). But on the other hand these facts are equally obvious: the general extension of their equity jurisdiction by all American courts today, whether State or federal; the indebtedness of the Supreme Court of the United States to state jurisprudence for its present view of the pregnant phrases of the Fourteenth Amendment; the evident readiness of the Supreme Court to enforce the same ideas against federal legislation under the sanction of the first eight amendments (*Adair* v. *U. S.,* 208 U. S. 161), and indeed the "general principles of constitutional law," where these may be needed to piece out the written Constitution (Dicta in the *Insular* and related cases); and finally the fact that the Supreme Court of the United States has never in the course of its existence bestowed authority upon the political branches of the federal government, though it has often been called upon to ratify an assumption of authority by those branches after the act. The truth of the matter is that the alleged issue between State power and federal power is largely imaginative, and in this connection at least quite pointless. The real issue is far different and traverses both State and federal governments. It is the issue between two theories of government, one of which, centering around the notion of sovereignty, regards government as the agent of society; the other of which, centering around the notion of natural rights, regards government as somewhat extrinsic to society. It is the issue also between two theories of law, the one of which regards law as an emanation from authority and as vested with a reformative function, the other of which holds that law ought to be conservative and ought to represent no more than a ratification of the custom of the community. The latter is plainly shown, for example, by the language of Justice Holmes' dissent just quoted to be the theory of our American courts, which indeed seem disposed to reduce legislative power to the function of finding the law rather than of making it. Nor is it impertinent to add in this connection that the maxim *sic utere tuo ut alienum non laedas,* which the courts today make the controlling principle of the police power, is the norm which the Common Law sets to private action.

My second remark I can put more briefly. The Court in its early fear for the federal balance denied the Fourteenth Amendment practically all efficacy as a limitation upon State power, save in the interest of racial equality before the law. Subsequently, however, the Court found reason to abandon its early conservative position and in the interest of private and particularly of property rights to take a greatly enlarged view of its supervisory powers over State legislation. As we have seen, the history of this change is the history particularly of the development of the phrase "due process of law." But now an interesting thing is to be noted. The *Berea College* decision makes it perfectly plain that the enlarged view of "due process of law" is not available against legislative classifications based on racial differences, such classifications being deemed prima facie reasonable. Thus it comes about that property, or, calling to mind the *Santa Clara* case, the corporations succeed to the rights which those who framed the Fourteenth Amendment thought they were bestowing upon the negro. This outcome is not entirely devoid of irony, but neither on the other hand, as I have above emphasized, is it devoid of historical justification, from our constitutional jurisprudence antedating the Fourteenth Amendment.

★ V ★

Constitution v. Constitutional Theory*

The Question of the States v. the Nation

If there still must be an appeal to the framers of the Constitution, let it be Marshall's appeal: "The Constitution was intended to endure for ages, and consequently to be adapted to the various crises of human affairs.

Like other branches of learning, constitutional interpretation pretends to a certain terminology or jargon of its own, but just how accurate this is, is indeed a question. And if it be inaccurate, this fact furnishes all the more reason why some attempt at defining terms should accompany a consideration of the question of the constitutional relationship of the states and the nation.

First, we have the term constitution, but even that is of ambiguous significance. In the formal sense the Constitution of the United States is the written instrument which was drafted at Philadelphia in 1787, plus the amendments which have been added since, in accordance with the forms laid down in the same instrument. In a material sense, however, the Constitution of the United States is much more than this. . . . [T]he Constitution of the United States in its material sense includes a vast bulk of "judicial decisions," particularly decisions of the national Supreme Court, which—at the behest of private interests for the most part—undertake to

* 19 *American Political Science Review* (May, 1925), 290.

define certain terms of the formal constitution. Nor can it be questioned that some of the terms which have furnished the basis of judicial decisions were inserted in the constitution for the direct end of safeguarding private interests through the medium of the courts; but it is also clear that the scope of judicial supervision of political power in our system has been greatly enlarged by the assumption that private interests are legally entitled to the immunities arising from mere defect of power in this, that, or other instrument of government. It results, hence, that judicial interpretations of the constitution are important, not only in the definition of the rights which are thereby recognized, but also for their effect upon the distribution of governmental power among the organs set up by the constitution.

We are thus brought to a . . . term of interest to our science, constitutional law. This, too, is ambiguous—indeed doubly so. . . . In the first place, the term law is ambiguous. . . . We may content ourselves with considering two definitions: (1) that law is a rule of action; (2) that it is a rule of judicial decision. The two ideas are not mutually exclusive, for a rule of judicial decision must still be a rule, unless we accept Professor Gray's apparent supposition that a court is incapable of apprehending a rule. On the other hand, there are rules which in fact determine constitutional procedure in our system, though they have never received judicial sanction, or have received it only incompletely. Indeed, it is demonstrable that in some instances the judicial theory of the constitution has finally thrown up its hands in despair and surrendered to some rule of action of the political branches. . . .

But the second ambiguity lurking in the term constitutional law is even more of a pitfall. It may be described as consisting of the indefiniteness of demarcation of constitutional law from constitutional theory. This indefiniteness furnished . . . the very foundation of Marshall's work as expounder of the constitution, and so it is not surprising that it is best illustrated in some of his opinions. Take, for instance, the case of *McCulloch* v. *Maryland*. In this case the court ruled that a certain tax which the State of Maryland had levied on certain operations of a branch of the Bank of the United States located in Baltimore was void, as representing a claim on the part of the state of a constitutional power to control or even destroy an instrumentality of the United States government. The opinion is compounded of theories as to the nature of the power to tax, of the intrinsic limits of state power, of the relation of the states to the national government under the constitution, of the nature of the constitution, and of the nature of its source. The constitution, it is asserted, comes from the people of the United States and not the states, and is therefore to be generously construed from the point of view of making it a useful instrument of popular government. Therefore, the terms "necessary and proper," construed in this context, mean simply convenient, and the bank being a convenient fiscal instrument, is an agency of the United States government, beyond the reach of all state powers which might be wielded in a hostile fashion, among such powers being that of taxation, which is a power of destruction. And so on—what part of this argument is constitutional law, what part is constitutional theory? . . . I must utter a caution against a possible inclination to regard constitutional theory as a deduction from constitutional law. The truth is rather the exact reverse of this; and particularly is this so within that field of either, which deals with the relationship of the nation and the states. The relation of constitution, constitutional law, and constitutional theory to one another—especially as they affect the problem just mentioned—may be shown diagrammatically—not that a diagram proves anything, except possibly the inability of the maker of it to express himself as well in some other way. You are, then, to conceive the constitution in the formal sense as the nucleus of a set of ideas. Surrounding this and overlapping it to a greater or less extent, is constitutional law, in the formal sense too of a rule of decision. Outside this, finally, but interpenetrating it and underlying it is constitutional theory, which may be defined as the sum total of ideas of some historical standing as to what the constitution is or ought to be. Some of these ideas do actually appear more or less clearly in the written instrument itself, as for example, that interpretation of the doctrine of the separation of powers which yields judicial review; others tend toward solidification in the less fluid mass of constitutional law; and still others remain in a more or less rarefied or gaseous state, the raw materials, nevertheless, from which national policy is wrought. But how wrought? In answering this question let us turn for a moment to the other phase of our subject—the relationship of the nation and the states.

Considered for its final result, the struggle which attended the adoption of the constitution was less a struggle over whether it should be adopted than over the interpretation which should be put upon the act once it was accomplished. The friends of the constitution were for the most part nationalists, and it was they who set the new government in operation. But the other point of view was early formulated in the Virginia and Kentucky Resolutions, which in time became a gloss upon the constitution fully as authoritative as the written instrument itself; and in 1838 the United States Senate adopted by the vote of 31 to 13 a resolution offered by Calhoun which declared the constitution to be a compact of sovereign states. Meantime, the other point of view had received reiterated statement from the Supreme Bench in the opinions of Chief Justice Marshall, whose greatest service perhaps was just this service of keeping the breath of life in the nationalistic tradition over a critical period. The Civil War, however, restored the idea of the national government as a territorial sovereign, though one of restricted powers. Then, two decades later, the development of industry on a national scale produced an alliance between the principle of nationalism and that of *laissez faire,* which operating through the commerce clause, shattered state control of business. But the commerce clause proved a two-edged sword, and the very precedents which relieved the railroads, for instance, from local regulation became the foundation of national regulation. The result has been a new turn of the kaleidoscope, a new combination of elements of constitutional theory, and some new constitutional law.

Of the issues between those who pose as the champions of nationalism today and those who take up the cudgels for states' rights, the most exigent and interesting one concerns the question of the allocation of the purposes of government in the United States. Both nationalists and states' righters are in general agreement that there are certain large purposes which any system of government should serve. The issue between them is of how these purposes are supposed to be served under the constitution of the United States. The one party holds that the purposes for which the national government may constitutionally exercise its powers are relatively few, and that the ultimate objectives of good government are for the most part, under our system, reserved to the states, whose police power has been defined always as the power to promote the public health, safety, morals and general welfare. The other party answers, however, that while the powers of government are divided in the United States, its broader purposes may be served by each government within the field of its powers, and that the purposes which the police power of the states is designed to serve are by no means reserved exclusively to that power, that it was no thought of the framers of the constitution in erecting a national government and assigning it certain powers to withdraw those powers from the service of the major objects of civilized society, that the preamble in the constitution itself proves the contrary purpose. The one theory may be termed the theory of competitive federalism; the other, the theory of coöperative federalism.

Just at the present writing it would seem that the competitive theory has the better of it. In interpreting the commerce clause, the Supreme Court has shown itself ready to permit the national government to make vast inroads upon what had been thought to be reserved powers of the states, so long as its object is the promotion of commercial prosperity. On the other hand, as the recent child labor cases show, once the national government operating on the same clause undertakes a program of humanitarian legislation, then the reserved rights of the states become a very grave consideration indeed.

Yet this was not always so. . . [It] was not so very many years ago that the Supreme Court itself, in sustaining the Mann White Slave Act, used the following language: "Our dual form of government has its perplexities, state and nation having different spheres of jurisdiction . . . but it must be kept in mind that we are one people, and the powers reserved to the states and those conferred on the nation are adapted to be exercised, whether independently or concurrently, to promote the general welfare material and moral." A better statement of the coöperative theory of the federal relationship could not be asked for.

So much for the national view-point; now for that of states' rights. It will be found underlying Chief Justice Taft's explanation, in the recent case of *Bailey* v. *The Drexel Furniture Company,* of the earlier decision in *Hammer* v. *Dagenhart,* in which the first Child Labor Act was held void. "When Congress," says the Chief Justice, "threatened to stop inter-state commerce in ordinary and necessary commodities, unobjectionable as subjects of transportation, and to deny the same to the people of a state in order to coerce them into compliance with Congress's regulation of state concerns, the court said this was not in fact a regulation of interstate commerce, but rather that of state concerns, and was invalid." "State concerns," "unobjectionable subjects of transportation"—in other words, Congress may prevent child labor from injuring transportation, but not *vice versa*.

Let us now turn back to the other phase of the topic announced: constitution v. constitutional theory. What I have been doing obviously is to seize the occasion to indoctrinate you with my favorite brand of constitutional theory on a certain current issue, while illustrating the relation of constitutional theory to the constitution and to constitutional law. But at this point I am likely to be met with an objection which, in the very act of anticipating it, I shall endeavor to appease. This will be that the real stimulus to the development of constitutional law comes not from constitutional theory, but from considerations of public policy, themselves the outgrowth of social change, and that the relationship of constitutional theory to such considerations, like that of constitutional law, is a purely instrumental one. Indeed, the objector may speak more bluntly, and declare that the judges are often at least the partisans of identifiable economic interests, and that precedent and theory are only a camouflage in the shadow of which matters of choice take on the delusive appearance of inevitability.

No student would care to deny altogether the force of these views. A full explanation of the growth of American constitutional law must recognize that the relatively compact universe of constitutional theory is bathed in a vastly wider atmosphere of social and economic activity, athwart which are constantly blowing the winds of change, set loose no man knows how. Here is the very realm of the "inarticulate major premise" of which Justice Holmes has spoken. Nor is Justice Holmes's the voice in the wilderness that it was once. Nowadays almost everybody admits, however grudgingly, that the judges make law, and that not merely in the sense of adding to or subtracting from the supposititious intention of a more or less supposititious law-giver, but also in the sense of determining such additions and subtractions by their own preferences. Those, therefore, have a certain amount of truth on their side who would make legal history a side issue of judicial biography.

Yet granting all this, does constitutional theory—by which I mean, let me repeat in substance, those generalized, and often conflicting views of what the constitution is or ought to be, which are often as old as the constitution itself—does constitutional theory in this sense lose its significance? Certainly not altogether; and in one respect it takes on a new importance. I refer again to the matter of judicial legislation. The question nowadays is not so much whether the judges do make law, but rather the extent of such law-making, a question which arises from the extremely elusive character of judicial legislation. How is it that intelligent judges can deny to this day that they do make law? In the field of our constitutional law the answer is furnished in great part by the relationship which I have already pictured as existing between constitutional law and theory. Almost from the beginning, as we have seen, two theories have been going as to the relationship of the states and the national government under the constitution. Each theory in turn has enjoyed its period of predominant influence with the court, and each in consequence has back of it a respectable line of supporting precedents. It results that when the court comes to deciding issues along the line which divides national and state power today, it finds itself in an extremely comfortable position. It has a free choice between two lines of precedents, so that once its choice is made, it becomes assimilated to the one or the other of these lines, and every appearance of choice is thus automatically occulted. . . .

In short, the existence of certain standardized, but conflicting views of the constitution both confers upon the judges perfect freedom of decision where the issue before them is one that can be stated in the terms of such views, and at the same time sets up a defence against any attack based on conventional notions of judicial function, which it is extremely difficult to break down. When John Randolph declared of one of Marshall's decisions, "All wrong, all wrong, but no man in the United States can say wherein wrong," he was only expressing the sense of bafflement that many other critics of judicial decisions have felt.

The question, however, remains whether the average judge takes quite so sophisticated an attitude toward constitutional theory; and on that point I venture to express a strong doubt. The average Supreme Court judge, I believe, takes his constitutional theory very seriously. As Justice Holmes has observed from a long experience of judges, "They are apt to be naïf, simple-minded men, with little of the spirit of Mephistopheles." To them such phrases as the separation of powers, check and balance, judicial independence, national supremacy, states' rights, freedom of contract, vested rights, police power, not only express important realities, they *are* realities—they are forms of thought with a vitality and validity of their own. Nor is it anything to the point that many of these ideas, when pressed to their logical extremes collide with others of them. The most ordinary function of a high court is to demark the limits of jurisdiction of conflicting principles of law. In the field of constitutional law the court may well feel that its highest duty is so to adjust the claims of contradictory ideas as to prevent either from being crowded to the wall. . . .

These observations bring us into contact once more with the other phase of our subject. Two questions suggest themselves: first, whether it would not be a good thing if constitutional theory could be abolished; secondly what effect its abolition would have on the question of the relation of national and state power? Toward the end of the nineteenth century a school of German theologians, which had its followers in this country, announced it to be their programme to get rid of what they called the incubus of the Pauline theology. Their argument was that while the authentic message of Christianity was as vital as ever, the harsh, stiff concepts of the Pauline teaching were unadjustable to modern needs and that, therefore, if Christianity was to survive, the screen which the Pauline theology obtruded between the modern believer and the pure faith must be kicked away. Might not a similar Puritanism be summoned to the defence of the constitution and against the gloss of constitutional theory that so often encumbers its provisions?

It is certainly true that the maxims which the courts have built up to guide them in the construction of laws and constitutions owe far too much to their work of construction in other and quite different fields where the public interest was not involved. A maxim especially in point in this connection is that which says that the court must give effect to the will of the law-giver. This maxim comes straight from the law of Wills. Naturally the intention which should govern the application of a will is that of its maker, although he is dead before the task of ascertaining his intention arises. But is there any reason why the intention of a law-maker, as distinct from that of the law itself should govern the law's interpretation? To be sure, the law-maker is dead the moment the statute is made; that particular law-maker—that is to say, that particular congeries, or consensus of individual wills—will never in all probability function again, legislatively or otherwise. Is there, however, any reason why weight should be given in the interpretation of the law to the fact that such a law-giver did for one single instant flash into existence and then with equal celerity pass into an unrecoverable oblivion?

Yet it is this maxim that the intention of the law-maker governs which has always been the principal, if not the sole viaduct, so to speak, between the constitution and constitutional theory. Constitutional theories the most contradictory have from the first claimed the attention of the official interpreters of the constitution on the score of representing the real honest-to-goodness intentions of the framers of the constitution, or if not of its framers, then of those who adopted it. Fortunately, the court has not always treated such arguments as relevant. Marshall in his opinion in *Gibbons* v. *Ogden* thought they should be heeded very rarely—though at other times his attitude is rather different. Not so many years ago the court dismissed an appeal to the intention of the framers in these brusque words: "The reasons which may have caused the framers of the Constitution to repose the power to regulate inter-state commerce in Congress do not . . . affect or limit the extent of the power itself."

And is not this the position which the court ought always to take in this year of grace, one hundred and thirty-five years after the framing of the Constitution? As a *document* the Constitution came from its framers, and its elaboration was an event of the greatest historical interest, but as a *law* the Constitution comes from and derives all its force from the people of the United States of this day and hour. In the words of the preamble, "We, the people of the United States, *do* ordain and establish this Constitution"—not *did* ordain and establish. The Constitution is thus always in contact with the source of its being—it is a living statute, to be interpreted in the light of living conditions. Resistance it offers to the too easy triumph of social forces, but it is only the resistance of its words when they have been fairly construed from a point of view which is sympathetic with the aspirations of the existing generation of American people, rather than that which is furnished by concern for theories as to what was intended by a generation long since dissolved into its native dust.

Finally, let me put the question, what would result from such a procedure to the notion that the constitution excludes the national government from the main purposes of good government? It can be confidently answered that this notion would fall and dwindle by the wayside. Again, the preamble is in point; for where could a better statement be found of the wider objectives sought by good government the world over, "to promote justice, insure domestic tranquillity, provide for the common defence and the general welfare"? Nor is this to say that the preamble is a grant of power; it is simply a catalogue of the ultimate ends to be served by the powers granted in the constitution itself. No gloss derived from speculative theories about the nature of the Union should have ever been permitted to obscure its clear import. . . .

The main argument may be summarized thus: For many practical purposes the *constitution* is the judicial version of it—*constitutional law*. The latter in turn derives in no small part from speculative ideas about what the framers of the constitution or the generation which adopted it intended it should mean—*constitutional theory*. Such ideas, nevertheless, whatever their historical basis—and that is frequently most precarious—have no application to the main business of constitutional interpretation, which is to keep the constitution adjusted to the advancing needs of the time. On the contrary, they frequently contribute to rendering the written instrument rigid and inflexible far beyond what is the reasonable consequence of its terms. The proper point of view from which to approach the task of interpreting the constitution is that of regarding it as a living statute, palpitating with the purpose of the hour, reënacted with every waking breath of the American people, whose primitive right to determine their institutions is its sole claim to validity as a law and as the matrix of laws under our system. . . . [If] there still must be an appeal to the framers of the constitution, let it be Marshall's appeal: "The constitution [was] intended to endure for ages, and consequently to be adapted to the various crises of human affairs."

★ VI ★

Social Planning Under the Constitution*

By Congress alone can the public interest which modern business purports to serve be safeguarded ordinarily, for it is the interest of the country as a whole.

. . . The present depression is the fifteenth major depression of the past century, and no other—in the absence of that fillip to creative thinking which bears the label "Moscow"—seems to have suggested to either Business or Government anything more than hand to mouth expedients. What is more, no single important measure of the past forty years meant to correct business practices in the interest of a wider public can be pointed to which had the support of Business. The Interstate Commerce Act did not, the Sherman Act did not, the Federal Trade Commission did not, the Clayton Act did not, the Federal Reserve Act did not. On the contrary, Business presented in every one of these instances an almost solid front of opposition.

Any viable plan affecting business in an important way must unquestionably consult business experience, in other words, the experience of business men. With equal certainty, it must rely in part upon sanctions which only government can supply; and that means ordinarily, in view of the present structure of business, sanctions which only the national government can apply effectively. And so the question presents itself, What sanctions does the Constitution, that is to say, constitutional law, permit?

* 26 *American Political Science Review* (February, 1932), 1.

I.

The present-day edifice of American constitutional law dates to an altogether unappreciated extent from this side of the year 1890, and so is fully a century younger than the Constitution itself; and especially is this true of those doctrines and principles concerning which the social planner needs feel special concern. These are not, in the main, the outgrowth of earlier precedents; more often they are the repudiation of them. They derive from a point of view which became dominant with the Court about 1890 and remained so for somewhat more than a decade and a half.

Never had "the American way of life" been in such peril as in the decade which is divided by the year 1890. The Federation of Labor, the Haymarket riots, the Chicago stockyards strike, the Homestead strike, the panic of 1893, "Coxey's army," the Pullman strike, "Free Silver," "Coin" Harvey, "Crown of Thorns and Cross of Gold," Altgeld, Pennoyer, "Bloody-Bridles" Wait, and so on and so forth; why continue? The country was in a state of riot, and, in the phraseology of the common law, "men of firm mind, with property in the neighborhood and women and children to protect," were alarmed.

To compensate, on the other hand, for this most distressing situation of fact, what may be termed the ideological situation was most reassuring to those to whom, in the contemporary words of the president of the Reading Railway, "God in His wisdom had confided the destinies of this great nation."[1] There was not a teacher of political economy of any reputation in the country who did not teach that economic activity was governed by laws of its own which, so long as government did not interfere with their operation, worked inevitably for human betterment. Then to back the teachings of the classical political economy was the lesson drawn from the current Darwinian biology. Evolution was a universal process which had all nature, including human nature, in its grip, and was tugging it along to some far off divine event willy-nilly. For evolution meant "the survival of the *fittest*"; only it must be *evolution,* that is, improvement by the slow accumulation of minute differences, not *revolution,* of which indeed the century had earlier had rather more than its fill.

[1] See W. J. Ghent, *Our Benevolent Feudalism.*

So when Mr. Gladstone uttered his well-intentioned eulogy of the Constitution of the United States as "the greatest work ever struck off at a given time by the brain and purpose of man," the pundits assailed him from every side. "Brain and purpose of man"—a gross heresy! The American Constitution was only a copy of the British Constitution "with the monarchy left out," and the British Constitution was the superlative embodiment of political wisdom which it was because in sooth it embodied no wisdom at all, being "a growth," "an accumulation." To consider the Constitution of 1789 as an instance of social planning was an utterly abhorrent notion to the generation of 1890.

But the mind which compacted the *laissez faire* political economy and biological evolutionism into a systematic philosophy was that of Herbert Spencer, whose *Social Statics* Mr. Justice Holmes once informed the Court, though unavailingly at the time, the Fourteenth Amendment was not intended to enact. There are few less humorous books in the language than Spencer's *Autobiography,* although this does not signify that it is entirely unamusing. Spencer's foible, along with omniscience, was originality, and indeed his claims on the latter score may usually be conceded. Educated in a haphazard fashion, he had developed something like genius for picking up information wherever he went and with whomever he conversed, and an equal genius, if so it should be termed, for combining facts and ideas into systems; whence Huxley's gibe that "Spencer's idea of a tragedy was a beautiful theory killed by an ugly fact." Had he been a mechanic, Spencer would have spent his days tinkering at perpetual motion; had he been a mathematician, he would have squared the circle, at least to his own satisfaction. Having, however, given his interest to social theory, or "Sociology," he did what was equivalent, reconciled—to his own satisfaction—the doctrine of natural rights, which he had imbibed in youth from the discourses of dissenting preachers, with the notion of society as an organism, an adoption and adaptation from the current Darwinism.

Society, being an organism, is, of course, subject to the evolutionary process, albeit in a manner somewhat peculiar. For the social organism, on examination, possesses two "organizations," the "nervous," which is the State or Government, and the "alimentary," or Industry. The former is "inferior," and therefore destined eventually to disappear through the operation of evolution on its constituent cells, that is, human beings, thus leading to increasing "individuation" and ultimately political anarchy. The evolution of the latter, on the other hand, is attended by progressive "integration of function" or "sympathy" among its cells, that is, these same human beings. So in the end the human family, pleasantly relieved of its nervous system, is absorbed into the social stomach, and along with this apotheosis universal peace and good will hold sway. In short, while political subordination is utterly antagonistic to the nature of man, economic subordination is not.[2]

Mr. Ernest Barker opines that Spencer is just the kind of political philosopher that England deserved, a statement which is not intended apparently to be especially complimentary to either of the parties mentioned. The apostle of Spencer to the American people—and a very fervent one—was John Fiske. Of Fiske, his rival, the historian Winsor, maliciously, and perhaps a bit enviously, declared that he was "the greatest of historians among philosophers and the greatest of philosophers among historians." And through Fiske or more directly, American judges and lawyers became indoctrinated with the Spencerian concept of "equal freedom," that is, "such measure of freedom for each as is compatible with the like freedom for all"—a conception which Mr. Al Capone would undoubtedly applaud, implying as it does, the right of anybody to become a gunman or racketeer so long as he refrains from "elbowing in" tactics.

At any rate, furnished with this endorsement of the "American way of life" as part and parcel of a universal, ineluctable, and all-beneficent process, "the naïf, simple-minded men" (the phrase is Justice Holmes's) who composed the Supreme Court of the years 1890 and following set to work, with the resolution which only consciousness of a righteous cause can lend, to remake our constitutional law, and within a decade and a half had succeeded in doing so with astonishing completeness.

II.

In the history of the Supreme Court, two terms of Court stand out above all others for the significance of their results to American constitutional law, the February term of 1819, when *McCulloch* v.

[2] See Ernest Barker's *Political Thought from Spencer to the Present Day* and Francis W. Coker's *Organismic Theories of the State*.

Maryland, Sturges v. *Crowninshield,* and *Dartmouth College* v. *Woodward* were decided; and the October term of 1894 when the *Sugar Trust* case, the *Income Tax* cases, and *In re* Debs were passed upon.[3] Nor would it be easy to conceive how three decisions could possibly have been more to the liking of Business than the three decisions last mentioned. In the Sugar Trust case, the recently enacted Sherman Anti-Trust Act was put to rest for a decade, during which period Capital, fulfilling the Pauline injunction of "diligence in business, serving the Lord," made the most of its opportunities. In the Income Tax cases, the Court, undertaking to correct what it termed a "century of error," ruled that the wealth of the country was to be no longer subject to national taxation. At the same time, when the said wealth was menaced with physical violence, it was entitled, by the decision in the Debs case, to have every resource of the national executive and judicial power brought to its protection.

The so-called Sugar Trust was a combination of manufacturers which, the Court admitted, controlled a vast portion of the sugar market of the United States; and, as the Government pointed out, a manufacturer manufactures in order to sell his product, and in the case of a necessary of life like sugar the overwhelming proportion of the product will be sold outside the state where it is produced, and, if the concern is a monopoly, on terms dictated by it. The Court answered, nevertheless, that "this was no more than to say that trade and commerce served manufacture to fulfill its function"! Thus the very process which the Anti-Trust Act was designed to govern, namely, commerce in the etymological sense of "buying and selling," was assimilated to the local process of manufacturing—in short, was held not to exist. The result is the more striking in view of the fact that in the first case to arise under the commerce clause, *Gibbons* v. *Ogden,* the question at issue was whether "commerce" ever meant anything but buying and selling.

And so the law stood until the *Swift* case of 1905,[4] when the Court announced that it would no longer permit "a course of business" which was essentially interstate to be characterized by its intrastate incidents for the purpose of rendering national control of it ineffective. This holding, in which Justice Holmes spoke for the

[3] 156 U. S. 1; 157 U. S. 429 and 158 U. S. 601; 158 U. S. 564.
[4] 196 U. S. 375.

Court, injected new life into the Anti-Trust Act just as the second Roosevelt administration was getting under way. But meantime most of the damage had been done, and the Court so realized. In the *Standard Oil* and *Tobacco* cases[5] of 1912, Chief Justice White announced the famous "rule of reason," which is properly to be interpreted as an attempt on the part of the Court to effect a *modus vivendi* between the resuscitated Sherman Act and the existing structure of American Big Business for which the Court itself was so largely responsible. The act had been restored to the statute books, to be sure, but there must be no "running amuck" with it.

Even more remarkable was the Court's correction of a "century of error" in the *Income Tax* cases. An error so venerable ought, one would think, to have become entitled long since to be regarded as truth, not to mention the fact that the trail of this particular error led to the very doors of the body which framed the Constitution. This was the idea that the term "direct taxes" comprehended only land and poll taxes, having been inserted in the Constitution, not for the purpose of reducing materially the complete power of taxation which elsewhere in the Constitution had been conferred on the national government, but for the very limited purpose of reassuring the Southern slave-holders that their broad acres and slaves would not be subjected to land and poll taxes. And the Court was equally dashing in its encounters with the precepts of the Aristotelian logic. The Chief Justice's opinion for the Court comprised the contention that a tax on income which is derived from property must be regarded as a tax on said property, and *so as a direct tax on it,* although if words be given their "ordinary meaning," as the Chief Justice was scrupulous to insist, it would seem clearly evident that a tax burden which reaches property in consequence of being imposed upon income derived from it reaches the property *indirectly*.

But the decision has also its "inarticulate major premise," save that, thanks to Justice Field, it did not remain inarticulate. In the words of his concurring opinion, the income tax was "but a beginning" of "an assault upon capital" which was bound to spread until "our political contests will become a war of the poor upon the rich"; and while Justice Gray, the other of the two Nestors of the Bench, kept silent—indeed very much so—he reversed the opinions of a

[5] 221 U. S. 1 and 106.

lifetime—"over night," as Mr. Bryan would have it—to help resist the assault *in principiis*. The school-boy who defined "property" as "what Socialists attack" had, it may be surmised, been reading the Income Tax decision.

And, while the regulatory and taxing powers centered in Congress were being thus seriously diminished, the protective powers centered in the President and the courts were undergoing a contrary process in the *Debs* case. Correcting another "century of error," the Court held in that case that the Executive has the prerogative right to enter the national courts independently of statutory authorization, and obtain an injunction to protect any widespread public interest of a proprietary nature, and to support the injunction with all requisite force. Should "the man on horseback" ever put in an appearance, he might well baptize his Bucephalus "In Re Debs."

Meantime, beginning with the first *Minnesota Rate* case, decided in 1890, our *laissez faire* Court had been struggling with the question of railway rate regulation, but did not achieve final results until *Smyth* v. *Ames*, seven years later.[6] . . . The theory underlying *Smyth* v. *Ames* is that a public regulation of charges is *pro tanto* an appropriation of property which up to that moment was *juris privati* only, a premise from which ensues almost mathematically the rule that rates which are set by public authority must yield a fair return on "the present value" of the property undergoing regulation. . . . But if *Smyth* v. *Ames* set up new restrictions on legislative power in control of business and property, by the same token it also enlarged judicial review in safeguard of those interests, and the decision in *Holden* v. *Hardy*[7] in the same term of court did so even more strikingly. In this case the Court, following some earlier backing and filling with respect to the matter, finally discarded the rule laid down in *Munn* v. *Illinois*[8] for the determination of cases arising under the due process clause, that "if a state of facts could exist justifying legislation, it must be presumed that they did exist," and gave unmistakable warning that it intended henceforth to require the state to show special justification in support of measures restrictive of the right of employers to make such terms as their economic advantage enabled them to in dealing with

[6] 134 U. S. 418; 169 U. S. 466.
[7] 169 U. S. 366.
[8] 94 U. S. 113.

employees and those seeking employment, that is, so-called "freedom of contract." . . .

The truly miraculous effect of *Smyth* v. *Ames* and *Holden* v. *Hardy* upon the Court's power of judicial review is not open to question. Anterior to that time, thirty years under the Fourteenth Amendment had given rise to one hundred and thirty-four cases under all clauses of the amendment. In the course of the next fifteen years, more than three times as many cases were decided under the due process of law and equal protection clauses alone. The Court had become a third house of every legislature in the country, or, as Justice Brandeis has expressed it, a "super-legislature."

Two other closely related lines of doctrine in this period may be dismissed more briefly, although they are of great importance for the protection which in combination they afford "the American way of life." The first is illustrated by the "Liquor cases,"[9] in which the Court for the first time projected the commerce clause sharply into the field of the states' police power. In these cases it was held that, liquor being "a good article of commerce," the states could not forbid interstate traffic in it, a doctrine which put the solution of the liquor question on a local basis out of the bounds of constitutional possibility, and so led finally to the Eighteenth Amendment, in somewhat the same way that the *Dred Scott* decision, by rendering a legislative solution of the slavery question constitutionally impossible, contributed to bring on the Civil War.

The other line of cases referred to was headed by the "Lottery case," *Champion* v. *Ames*.[10] In that case the Court, after three arguments, sustained, by a vote of five to four, an act of Congress excluding lottery tickets from interstate transportation, but did so on grounds which strongly implied that all efforts on the part of Congress to control concerns engaged in interstate business by the threat of stopping their interstate trade would be likely to be frustrated by the Court. The culmination of the course of reasoning adopted by the Court in *Champion* v. *Ames* is to be seen in the first *Child Labor* case, *Hammer* v. *Dagenhart*.[11] There Congress was informed that it could not prohibit the interstate transportation of child-made goods, since to do so would be to invade the police powers of the states; although by the Liquor cases just referred to any

[9] 125 U. S. 465; 135 U. S. 100.

[10] 188 U. S. 321.

[11] 247 U. S. 251.

attempt by a state to do the same thing would amount to an invasion of the power of Congress to regulate interstate commerce.

Once again the Court was correcting a "century of error." That the power to regulate commerce comprises the power to prohibit it appears to the point of demonstration from the simple consideration that when prohibition is for any reason essential, it is the regulatory power which must provide it. And so it was assumed by the Federal Convention; otherwise, why the provision that the slave trade was not to be prohibited until 1808? As Judge Davis pointed out in the early case of the *William*,[12] growing out of Jefferson's embargo, this provision shows that "the national sovereignty" was thought to be authorized to abridge commerce "in favor of the great principles of humanity and justice," and for "other purposes of general policy and interest." Indeed, Hamilton in the *Federalist* had listed the commercial power as one of the powers which are vested in Congress "without any limitation whatsoever"; and Marshall's later consideration of the same subject in *Gibbons* v. *Ogden*[13] is to like effect: "The wisdom and discretion of Congress, their identity with the people, and the influence which their constituents possess at elections, are, in this, as in many other instances, as that, for example, of declaring war, the sole restraints on which they have relied to secure them from its abuse."

The issue raised by the confrontation of these words with those of the Court in *Champion* v. *Ames* and *Hammer* v. *Dagenhart* is of the utmost importance from the point of view of any considerable program of social planning. As we have seen, planning means coercion for intransigent minorities—that at least—and if coercion is to be applied by the national government, it must usually be under the commerce clause.

I do not mean to suggest, however, that to Congress should be attributed an unconditional power over everybody's privilege of engaging in interstate commerce in all situations and for all purposes—that, for instance, of controlling marriage and divorce. What I do mean is that *all businesses whose operations extend beyond the boundary lines of a single state should be regarded as subject through their interstate commercial activities to the control of Congress fairly and reasonably exercised.* Commerce is business, and

[12] 28 Fed. Cas. No. 16,700.
[13] 9 Wheat. 1.

today business is dominated by its interstate characteristics—buying and selling across state lines, transportation across state lines, communication across state lines. So, in "the typical and actual course of events," even manufacturing becomes but a stage in the flow of the raw product to the mill and the out-flow of the finished product from the mill to the market; and while checking momentarily the current of interstate commerce, is at the same time, to adapt the words of Chief Justice Taft in *Stafford* v. *Wallace,*[14] "indispensable to its continuity." In short—to reverse the expression of the Court in the *Sugar Trust* case—manufacturing today serves trade and commerce to fulfil *their* function.

Over business thus organized the states are unable, in point both of law and of fact, to exert any effective control; nor would interstate compacts assist them materially in the attempt to do so if unaccompanied by extensive delegations of power from Congress. By Congress alone can the public interest which modern business purports to serve be safeguarded ordinarily, for it is the interest of the country as a whole.

III.

"What proximate test of excellence can be found," asks Justice Holmes in his essay on Montesquieu, "except correspondence to the actual equilibrium of forces in the community—that is, conformity to the wishes of the dominant power?" "Of course," he adds, "such conformity may lead to destruction, and it is desirable that the dominant power be wise. But, wise or not, the proximate text of good government is that the dominant power have its way." Hence, "the true science of the law," as he elsewhere remarks, "consists in the establishment of its postulates from within upon accurately measured social desires"—a point for our statisticians.[15]

Justice Holmes brought his pragmatic outlook—perhaps it should be spelled with a capital "P"—to the Bench in December, 1902, although it was some years before its leaven began to affect perceptibly the heavy theological Spencerianism of that tribunal. Indeed, his opinion in the *Swift* case is the first clear assertion of the new point of view. And to his Pragmatism—wherein he was the

[14] 258 U. S. 495.

[15] *Collected Legal Papers,* pp. 224–26 and 258.

teacher rather than the disciple of his fellow Cantabrigian, William James—Holmes the legal philosopher added the contribution of Holmes the historian of the Common Law—the discovery, revolutionary at the time, that the judges are not the mere automata of established rules of law, but are law-makers, whether they would be or not, and so must accept responsibility for the kind of law they make.

And yet—and this is the third point in the Holmesian credo—the traditions of their office should inspire judges with a certain aloofness toward the issues of the day. They should endeavor to look at things *sub specie quasi aeternitatis,* so to speak, and not be in a bustle to align themselves with either "the dominant forces of society" or the contrary forces. They should, indeed, let such forces have a fair field, and only come in at the end when their craftsmanship is needed to record the terms of settlement.

"It is a misfortune," he once asserted, with both our constitutional law and our common law in mind, "if a judge reads his conscious or unconscious sympathy with one side or the other prematurely into the law, and forgets that what seem to him to be first principles are believed by half his countrymen to be wrong. . . . When twenty years ago a vague terror went over the earth and the word Socialism began to be heard, I thought and still think that fear was translated into doctrines that had no place in the Constitution or the common law. Judges are apt to be naïf, simple-minded men, and they need something of Mephistopheles."[16]

Thus Justice Holmes became the mouthpiece on the Bench of a new gospel of *laissez faire,* namely, of *laissez faire* for legislative power, because legislative power is, or under the democratic dispensation ought to be, the voice of "the dominant power" of society.

At about the same time, moreover, the Court was also introduced to a new technique in the weighing of constitutional issues. This occurred when Mr. Louis D. Brandeis handed the Court, in defense of an Oregon statute limiting the working hours of women,[17] his famous brief, three pages of which were devoted to a statement of the constitutional principles involved and 113 pages of which were devoted to the presentation of facts and statistics, backed by scien-

[16] *Ibid.,* p. 295.
[17] *Muller* v. *Ore.,* 208 U. S. 412.

tific authorities, to show the evil effects of too long hours on women, "the mothers of the race." The act was sustained, Justice Brewer, the arch-conservative of the Court, delivering the opinion. And the work thus begun by Attorney Brandeis has been continued by Justice Brandeis. The Court's function, under the due process of law clause, he has defined as that of determining the reasonableness of legislation "in the light of all facts which may enrich our knowledge and enlarge our understanding."[18] Indeed, this technique has imparted a new flexibility to the concepts of constitutional law in almost every one of its more important departments, and to have given it scope is the really valuable aspect of the modern doctrine of due process of law.

For our purposes, no detailed consideration of the work of the Court from 1905 to 1920 is essential. In the field of state legislation, the outstanding achievement was workmen's compensation; in that of national legislation, it was the reconstitution of the Interstate Commerce Commission and the immense augmentation of its powers, and in both instances the Court lent a helpful hand. A few dicta of the period are, however, so much to our purpose as to warrant quotation, notwithstanding limitations of time and space.

Speaking for the Court in the *Workmen's Compensation* cases, Justice Pitney hinted the premise of a much more comprehensive scheme of social insurance, characterizing the worker as "the soldier of industry" and industry as "the joint enterprise" of capital and labor.[19] Voicing the Court's approval of an act of Kansas regulating insurance rates, Justice McKenna protested "against that conservatism of the mind which puts to question every new act of regulating legislation and regards the legislation as invalid or dangerous until it has become familiar." In the face of this, said he, "government—state and national—has pressed on in the general welfare and our reports are full of cases where in instance after instance the exercise of regulation was resisted and yet sustained against attacks asserted to be justified by the Constitution of the United States. The dread of the moment having passed, no one is now heard to say that rights were restrained or their constitutional guarantees impaired."[20]

To the same Justice must also be credited a notable statement,

[18] 264 U. S. 504, 534.
[19] 243 U. S. 188 and 219.
[20] 233 U. S. 389.

in support of the White Slave Act, of the concept of coöperative federalism: "Our dual form of government has its perplexities, state and nation having different spheres of jurisdiction . . . but it must be kept in mind that we are one people; and the powers preserved to the states and those conferred on the nation are adapted to be exercised, whether independently or concurrently, to promote the general welfare, material and moral"[21]—a sentiment which, unfortunately, precisely one-half of one Justice too many was to forget or ignore when it came to deciding the first *Child Labor* case.

To the same period also belong the memorable words of Justice Holmes in sustaining the migratory game treaty with Canada:

> When we are dealing with words that are also a constituent act like the Constitution of the United States, we must realize that they have called into life a being the development of which could not have been foreseen completely by the most gifted of its begettors. It was enough for them to realize or to hope that they had created an organism. . . . The case before us must be considered in the light of our whole experience and not merely in the light of what was said a hundred years ago.[22]

Such statements evidence an inclination of mind, and one never can tell of what value they may be in imparting to a puzzled Court the same favorable inclination again.

IV.

Chief Justice White's presidency of the Court was, therefore, in the main, one of the expansive views of governmental power, although not always; Chief Justice Taft's period, on the other hand, was one, frequently, of reaction toward earlier concepts, sometimes indeed of their exaggeration. Yet even when the more advanced positions of the earlier period were later relinquished, they were not therefore obliterated. In the corporate memory of Bench and Bar and Jurists—to say nothing of the dissents of Justices Holmes and Brandeis, reinforced later on by Justice Stone—they still survive as *points d'appui* for the Court of today and tomorrow.

[21] 227 U. S. 308.
[22] 252 U. S. 416.

The *chef d'oeuvre* of the Taft Court was its decision in the Minimum Wage case, to which the Chief Justice himself dissented.[23] In the course of the war with Germany, the Court had sustained several measures, both state and national, on the ground that they met an existing emergency. From this circumstance the new membership of the Court proceeded to draw the rather questionable conclusion that an emergency must be forthcoming to justify even legislation designed to remedy long-standing conditions; and naturally in an era of "return to normalcy" a justifying emergency was often hard to produce.

For the rest, the Court's disposition of the Minimum Wage case reduces to this: that whatever might be urged on behalf of the statute on the score of the public interest involved or of widespread popular approval, inasmuch as it invaded fundamental property rights, it was null and void. Incontestably this is a position for which much may be said on historical grounds. The doctrine of vested rights, as applied in a number of the state courts before the Civil War, was to the general effect that the property right was subject to regulation primarily for the purpose of making the subject-matter of the right more secure in the hands of the owner and more useful to him in the long run; if the state wished to venture beyond this, it must employ the power of eminent domain. But the property right then thought of was, for the most part, a right of direct control over definite, tangible *things* and belonged to natural *persons,* parties to the social contract and endowed with the inalienable rights of man. Today the ownership of the vast proportion of the wealth of the country, probably of all of it of which the social planner would have to take account, is vested in corporations; and a corporation, in the language of that notable conservative, Justice Brewer, "while by fiction of law recognized for some purposes as a person . . . is not endowed with the inalienable rights of a natural person."[24]

Ownership, in a word, has become *depersonalized;* and this signifies, so far as the individual owner is concerned, a transference of control over his property which, were it to government, would amount to outright confiscation. . . .

But not only has ownership become depersonalized through absorption of its active elements into the rapidly expanding pre-

[23] 261 U. S. 525.

[24] 193 U. S. 197, 362.

rogatives of corporation management; property of all kinds has, as it were, become *dematerialized,* by which I mean merely that economic value is today a function of social arrangement as never before, so that when social process falters, value simply takes to itself wings. Within the last twenty-seven months, it has been estimated, anywhere between one-half and two-thirds of the "property," so-called, in this country has simply evaporated. The circumstance is of too impressive dimensions to leave constitutional theory respecting the property right unaffected. Nor should we overlook the concessions which the Court itself has made in recent years to governmental power in times of emergency—emergency being just what life nowadays "ain't nothing but."[25]

The truth is that even judicial conservatism is not always obdurate to ideas of social planning. The same Court which decided the *Minimum Wage* case, speaking through the same Justice, upheld, in *Euclid* v. *Ambler Realty Company,*[26] a zoning ordinance which the company asserted would reduce the market value of land owned by it from ten thousand to twenty-five hundred dollars per acre. "A belief, no matter how fervently or widely entertained, that municipal authorities can assert some sort of communal control over privately owned land," said counsel "is at variance with the fundamental nature of private ownership"; to which the Court responded: "The constantly increasing density of our urban populations, the multiplying forms of industry and the growing complexity of our civilization make it necessary for the state . . . to limit individual activities to a greater extent than formerly." Ownership, then, is not something static but an *activity,* and one that must be adjusted to other activities.

And in the meantime the same Court had endorsed a definition of "liberty" under the Fifth and Fourteenth Amendments the logical possibilities of which are at least challenging. In *Holden* v. *Hardy* and the *Lochner* case, "liberty" was defined as "liberty of contract"—a necessary adjunct, to the mind of a *laissez faire* Court, of the property right. Recent cases, however, bring within its protection freedom of speech and of the press; and if these, why not other comparable interests?[27] *The day may come, in other words,*

[25] 243 U. S. 332; 252 U. S. 135 and 170.

[26] 272 U. S. 365. See also 254 U. S. 300, sustaining a "conservation" statute; also 260 U. S. 393, both opinions.

[27] 283 U. S. 697, and cases there cited.

when the Court will treat the term "liberty" as itself embodying constitutional recognition of the entire range of those personal and humane values which enlightened social legislation is designed to promote.

The *Child Labor Tax* case,[28] also decided by the Taft Court, merits a briefer word. Like the earlier *Child Labor* case, it proceeds on the assumption that the Court has a special mandate from the Constitution to refrigerate the distribution of power between the states and the national government as it exists at any particular time—in other words, a mandate to stereotype the so-called "federal equilibrium." Obfuscated by its sense of mission, the Court adopted in both these cases the very procedure against which Marshall protests in *Gibbons* v. *Ogden*. "In support of a theory not to be found in the Constitution," they denied "the government powers which the words of the grant, as usually understood, import."

Such a procedure indicates a serious misapprehension on the part of the Court of certain realities. It is by no means the case that any extension of national power into fields which were once occupied solely by the states necessarily spells a weakening of state power. One of the most evident extensions of national power within recent years is that which takes the form of so-called "federal grants-in-aid," and far from having proved annihilative of state power, these have generally proved stimulative of it—rather too much so in some instances. Indeed, it may be said broadly that under modern conditions more power to the national government means more actually effective power to the states, the cause of effective government being confronted by the same hostile interests in both fields. Nor have our administrators overlooked this fact, with the result that a man can hardly commit murder in either Chicago or New York these days without having his income tax record ransacked by the federal authorities. There may still be cases, no doubt, in which the aggrandizement of national power may be justifiably regarded as taking place at the expense of the states; but even in such cases the question remains whether, with industry and crime both organized on the national scale that they are, the state can make efficacious use of its theoretical powers. If the answer is no, then such powers are to all honest intents and purposes nonexistent, and a realistic jurisprudence will so adjudge them.

[28] 259 U. S. 20.

V.

What is the Court's outlook today—its cosmology? Fortunately, the preachments of our present-day scientific pontiffs are quite incapable of impelling the thought even of "naïf, simple-minded" men along a single track as did Laissez Faireism backed by Evolutionism, backed in turn by belief in a benevolent Unknown. . . . The truth of the matter seems to be that modern science throws man back on his own resources once more. Law, even in the scientific sense, is held to be a creation of the human mind, rather than a datum conferred by a benevolent Providence; it is an instrument of human power and control, as is the human mind itself. . . . We are no longer headed for Heaven in a perambulator labeled Evolution, *Laissez Faire,* or any other uncomprehended force. If we get there, it will be on our own power.

Pertinent in this connection are the words of Mr. Justice Brandeis, then plain Mr. Brandeis:

I see no need to amend our Constitution. It has not lost its capacity for expansion to meet new conditions, unless it be interpreted by rigid minds which have no such capacity. Instead of amending the Constitution, I would amend men's economic and social ideas. . . . Law has always been a narrowing, conservatising profession. . . . What we must do in America is not to attack our judges but to educate them.[29]

Or, harking back some two hundred and fifty years, we may recall the words of Lord Halifax, spoken with reference to the English Constitution: "The Constitution cannot make itself; somebody made it, not at once but at several times. It is alterable; and by that draweth nearer Perfection; and without suiting itself to differing Times and Circumstances, it could not live. Its Life is prolonged by changing seasonably the several Parts of it at several Times."[30] Whereto it needs only be added that the body whose task it is to keep the Constitution of the United States adjusted to time and circumstance, that is to say, *alive,* is ordinarily the Supreme Court.

[29] A. T. Mason, in 79 *Pennsylvania Law Review,* at p. 693.

[30] *Works of George Saville, First Marquess of Halifax* (Raleigh ed.), 211, quoted by Professor Frankfurter in 45 *Harvard Law Review,* at p. 85.

★ VII ★

Curbing the Court*

Let us give the Constitution a chance to function.

The power of the Court in relation to legislation, both state and national, *has* increased vastly during the last half-century, and certain aspects of this increase are to be deplored as out of harmony with democratic institutions. As to these, the power of the Court ought to be, if not diminished, at least brought under control —the question is, *how?*

Theoretically, the Court's power of judicial review rests upon the Constitution. Actually, judicial review of acts of Congress—quite in contrast, for instance, to the President's veto power—can be articulated with the constitutional document only by a course of reasoning, and one which rejects *pro tanto* one of the most fundamental principles of the constitutional theory of the framers, namely, that of legislative supremacy. Yet that most of the framers did in 1787 believe that there would be judicial review of acts of Congress seems certain. As Professor McLaughlin puts the matter:

> There was no complete and definite announcement by the [Philadelphia] Convention of a court's duty to pronounce Congressional acts void. And still it may be fair to say, the existence of this judicial power was by most of the delegates taken for granted.[1]

* *Annals of the American Academy of Political and Social Science* (May, 1936), Vol. 185, p. 45.

[1] A. C. McLaughlin, *A Constitutional History of the United States,* 1935, p. 185.

But the question of the existence of judicial review is one thing; that of its desirable scope and effect in an institutional setup which is otherwise democratic is a different, although related thing.

I.

The question of curbing the Court is at basis the question of properly defining judicial review, and for this the history of constitutional theory affords ample materials. In form and method a judicial function, judicial review has become today, so far as it affects national legislative power, the function of a superlegislature —the function, to borrow Woodrow Wilson's description of the Court, of "a constitutional convention in continuous session." The provisions of the Constitution upon which national legislative power principally depends are the commerce clause and the due-process-of-law clause of Amendment V. These, however, have been interpreted from time to time from such widely divergent points of view that today "alternative principles of construction and alternative lines of precedent constantly vest the Court with the utmost freedom in choosing the values which it shall promote" through its reading of these provisions.

Nor is this all. If there is one single principle which serves to differentiate judicial discretion from legislative discretion, it is the principle of *stare decisis;* and, as was pointed out above, its observance today in the field of constitutional law is also a matter of freest choice on the part of the Court. Nor, in fact, has this principle ever been regarded as applying to the broader instruments of constitutional exegesis or as interfering in any way with the Court's selection among these. Thus the present Court feels itself at entire liberty to utilize Marshall's doctrine of *adaptative* interpretation one day, and Taney's doctrine of *historical* interpretation the next. It all depends on the job needing to be done.[2]

The American Liberty League . . . would like to make people believe that there is never but one possible version of the Constitution on any question that may arise under it—the one to be presently announced by the Court. In other words, owing to some clairvoyant faculty which enters into a man when he becomes a justice of the Supreme Court, or on account of some mystical con-

[2] See my *Twilight of the Supreme Court,* 1934, pp. 112–22.

nection between the Court and Deity, the Court is able at all times to speak the authentic Constitution, with the result, of course, that all who are bound by the Constitution (Congress, President, *et al.*) are bound by the Court's version of it.

It is not possible, of course, to disprove such a theory of plenary inspiration, any more than it is possible to disprove that Moses was—as Coke asserted—"God's amanuensis." But there are some facts, none the less, that furnish grounds for skepticism. To recur once more to the phenomenon of overruled cases: which Court was it that enjoyed divine inspiration—the one that did the overruling, or the one that was overruled? And why this discrimination in the distribution of divine favor? And when a decision disallowing an act of Congress is a five-to-four decision, is the inspiration enjoyed by all the majority judges, or only by the odd man?[3] And why should a judge who has proved a worthy vessel of divine inspiration one day be turned away unfilled another day? At least, these be disturbing questions.

The view stated by Lord Bryce in his *American Commonwealth* seems more realistic, to say the least:

> The Supreme Court has changed its color i.e., its temper and tendencies, from time to time according to the political proclivities of the men who composed it. . . . Their action flowed naturally from the habits of thought they had formed before their accession to the bench and from the sympathy they could not but feel for the doctrines on whose behalf they had contended.[4] . . .

Dismissing, then, the theory of a mystical identity between the Constitution and whatever view the Court takes at any particular moment of any of its provisions, we still have before us the possibility that the Constitution itself requires that the latter be taken for the former by everybody *except the Court itself.*—Is this so?

It would certainly be difficult to show that it was so to John Marshall's way of thinking. Judicial review of acts of Congress became a part of American constitutional law with the decision in *Marbury* v. *Madison,* in 1803. In the course of his opinion Marshall said:

[3] On the inspiration of "the odd man," see the remarks culled by Professor Powell from Selden's "Table Talk," in *Annals of the Am. Acad. of Pol. and Soc. Sci.,* Sept. 1935, p. 149.

[4] 2nd Ed. revised, vol. I, p. 268.

> Why otherwise does it [the Constitution] direct the judges to take an oath to support it? This oath certainly applies, in an especial manner, to their conduct in their official character. How immoral to impose it on them, if they were to be used as the instruments, and the knowing instruments, for violating what they swear to support! . . . Why does a judge swear to discharge his duties agreeably to the Constitution of the United States . . . if it is closed upon him and cannot be inspected by him?[5]

But members of Congress and the President, too, take an oath to support the Constitution. Is then the Constitution, in contradistinction to the judicial version of it, closed to them? If so, "how immoral" to require such an oath of them!

II.

The finality, therefore, which attaches to a judicial construction of the Constitution for the purpose of deciding a case ought, it would seem, to be confined in strict theory, to the case thus decided. However, constitutional usage has . . . come to require that the President, as chief executive, should not attempt further to enforce an act of Congress which the Court has, in the course of deciding a case involving the act, stigmatized as "unconstitutional" and "void." On the other hand, it was asserted again and again in earlier years, and so long before judicial review had become the power of a superlegislature that it is today, that the legislative power of the Union was not to be confined by previous judicial constructions of the Constitution. This was the position of both Jefferson and Jackson. Said the latter, in his famous Veto Message of July 10, 1832:

> The Congress, the Executive, and the Court must each for itself be guided by its own opinion of the Constitution. Each public of-

[5] 1 Cranch, 137, 180. It ought to be recalled that Marshall was ready, at the time of Chase's impeachment, to concede to Congress the right to reverse "those legal opinions deemed unsound" by it, if Congress in turn would give up the power of impeachment. This exchange of prerogatives was, apparently, to be effected by a sort of informal understanding, as Marshall was much perturbed lest, if the impeachment of Chase succeeded, he would be the next victim. See Beveridge, *Life of John Marshall,* II, 176–77.

ficer who takes an oath to support the Constitution swears that he will support it as he understands it, and not as it is understood by others. It is as much the duty of the House of Representatives, of the Senate, and of the President to decide upon the constitutionality of any bill or resolution which may be presented to them for passage or approval as it is of the supreme judges when it may be brought before them for judicial decision. The opinion of the judges has no more authority over Congress than the opinion of Congress has over the judges, and on that point the President is independent of both. The authority of the Supreme Court must not, therefore, be permitted to control the Congress or the Executive when acting in their legislative capacities, but to have only such influence as the force of their reasoning may deserve.[6]

Jefferson expressed himself more curtly: "To consider the judges as the ultimate arbiters of all constitutional questions would place us under the despotism of an oligarchy."[7]

Nor was the view of the "Father of the Constitution" substantially different. Madison even contested . . . the notion that an adverse judicial decision determined the final quality of a legislative act; though on this point history has overruled him. He also contended that Congress could at times construe the Constitution in a way to bind the Court—a position which has been watered down today into the very innocuous doctrine of "political questions." Furthermore, he was willing to concede that the Constitution had been *finally* construed on the subject of internal improvements in a way contrary to his own earlier views, by "the will of the Nation" manifested through a long term of years. . . .

Dealing with the subject in his first Inaugural, Lincoln did not deny that a decision of the Court finally disposed of the particular

[6] J. D. Richardson, *A Compilation of the Messages and Papers of the Presidents, 1789–1897* (10 vols.), Vol. II, p. 582.

Bancroft and Curtis both accept Jackson's position as the correct one. See the former's *History* (author's last revision), VI, 350; and the latter's posthumous second volume (1896), pp. 69–70. "However the Court may interpret the provisions of the Constitution, it is still the Constitution which is the law and not the decision of the Court." Warren, *The Supreme Court in United States History*, II, 749.

[7] *Writings* (Mem. ed.), XV, 276–78. Jefferson, in general, held that each department had "equal right" to construe the Constitution "in cases submitted to its action," "without regard to what the others may have decided for themselves under a similar question." See *Writings* (Ford, Ed.), X, 140–42.

case and to that extent was legally binding on all and sundry. Nor did he question that a reading of the Constitution made by the Court for the purpose of deciding a case was further entitled to "very high respect" from the other departments of the Government "in all parallel cases." But he continued:

At the same time, the candid citizen must confess that if the policy of the Government upon vital questions affecting the whole people is to be irrevocably fixed by decisions of the Supreme Court, the instant they are made in ordinary litigation between parties in personal actions, the people will have ceased to be their own rulers, having to that extent practically resigned their Government into the hands of that eminent tribunal. Nor is there in this any assault upon the Court or the judges. It is a duty from which they may not shrink to decide cases properly brought before them, and it is no fault of theirs if others seek to turn their decisions to political purposes.[8]

In short, while the Court can and must decide *cases* according to its own independent view of the Constitution, it does not in so doing decide *questions*. . . .

IV.

We now return to the question of curbing the Court. That nine elderly gentlemen holding office for life should exercise, without considerable responsibility and responsiveness to the political forces

[8] Richardson, *op. cit.,* VI, 9–10. It is to this passage that Theodore Roosevelt referred when he remarked: "Judges and lawyers are merely instruments for procuring the right solution on certain problems with which all good citizens are equally concerned. How completely the self-styled Republican leaders have wandered today from the principles of Abraham Lincoln is shown by their refusal to apply to this question the principles which Lincoln laid down in discussing the Dred Scott decision. He scornfully refused to treat the decision of the Supreme Court in that case as permanently binding upon the people, or as a matter only for judges and lawyers; and he explicitly laid down the doctrine that the people were the masters of the Court, and that it was for the people and not for the courts to determine the principles and policies in accordance with which our Constitution was to be interpreted and our Government administered." *Congressional Record,* Aug. 23, 1935, p. 14694. Slavery was prohibited in the territories by an act of Congress in 1862, in the face of the Dred Scott decision. Rhodes, *History,* III, 630–31.

of the Nation, the sweeping powers which the Court today exercises over the national legislative power, would be a preposterous idea and one in nowise to be reconciled with the notion of "a government of the people, by the people, and for the people." . . . Wise statesmanship consists in using existing institutions as far as possible, and especially is this so in times of stress, since it is the *visible continuity of institutions* upon which the maintenance of social discipline most immediately depends and which therefore constitutes the strongest barrier against revolutionary violence.

The thing which, I am convinced, more than anything else today menaces the due influence of public opinion upon the Court is the doctrine of the *finality* of its readings of the Constitution—their finality, that is to say, as regards every organ of government except the Court itself. But, as we have seen, this doctrine is logically inconsistent with the very course of reasoning by which, in *Marbury* v. *Madison,* judicial review of acts of Congress was derived from the Constitution. We also have convincing grounds for believing that Madison would not have tolerated such a theory of judicial review; and it is highly improbable that Hamilton would have done so. In point of fact, the Hamiltonian doctrine of broad construction of the national legislative power, which was taken over by Marshall in *McCulloch* v. *Maryland,* really reduced judicial review of acts of Congress to a minimum; and throughout the fifty-four years between *Marbury* v. *Madison* and the *Dred Scott* case, not a single act of Congress was disallowed by the Court. Finally, as we have seen, Jefferson, Jackson, and Lincoln are all definitely on record as denying that a construction of the Constitution made by the Court in the exercise of its *judicial* duty of deciding a case, becomes henceforth a part of the Constitution by which the national legislative power is bound.

Discarding then, this spurious gloss upon the principle of judicial review, where do we arrive? We arrive at clear recognition that the national legislative organ, Congress and the President, are vested not only with the *power* but with the *duty* to read the Constitution for themselves. To be sure, they are entitled to consult the opinions of the Court for such light as these may shed on particular questions of constitutional power; and indeed they ought to do so, not only out of respect for a coördinate branch of the Government, but also because the Court has had great experience in these matters. For all that, they are not entitled to abdicate their own official function of independent judgment on the plea that such opinions are the authentic Constitution. . . .

There can certainly be no sound objection to a course of action which requires the Court to clarify its precise position with regard to grave questions of constitutional power. But I go further, and contend that there can be no sound objection to a course of action which is calculated to enable the electorate to choose between the Court's view of the Constitution and Congress's view, when these conflict. And if, as some have claimed, this would put the Court "on the spot," so also would it put Congress "on the spot."

In other words, the above view of the constitutional duty of Congress brings both the Court's and Congress's interpretations of the Constitution to the test of public opinion and so leaves the issue of finality to be settled by what Madison termed "the will of the Nation." In "a government of the people, by the people, and for the people," that is just how it ought to be settled.

★ VIII ★

Statement of March 17, 1937 before the Senate Judiciary Committee on Court Reorganization*

Mr. Roosevelt did a good thing to fall back upon the Constitution and to summon forth from the document itself an indisputable power in Congress, capable of correcting this unduly extended power of the Court.

I am going to speak about my reaction and reflections on the President's proposal. When I first saw *The New York Times* with the headlines announcing it I was a bit startled. On further reflection I became convinced that the President has grasped the realities of the situation. I have not read anything or found anything in the course of the various discussions that have taken place that has led me to change that opinion; rather I have been confirmed in it.

I think the realities of the situation are these: In the first place, the doctrines of constitutional law of the majority of the Court involve the entire program of the administration in a fog of doubt as to constitutionality; and second, that cloud or doubt can be dispelled within a reasonable time only by reestablishing that mode of reading the Constitution which adapts it to present needs in harmony with its intent as announced by its earliest expounders, that it should "endure for ages to come, and consequently be adapted to various crises in human affairs." Those are the words

* Reorganization of the Federal Judiciary. *Hearings* before the Committee on the Judiciary. U. S. Senate. 75th Cong. 1st Sess., pp. 167–174 *passim*.

of Chief Justice Marshall. And also in harmony with the idea that the Constitution was intended for an "indefinite and expanding future."

The controlling majority of the Court has turned its back upon this point of view. Also, it has forgotten the principal maxim to which the Court adhered for nearly 100 years, that all reasonable doubts are to be resolved in favor of challenged legislation.

Senator Beveridge, in his book on *The State of the Nation,* said:

When five able and learned judges think one way, and four equally able and learned judges all on the same bench think the other way, and express their dissent in powerful argument and sometimes with warm feeling, is it not obvious that the law in question is not a plain infraction of the written Constitution beyond any question?

There is no doubt but that many parts of the New Deal could have been sustained on the basis of doctrines which have been approved by the Court in the past, doctrines equally reputable—more reputable—than the doctrines by which it was overthrown. Modern principles of constitutional law confront the Court with great political questions. It is desirable that they should be decided by men whose social philosophy is modern; at least, by men who are willing to pursue a hands-off policy unless clearly agreed principles leave them no option but to interfere.

The present Court has not been content to do that. It has repeatedly, when it had a free choice, chosen the alternative which set it against the other branches of the Government. And why? There is only one explanation that fits the situation. It has been endeavoring to elevate into constitutional law a particular economic bias of its own: the theory of political economy that government must keep its hands off of business and, particularly, must not interfere with the relations of employer and employee. The latter, it would have us believe, were placed by the Constitution beyond the reach of Government in this country, either State or National. . . .

Now, I wish to speak briefly about the possibility of meeting the situation by amendment. That method is very hazardous. The Gallup poll revealed the fact that the child-labor amendment is favored by 76 percent of the voters, by a majority in every State, and by 83 percent of the voters of the State of New York, but it was recently defeated in that State. It has been pending for 13 years and is still a long way from being ratified. No doubt the constitutional-convention method might prove more feasible, but one-twenty-fifth of the population in 13 States can defeat an amendment. The people who talk about an amendment being the only square and honest way to meet the situation should answer this question: Suppose an amendment is clearly desired by a majority of the people, and still is defeated; what are they going to do about it? Do they have any plan in respect to that? Many of the amendments within recent years were the culmination of long-drawn-out periods of agitation reaching back as far as the Civil War. To rely solely on an amendment, to make that the sole reliance, would be extremely hazardous. If the President's proposal succeeds, the resisting power of those who are likely to resist amendments will be so weakened that it will not be as effective as it would be otherwise. They will be more apt to listen to reason, and it is possible that the extravagances of the campaign against the child-labor amendment, which involves the idea that the political branches are not to be trusted to use common sense, will be somewhat diminished.

What form is the amendment to take? Adding power to Congress? What powers are to be added? And what is to happen to the amendments, once they are within the Constitution? Are they to be exposed to the same type of interpretation as made them necessary in the first place? If so, how long will these amendments prove sufficient? If liberal principles and constitutional interpretations are reestablished, on the other hand, an amendment may not be necessary. Let us give the Constitution a chance to function. . . .

The President's proposal has centered attention on the Court, and rightly so. The present situation is not due to the inadequacy of the Constitution, but is due to interpretations of the Constitution by the Court which do not meet present-day needs.

In the second place, the President's proposal, or something equivalent to it, was required to correct a serious unbalance in the Constitution, resulting from the undue extension of judicial review.

The *Dred Scott* case was the first case in which the Court began to apply constitutional tests not statable in plain language. The first Legal Tender decision was an example of the same sort of doctrine producing a situation which had to be met by somewhat special means. Within the last 40 or 50 years the Court has in the exercise of judicial review dissolved every limitation upon the exercise of its power. I want to read in that connection a statement of Professor Powell in 1932:

> Nine men in Washington have a pretty arbitrary power to annul any statute or ordinance or administrative order that is properly brought before them. The power is an arbitrary power, even though it may not be arbitrarily exercised. It is arbitrary in the sense that in the last analysis it is exercised as five or more of the nine men think best.
>
> The Supreme Court can hardly be said to be controlled by the Constitution because so seldom does the Constitution clearly dictate a decision. It is not controlled by its own precedents, for it feels free to overrule them. It feels even more free to make distinctions that no sensible person would think of making except to avoid confession that a precedent is being disregarded. All this remains true even though in most of the cases it is also true that applicable precedents are either followed or are not there to be invoked. The Supreme Court does what it prefers to do when it prefers to do as nearly as possible what it has done before.

Of course, we have ample testimony from the bench itself as to the illimitable character of judicial review. We have the statement of Chief Justice Hughes in Elmira in 1908, "We live under the Constitution but the Constitution is what the judges say it is." And Senator Borah's statement in February 1930, in the debate on the approval of the nomination of Mr. Hughes for Chief Justice, that the Supreme Court had made itself "Economic dictator of the United States." And Justice McReynolds' statement in the *Nebbia* case that the Court must pass on the wisdom of statutes; Justice Stone's statement in the *A.A.A.* case that the Court is subject only to its own sense of self-restraint, while the other branches of the Government are subject to the courts; and so on and so forth. These might be multiplied. . . .

So it is my own belief that Mr. Roosevelt did a good thing to fall back upon the Constitution and to summon forth from the document itself an indisputable power in Congress, capable of correcting this unduly extended power of the Court.

It must be remembered that the framers of the Constitution were brought up on Locke and Blackstone, whose very definition of constitutional government was a government in which the legislative power is virtually supreme. Judicial review was at first confined to a pretty definite basis. But there were those who early came to see its possibilities, and when they did so they drew back from it. . . .

Mr. Hughes says in his book on the Supreme Court that the Court has inflicted three self-wounds. One was the Dred Scott decision, another was the Legal Tender decision in 1870, and another was the Income Tax decision in 1895. The aged Chief Justice Taney, was at first opposed in the *Dred Scott* case to allow the constitutional question to be considered. In fact, an opinion had been already written for the Court by one of the Justices deciding the case without any reference to the constitutional question. In 1870 it was Justice Grier's senility which produced confusion. In 1895 we had Justice Field's remarkable opinion, which was one of the last opinions he wrote, though he continued on the bench some years longer.

Elderly men look backward. The experience that elderly judges have had in life is inapplicable to changing conditions. There ought to be constant refreshment of knowledge of life and of new currents of thought available to the entire bench. The 70-year age limit would appear to be reasonable. In the past, too large a proportion of the judges had already completed a career at the bar when appointed to the Court. I want to read what Justice Miller said about that kind of judge in 1874. Justice Miller was one of the ablest men who ever sat on the Court. He said:

> It is in vain to contend with judges who have been at the bar the advocates for 40 years of railroad companies, and all the forms of associated capital, when they are called upon to decide cases where such interests are in contest. All their training, all their feelings are from the start in favor of those who need no such influence.

I think that applies today as well as it did then. That is not to say that these judges are not upright and honorable men. They are. But, as somebody has said, the greatest pressure of all is the pressure of atmosphere, which would be intolerable except that it is inside of us as well as outside. The pressure a judge is subjected to from his own personal experience, his own education, his own training, is a pressure which is exceedingly difficult to withstand.

I do not believe that the President's proposal is satisfactory as a permanent solution. It does not guard against a recurrence of the situation which called it forth primarily. How should that problem be met? What the people demand of the Court is "a reasonable contemporaneity," in the words of *The New York Times.* How are we going to get that? I think a 70-year age limit will help. I think a more regular system of appointments will help. Let us suppose we have a Court of 15. I have gone through the statistics on that subject, and I find if you have a Court of 15 the Court could be kept approximately at that size by according each successive administration the appointment of four judges. Mr. Irving Dilliard pointed out in the November Harper's the fact that since the question of the constitutionality of minimum-wage legislation has been before the Court there have been 17 judges on the Court, and 10 of them believed the minimum wage was constitutional and 7 believed it was unconstitutional, but those 7 happened to have a majority on the Court at the critical moments. That is not a Government of laws, but a Government of chance. Whether a further reform is desirable, I am somewhat skeptical. The President's proposal is very moderate. It is the best thing that could have been proposed, as far as I can think, to maintain the general continuity of our Constitution undisturbed. The President's proposal tends to rescue the Constitution from a disabling and nullifying gloss.

★ IX ★

Statesmanship on the Supreme Court

Liberty is something which can be threatened by economic as well as political power; and the latter may interpose against the former.

"We are very quiet there," Justice Holmes once wrote, referring to the Supreme Court, "but it is the quiet of a storm centre, as we all know." To remain at the center of a storm one has to keep moving, and there have been times, as for instance in the early days of the New Deal, when the Court was not as spry as it should have been, with the result that it lost a few plumes. Within the last three years, however, it seems to have again caught up with the tumultuous procession of which it is so essential a part—to be once more at the center of the storm and prepared to serve it as a stabilizing rather than a retarding agency. "The recent revolution in our constitutional law" has already become more or less of a commonplace; therefore understanding of its nature and probable import for the future is likely to have escaped attention.

We start from certain elementary propositions. One is that the Constitution is the supreme law of the land and that all other laws have to conform to its requirements; another is that all laws involve the courts sooner or later in their enforcement; still another is that the courts enforce the laws, and hence the Constitution, as *they* understand them; and yet another is that no law will be enforced by the courts which they, following the lead of the Supreme Court, deem to be in conflict with the Constitution. Also, it is agreed that the national government is a government of "enumerated powers,"

* *The American Scholar* (Spring 1940) IX, 159–163.

which means practically that Congress may legislate effectively only on matters which a majority of the Supreme Court regard as falling within the "enumerated powers." Furthermore, Congress may not pass laws even on such matters and get judicial support for the legislation if it violates the Court's reading of certain prohibitions of the Constitution—for instance, the one which says that "no person shall be deprived of life, liberty, or property without due process of law."

At this point, however, we leave the area of agreed principles and enter the field in which the "revolution" in our constitutional law has occurred. "The Congress," says the Constitution, "shall have power . . . to regulate commerce . . . among the states." But what is "commerce"? At the time the Constitution was adopted the term was sometimes used as virtually synonymous with business and as including even manufacturing. Yet a hundred years later it had come to be confined in some of the Court's decisions to transportation merely. And when is commerce "commerce among the states"? Does this phrase imply that in regulating commerce Congress must be careful not to regulate acts, like production, which take place exclusively within particular states; or may Congress on the other hand regulate commerce among the states, entirely regardless of the repercussions of its laws on intrastate affairs? And what is meant by "regulating" commerce in the sense of the Constitution? Must Congress' regulations be designed primarily to favor the development of "commerce among the states" or may they even prohibit such commerce in the furtherance of other interests, such as the repression of child labor?

Then there is that clause of the Constitution which says that "The Congress shall have power . . . to lay and collect taxes . . . to provide for the . . . general welfare of the United States." It is agreed, of course, that Congress may spend the proceeds from the taxes which it is entitled to lay and collect; the point in dispute is the meaning of the term "general welfare of the United States." Is "the general welfare of the United States" provided for when Congress hands over funds to the states to aid them in carrying out projects—vocational education, for example—which the national government could not otherwise promote; and is "the general welfare" provided for when Congress votes money primarily for private benefit, as in Old Age Assistance or Unemployment Compensation?

Now it is evident that every one of the questions posed in the preceding paragraphs is capable of being answered unfavorably to national power and is equally capable of being answered favorably to national power. In fact, every such question has been answered in these contradictory ways at different times by very respectable authorities, including frequently the Court itself. So, when the New Deal first appeared on the political horizon, the Supreme Court had available to it a double set of answers to each of these questions—answers from which, without departing from its judicial role in the least, it could choose. And the "revolution" in our constitutional law consists simply in this: that whereas the Court between 1934 and 1936 chose its answers, in passing upon the constitutionality of New Deal legislation, largely from those which are unfavorable to national power, it has since, when confronted with similar questions, chosen them largely from those which are favorable to national power. In a word, the "revolution" is a revolution in the point of view of the Court itself. How is this to be accounted for?

The decisions of the Court in 1935 and 1936 setting aside the NIRA, the AAA and the Guffey Coal Act were the result of inertia in the precise sense of the tendency of a body to continue in the same direction unless and until it is interfered with by some outside force. For nearly a half-century prior to the *Poultry* case, in which the NIRA was thrown out, our constitutional law—that is, the Court—had pursued, not without some interruptions and unevennesses, one general trend in cases touching the relation of government to business. This was the trend which is termed laissez faireism, the practical purport of which was that government—state as well as national—should not interfere with the employer-employee relationship; and especially that the national government ought not to interfere with the employer-employee relationship in *productive industry*. But following these decisions three things happened, the accumulated effect of which on the Court was precisely that of an outside force and one of increasing momentum. These were: first, Mr. Roosevelt's overwhelming reelection; second, the CIO strikes in Detroit—giving the lie direct to the idea that great industry could be effectively governed by the states; and third, the President's Court Proposal. The relative influence of these developments in shocking the Court out of its inertia and in persuading it to reconsider its position in our system of popular government it is, of course, impossible to determine, if it were worth while to do so. The essential thing is that the Court did reconsider its position, thus putting itself in line with the rest of the government—back in the center of the tornado.

The two groups of holdings which signalize the Court's new point of view, which comprise indeed the essential core of the "revolution" in our constitutional law, were those sustaining the Wagner Labor Act and those sustaining the Social Security Act. The former invoke those answers respecting Congress' power over commerce that are favorable to national power; the latter those answers respecting Congress' power in taxing and spending for "the general welfare" that are similarly favorable. But there is a larger implication of these holdings which must be taken account of in evaluating the recent "constitutional revolution." Simply put, this is that state lines no longer count greatly in determining the extent of Congress' powers over business activities and social and economic conditions which themselves ignore state lines. That is to say, in the field of business, governmental power marches abreast with economic and industrial organization.

There are, of course, those who complain that this means the end of States' Rights, and indeed of individual liberty; but the complaint is justifiable only from the point of view of the laissez-faire conception of these. As to States' Rights, the truth is that the states were no longer capable of exercising the powers which this conception attributed to them. Furthermore, such legislation as the Social Security Act, far from diminishing the usefulness of the states, has stimulated them to new tasks, to new usefulness—has endowed them with a new lease on life.

And it is much the same as to Liberty. What is "liberty," and what is it "liberty" from? Laissez faireism defined "liberty" as, above everything else, freedom of contract—that is, the freedom of employers to dictate the terms of employment; and the thing which it particularly feared was governmental interference with this. The Wagner Act, however, was sustained by the Court as a measure designed to protect "a fundamental right" of labor, the right of collective bargaining, against the superior bargaining power of employers. Liberty, in other words, is something which can be threatened by economic power as well as by political power; and when it is so threatened the latter may interpose in its favor against the former.

Further than this, recent decisions show the Court thoroughly alive to the importance of "liberty" in that enlarged sense which embraces freedom of speech, press and assembly, and alert to protect unpopular minorities from the encroachment of local tyrannies, state and municipal, upon the enjoyment of this liberty. Likewise, as in the *Scottsboro* cases, in which it came to the defense of the helpless victims of race prejudice, the Court has shown itself the champion of "due process of law" in the sense of a fair trial as against the mere forms thereof.

Projecting these results into the future we may arrive at some understanding of what the Court's position in our system of government is likely to be in the days to come. Its importance as defender of the "Federal Equilibrium" will be greatly diminished—it will no longer play States' Rights against National Power and vice versa as it often did throughout the half-century between 1887 and 1937. It will no longer be the makeweight, that it was during that period, of economic power against political power. It will not, in brief, play the role that it has done at times in the past in the shaping of governmental policy in the broader sense of that phrase. On the other hand, released from suspicion of political or partisan entanglement, it will be free as it has not been in many years to support the humane values of free thought, free utterance and fair play. The recent "revolution" in our constitutional law turns out, therefore, to be a superior act of statesmanship on the part of the Court itself—one than which there is no greater to its credit.

★ X ★

The Passing of Dual Federalism*

. . . what was once vaunted as a Constitution of Rights, both State and private, has been replaced by a Constitution of powers.

Within the generation now drawing to a close this nation has been subjected to the impact of a series of events and ideological forces of a very imperative nature. We have fought two world wars, the second of which answered every definition of "total war," and have submitted to the regimentation which these great national efforts entailed. We have passed through an economic crisis which was described by the late President as "a crisis greater than war." We have become the exclusive custodian of technology's crowning gift to civilization, an invention capable of blowing it to smithereens, and we greatly hope to retain that honorable trusteeship throughout an indefinite future. Meantime we have elected ourselves the head and forefront of one of two combinations of nations which together embrace a great part of the Western World and in this capacity are at present involved in a "cold war" with the head of the opposing combination; and as one phase of this curious and baffling struggle we find ourselves driven to combat at obvious risk to certain heretofore cherished constitutional values, the menace of a hidden propaganda which is intended by its agents to work impairment of the national fiber against the time when the "cold war" may eventuate in a "shooting war." Lastly, though by no means least,

* 36 *Virginia Law Review* (February, 1950).

the most wide-spread and powerfully organized political interest in the country, that of organized labor, has come to accept unreservedly a new and revolutionary conception of the role of government. Formerly we generally thought of government as primarily a policeman, with an amiable penchant for being especially helpful to those who knew how to help themselves. By the ideological revolution just alluded to, which stems from the Great Depression and the New Deal, it becomes the duty of government to guarantee economic security to all as the indispensable foundation of constitutional liberty.

Naturally, the stresses and strains to which the nation has been subjected by these pressures has not left our Constitutional Law unaffected. In general terms, our system has lost resiliency and what was once vaunted as a Constitution of Rights, both State and private, has been replaced by a Constitution of Powers. More specifically, the Federal System has shifted base in the direction of a consolidated national power, while within the National Government itself an increased flow of power in the direction of the President has ensued. In this article I shall deal with the first of these manifestations of an altered constitutional order.

I.

The medium by which social forces are brought to bear upon constitutional interpretation, by which such forces are, so to speak, rendered into the idiom of Constitutional Law, is Judicial Review, or more concretely, the Supreme Court of the United States. This of course is a commonplace. The nature, on the other hand, of the materials with which the Court works is often a more recondite matter; and it is definitely so in the present instance.

Thus, for one thing, the Court has not been called upon, in adapting the Federal System to the requirements of Total War and other recent exigencies, to assimiliate new amendments to the constitutional structure, as was the case after the Civil War. The period in question witnessed, it is true, the adoption of no fewer than four such amendments, the eighteenth, nineteenth, twentieth and twenty-first; and the first of these, the Prohibition Amendment, contemplated a considerable augmentation of national power at the expense of the States—so much so, indeed, that some people argued that it transcended the amending power itself. Although the

Supreme Court in due course rejected that contention, the controversy continued for some thirteen or fourteen years, when it was terminated in the same abrupt and drastic manner as that in which it had been precipitated, namely, by constitutional amendment. By repealing outright the Eighteenth Amendment, the Twenty-first Amendment restored the *status quo ante* so far as national power was concerned. Nor is the Nineteenth Amendment establishing woman suffrage, or the Twentieth, changing the dates when a newly elected President and a newly elected Congress take over, relevant to our present inquiry.

Nor again has judicial translation of the power requirements of national crisis into the vocabulary of Constitutional Law been effected for the most part by affixing new definitions to the phraseology in which the constitutional grants of power to the National Government are couched. One thinks in this connection especially of the "commerce clause." The phrase "commerce among the States" was held by the Court five years ago to embrace the making of insurance contracts across State lines,[1] but the ruling in question—negligible in itself so far as our purpose goes—was presently considerably diluted in effect by act of Congress.[2] Such expansion of the commerce power as is of relevance to this inquiry has been a *secondary,* even though important, consequence of other more immediate factors of constitutional interpretation.

Finally, the *structural* features of our Federal System still remain what they have always been, to wit: 1. A written Constitution which is regarded as "law" and "supreme law"; 2. As in all federations, the union of several autonomous political entities or "States" for common purposes; 3. The division of the sum total of legislative powers between a "general government," on the one hand, and the "States," on the other; 4. The direct operation for the most part of each center of government, acting within its assigned sphere, upon all persons and property within its territorial limits; 5. The provision of each center with the complete apparatus, both executive and judicial, for law enforcement; 6. Judicial review, that is, the power and duty of all courts, and ultimately of the Supreme Court of the Union, to disallow all

[1] *United States* v. *South-Eastern Underwriters Ass'n,* 322 U. S. 533, 64 Sup. Ct. 1162, 88 L. Ed. 1441 (1944).

[2] 59 STAT. 33, 34 (1945), 15 U. S. C. §§ 1011–1015 (1946); see *Prudential Ins. Co.* v. *Benjamin,* 328 U. S. 408, 66 Sup. Ct. 1142, 90 L. Ed. 1342 (1946).

legislative or executive acts of either center of government which in the Court's opinion transgress the Constitution; 7. An elaborate and cumbersome method of constitutional amendment, in which the States have a deciding role.

Not only have these features of the American Federal System never been altered by constitutional amendment in any way that requires our attention, none has within recent years been *directly* affected by judicial interpretation of the words of the Constitution in a way that need interest us. So far as the form and actual phraseological content of the Constitutional Document are concerned, Profesor Dicey's dictum that federalism implies "a legally immutable Constitution," or one nearly immutable, has been fully realized in the American experience.[3]

In just what fashion then has the shift referred to above of our Federal System toward consolidation registered itself in our Constitutional Law in response to the requirements of war, economic crisis, and a fundamentally altered outlook upon the purpose of government? The solution of the conundrum is to be sought in the changed attitude of the Court toward certain postulates or axioms of constitutional interpretation closely touching the Federal System, and which in their totality comprised what I mean by Dual Federalism. These postulates are the following: 1. The national government is one of enumerated powers only; 2. Also the purposes which it may constitutionally promote are few; 3. Within their respective spheres the two centers of government are "sovereign" and hence "equal"; 4. The relation of the two centers with each other is one of tension rather than collaboration. Here I shall sketch briefly the history of each of these concepts in our Constitutional Law and show how today each has been superseded by a concept favorable to centralization.

II.

. . . Today the operation of the "enumerated powers" concept as a canon of constitutional interpretation has been curtailed on all sides. Nor in fact did it ever go altogether unchallenged, even from the first.

[3] A. V. Dicey, *Introduction to the Study of the Law of the Constitution* 142 (7th ed. 1903).

Article I, section 8, clause 1 of the Constitution reads:

> The Congress shall have power to lay and collect taxes, duties, imposts and excises, to pay the debts and provide for the common defense and general welfare of the United States . . .

What is "the general welfare" for which Congress is thus authorized to "provide," and in what fashion is it authorized to provide it? While adoption of the Constitution was pending some of its opponents made the charge that the phrase "to provide for the general welfare" was a sort of legislative joker which was designed, in conjunction with the "necessary and proper" clause, to vest Congress with power to provide for whatever it might choose to regard as the "general welfare" by any means deemed by it to be "necessary and proper." The suggestion was promptly repudiated by advocates of the Constitution on the following grounds. In the first place, it was pointed out, the phrase stood between two other phrases, both dealing with the taxing power—an awkward syntax on the assumption under consideration. In the second place, the phrase was coordinate with the phrase "to pay the debts," that is, a purpose of money expenditure only. Finally, it was asserted, the suggested reading, by endowing Congress with practically complete legislative power, rendered the succeeding enumeration of more specific powers superfluous, thereby reducing "the Constitution to a single phrase."

In the total this argument sounds impressive, but on closer examination it becomes less so, especially today. For one thing, it is a fact that in certain early printings of the Constitution the "common defense and general welfare" clause appears separately paragraphed, while in others it is set off from the "lay and collect" clause by a semicolon and not, as modern usage would require, by the less awesome comma. To be sure, the semicolon may have been due in the first instance to the splattering of a goose quill that needed trimming, for it is notorious that the fate of nations has often turned on just such minute *points*.

Then as to the third argument—while once deemed an extremely weighty one—it cannot be so regarded in light of the decision in 1926 in the case of *Myers* v. *United States*.[4] The Court held that the opening clause of Article II of the Constitution which says that

[4] 272 U. S. 52, 47 Sup. Ct. 21, 71 L. Ed. 160 (1926).

"the executive power shall be vested in a President of the United States," is not a simple designation of office but a grant of power, which the succeeding clauses of the same article either qualify or to which they lend "appropriate emphasis." Granting the soundness of this position, however, why should not the more specific clauses of Article I be regarded as standing in a like relation to the "general welfare" clause thereof? Nor is this by any means all that may be said in favor of treating the latter clause as a grant of substantive legislative power, as anyone may convince himself who chooses to consult Mr. James Francis Lawson's minute and ingenious examination of the subject.[5]

Despite these considerations, or such of them as he was aware of, the great Chief Justice Marshall in 1819 stamped the "enumerated powers" doctrine with his approval. This was in his opinion in *McCulloch* v. *Maryland*,[6] where, in sustaining the right of the National Government to establish a Bank, he used the following expressions:

> This government is acknowledged by all to be one of enumerated powers. The principle, that it can exercise only the powers granted to it, would seem too apparent to have required to be enforced by all those arguments which its enlightened friends, while it was depending before the people, found it necessary to urge. That principle is now universally admitted.[7]

At the same time, however, Marshall committed himself to certain other positions in that same opinion which in their total effect went far in the judgment of certain of his critics to render the National Government one of "indefinite powers." One of these was the dictum that "the sword and the purse, all external relations, and no inconsiderable portion of the industry of the nation, are entrusted to its government." Another was his characterization of "the power of making war," "levying taxes," and of "regulating commerce," as "great, substantive and independent" powers. A third was his famous and for the purposes of the case, decisive construction of the "necessary and proper" clause as embracing "all [legis-

[5] The three preceding paragraphs are drawn largely from Corwin, *Twilight of the Supreme Court* 152–54 (1934).

[6] 4 Wheat. 316, 4 L. Ed. 579 (U. S. 1819).

[7] *Id.* at 405, 4 L. Ed. at 601.

lative] means which are appropriate" to carry out "the legitimate ends" of the Constitution.[8]

Approaching the opinion from the angle of his quasi-parental concern for "the balance between the States and the National Government," Madison declared its central vice to be that it treated the powers of the latter as "sovereign powers," a view which must inevitably "convert a limited into an unlimited government" for, he continued, "in the great system of political economy, having for its general object the national welfare, everything is related immediately or remotely to every other thing; and, consequently, a power over any one thing, not limited by some obvious and precise affinity, may amount to a power over every other." "The very existence," he consequently urged, "of the local sovereignties" was "a control on the pleas for a constructive amplification of national power."[9]

So also did Marshall's most pertinacious critic, John Taylor of Carolina, pronounce the Chief Justice's doctrines as utterly destructive of the constitutional division of powers between the two centers of government.[10] A third critic was the talented Hugh Swinton Legaré of South Carolina, who in 1828 devoted a review of the first volume of Kent's *Commentaries* to a minute and immensely ingenious analysis of Marshall's most celebrated opinion. "That argument," he asserted, "cannot be sound which necessarily converts a government of enumerated into one of indefinite powers, and a confederacy of republics into a gigantic and consolidated empire." Nor did one have to rely on reasoning alone to be convinced of this; one needed only to compare the Constitution itself as expounded in the *Federalist* with the actual course of national legislation. For thus, he wrote:

> He will find that the government has been fundamentally altered by the progress of opinion—that instead of being any longer one of enumerated powers and a circumscribed sphere, as it was beyond all doubt intended to be, it knows absolutely no bounds but the will of a majority of Congress—that instead of confining itself in time of peace to the diplomatic and commercial relations of the country, it is seeking out employment for itself by interfering in the domestic concerns of society, and theatens in the course of a very few years,

[8] *Id.* at 421, 4 L. Ed. at 605.

[9] 8 *Writings of James Madison* 447–53 (Hunt ed. 1908); 2 *Letters and Other Writings of James Madison* 143–47 (Phila. 1867).

[10] Taylor, *Construction Construed and Constitutions Vindicated* 9–28 *passim*, 77–89 *passim* (1820).

to control in the most offensive and despotic manner, all the pursuits, the interests, the opinions and the conduct of men. He will find that this extraordinary revolution has been brought about, in a good degree by the Supreme Court of the United States, which has applied to the Constitution—very innocently, no doubt, and with commanding ability in argument—and thus given authority and currency to, such canons of interpretation, as necesarily lead to these extravagant results. Above all, he will be perfectly satisfied that that high tribunal affords, by its own shewing, no barrier whatever against the usurpations of Congress—and that the rights of the weaker part of this confederacy may, to any extent, be wantonly and tyrannically violated, under colour of law, (the most grievous shape of oppression) by men neither interested in its destiny nor subject to its control, without any means of redress being left it, except such as are inconsistent with all idea of order and government.[11]

These words purported one hundred and twenty years ago to be history; they read today much more like prophecy. . . .

III.

We turn now to the second of the above postulates. The question raised is whether it was the intention of the Framers of the Constitution to apportion not only the powers but also the purposes of government between the two centers, with the result of inhibiting the National Government from attempting on a national scale the same ends as the States attempt on a local scale? In view of the latitudinarian language of the Preamble to the Constitution, an affirmative answer to this question might seem to encounter ineluctable difficulties. For all that, it has at times received countenance from the Court. Even in the pages of the *Federalist* can be discerned the beginings of a controversy regarding the scope of Congress's taxing power which was still sufficiently vital 150 years later to claim the Court's deliberate attention, although the substance of victory had long since fallen to the pro-nationalist view.[12] In brief the question at issue was this: Was Congress entitled to levy and collect taxes to further objects not falling within its other powers to advance? Very early the question became dichotomized into two

[11] 2 *The Southern Review* 72–113, No. 1 (1828); 2 *Writings of Hugh Swinton Legaré* 102, 123–33 (1846).

[12] *The Federalist*; Nos. 30, 34, 41.

questions. First, was Congress entitled to lay and collect tariffs for any but revenue purposes; secondly, was it entitled to expend the proceeds from its taxes for any other purpose than to provision the government in the exercise of its other enumerated powers, or as Henry Clay once put the issue, was the power to spend the *cause* or merely the *consequence* of power?

The tariff aspect of the general question was, for instance, debated by Calhoun, speaking for the States Rights view, and by Story in his *Commentaries* by way of answer to Calhoun.[13] Yet not until 1928 did the Court get around to affix the stamp of its approval on Story's argument, and then it did so only on historical grounds. Said Chief Justice Taft for the unanimous Court:

It is enough to point out that the second act adopted by the Congress of the United States July 4, 1789 . . . contained the following recital:

"Sec. 1. Whereas it is necessary for the support of government, for the discharge of the debts of the United States, and the encouragement and protection of manufactures, that duties be laid on goods, wares and merchandises imported:

"Be it enacted, . . . "

In this first Congress sat many members of the Constitutional Convention of 1787. This court has repeatedly laid down the principle that a contemporaneous legislative exposition of the Constitution when the founders of our government and framers of our Constitution were actively participating in public affairs, long acquiesced in, fixes the construction to be given its provisions. . . . The enactment and enforcement of a number of customs revenue laws drawn with a motive of maintaining a system of protection since the Revenue Law of 1789 are matters of history.[14]

In short, the constitutional case against the tariff went by default; and substantially the same is true also of the restrictive conception of the spending power. The classical statement of the broad theory of the spending power is that by Hamilton, in his *Report on Manufactures* in 1791. Reciting the "lay and collect taxes" clause of Article I, section 8 he says:

[13] See *Commentaries* § 1090.

[14] *Hampton & Co.* v. *United States,* 276 U. S. 394, 411, 48 Sup. Ct. 348, 353, 72 L. Ed. 624, 631 (1928).

The phrase is as comprehensive as any that could have been used, because it was not fit that the constitutional authority of the Union to appropriate its revenues should have been restricted within narrower limits than the "general welfare," and because this necessarily embraces a vast variety of particulars which are susceptible neither of specification nor of definition. It is therefore of necessity left to the discretion of the National Legislature to pronounce upon the objects which concern the general welfare, and for which, under that description, an appropriation of money is requisite and proper. And there seems to be no room for a doubt that whatever concerns the general interests of learning, of agriculture, of manufactures, and of commerce, are within the sphere of the national councils, *as far as regards an application of money.*[15]

Endorsed contemporaneously by Jefferson, stigmatized by him on further reflection, rebutted by Madison in his veto of the Bonus Bill in 1806, rejected by Monroe in the early years of his Presidency, endorsed by him in his famous message of May 4, 1822, Hamilton's doctrine has since the Civil War pointed an ever-increasing trend in Congressional fiscal policy. Yet even as recently as 1923 we find the Court industriously sidestepping the constitutional question and displaying considerable agility in doing so.[16] . . . In the *A.A.A.* case [of 1936] the Court at last came to grips with the constitutional issue, which it decided in line with the Hamiltonian thesis. Said Justice Roberts for the Court:

Since the foundation of the Nation sharp differences of opinion have persisted as to the true interpretation of the phrase, ["lay and collect taxes to . . . provide for . . . the general welfare"]. Madison asserted it amounted to no more than a reference to the other powers enumerated in the subsequent clauses of the same section; that, as the United States is a government of limited and enumerated powers, the grant of power to tax and spend for the general national welfare must be confined to the enumerated legislative fields committed to the Congress. In this view the phrase is mere tautology, for taxation and appropriation are or may be necessary incidents of the exercise of any of the enumerated legislative powers. Hamilton, on the other hand, maintained the clause confers a power separate and distinct from those later enumerated, is not restricted in mean-

[15] 4 *Works of Alexander Hamilton* 151 (Federal ed. 1904).

[16] *Massachusetts* v. *Mellon,* 262 U. S. 447, 43 Sup. Ct. 597, 67 L. Ed. 1078 (1923).

ing by the grant of them, and Congress consequently has a substantive power to tax and to appropriate, limited only by the requirement that it shall be exercised to provide for the general welfare of the United States. Each contention has had the support of those whose views are entitled to weight. This court has noticed the question, but has never found it necessary to decide which is the true construction. Mr. Justice Story, in his *Commentaries,* espouses the Hamiltonian position. We shall not review the writings of public men and commentators or discuss the legislative practice. Study of all these leads us to conclude that the reading advocated by Mr. Justice Story is the correct one. While, therefore, the power to tax is not unlimited, its confines are set in the clause which confers it, and not in those of § 8 which bestow and define the legislative powers of the Congress. It results that the power of Congress to authorize expenditure of public moneys for public purposes is not limited, by the direct grants of legislative power found in the Constitution.[17]

In short, the Court once more ratified the history that Congressional practice had made. . . .

IV.

Our third postulate is addressed particularly to this question: By what rule are collisions between the respective powers of the two centers of government supposed by the Constitution to be determined? In answer two texts of the Constitution itself compete for recognition, Article VI, clause 2, which reads as follows:

This Constitution, and the laws of the United States which shall be made in pursuance thereof, and all treaties made, or which shall be made, under the authority of the United States, shall be the supreme law of the land; and the judges in every State shall be bound thereby, anything in the Constitution or laws of any State to the contrary notwithstanding.

and the Tenth Amendment, which says:

The powers not delegated to the United States by the Constitution, nor prohibited by it to the States, are reserved to the States respectively, or to the people.

[17] *United States* v. *Butler,* 297 U. S. 1, 65, 56 Sup. Ct. 312, 319, 80 L. Ed. 477, 488.

It was quite plainly the intention of the Federal Convention that national laws, otherwise constitutional except for being in conflict with State laws, should invariably prevail over the latter,[18] or, as Madison later phrased the matter, State power should be "no ingredient of national power"[19] This was also Marshall's theory.[20] Indeed, the principle of "national supremacy" was in his estimation the most fundamental axiom of constitutional interpretation touching the federal relationship. . . .

Whence came the notion of National-State "equality," and what effect did it have on the Court's jurisprudence? The germ of it is to be found in the theory of the Constitution's origin developed in the Virginia and Kentucky Resolutions, that it was a compact of "sovereign" states, rather than an ordinance of "the people of America." The deduction from this premise that the National Government and the States, both being "sovereign," faced each other as "equals" across the line defining their respective jurisdictions, was made by John Taylor of Carolina in his critique of the decision in *McCulloch* v. *Maryland.* But earlier, the Virginia Court of Appeals had contributed to Taylor's system of constitutional interpretation the notion that under the "supremacy" clause itself, the State judiciaries were the constitutionally designated agencies for the application of the principle of supremacy.[21] It followed that the Supreme Court no more than Congress was able to bind the "equal" States, nor could they on the other hand bind Congress or the Court.

The notion of National-State equality became in due course a part of the constitutional creed of the Taney Court, but stripped of its anarchic implications and reduced to the proportions of a single thread in a highly complicated fabric of constitutional exegesis. It was early in this period that the concept of the Police Power emerged.[22] This, broadly considered, was simply what Taney termed "the power to govern men and things" defined from the point of

[18] See 1 *Records of the Federal Convention* 21–22 (Farrand ed. 1911).

[19] 2 *Annals of Congress* col. 1891 (1790–91). See Corwin, *Commerce Power Versus States Rights* 117–72 (1936).

[20] See *McCulloch* v. *Maryland,* 4 Wheat. 316 (U. S. 1819) and *Gibbons* v. *Ogden,* 9 Wheat. 1 (U. S. 1824).

[21] See *Hunter* v. *Martin,* 4 Munf. 1, 11 (Va. 1814), rev'd, *Martin* v. *Hunter's Lessee,* 1 Wheat. 304, 4 L. Ed. 97 (U. S. 1816).

[22] See *New York* v. *Miln,* 11 Pet. 102, 9 R. Ed. 648 (U. S. 1837).

view of the duty of the State to "promote the happiness and prosperity of the community"; more narrowly, it was a certain central core of this power, namely the power of the States to "provide for the public health, safety, and good order." Within this latter field at least, the powers reserved to the States by the Tenth Amendment were "sovereign" powers, "complete, unqualified, and exclusive." Yet this did not signify that the States, acting through either their legislatures or their courts, were the final judge of the scope of these "sovereign" powers. This was the function of the Supreme Court of the United States, which for this purpose was regarded by the Constitution as standing outside of and over both the National Government and the States, and vested with authority to apportion impartially to each center its proper powers in accordance with the Constitution's intention. And the primary test whether this intention was fulfilled was whether conflict between the two centers was avoided.[23] In Judge Cooley's words, "The laws of both [centers] operate within the same territory, but if in any particular case their provisions are in conflict, one or the other is void," that is, void apart from the conflict itself.[24]

Thus the principle of national supremacy came to be superseded by an unlimited discretion in the Supreme Court to designate this or that State power as comprising an independent limitation on national power. In only one area was the earlier principle recognized as still operative, and that was the field of interstate commercial regulation. This field, indeed, was not properly speaking a part of the "reserved powers" of the States at all; it belonged to Congress's enumerated powers. The States, however, might occupy it as to minor phases of commerce unless and until Congress chose to do so, in which case Article VI, paragraph 2 came into play and conflicting state legislation was superseded.[25]

While, as we have seen, the Police Power was defined in the first instance with the end in view of securing to the States a near monopoly of the right to realize the main *objectives* of government, the concept came later to embrace the further idea that certain *subject-*

[23] On this system of constitutional interpretation, see especially *New York* v. *Miln*, 11 Pet. 102, 9 L. Ed. 648 (U. S. 1837); see also *License Cases*, 5 How. 504, 527–37, 573–74, 588, 613, 12 L. Ed. 256, 266–71, 387–88, 294, 305 (U. S, 1847) *passim*.

[24] Cooley, *Principles of Constitutional Law* 152 (3d ed. 1898).

[25] *Cooley* v. *Board of Wardens*, 12 How. 299, 13 L. Ed. 996 (U. S. 1851).

matters were also segregated to the States and hence could not be reached by any valid exercise of national power. That production, and hence mining, agriculture, and manufacturing, and the employer-employee relationship in connection with these were among such subject-matters was indeed one of the basic postulates of the Court's system of Constitutional Law in the era of *laissez faire*.[26]

This entire system of constitutional interpretation touching the Federal System is today in ruins. It toppled in the *Social Security Act* cases and in *N.L.R.B.* v. *Jones & Laughlin Steel Corporation,* in which the Wagner Labor Act was sustained.[27] This was in 1937 while the "Old Court" was still in power. In 1941 in *United States* v. *Darby,*[28] the "New Court" merely performed a mopping-up operation. The Act of Congress involved was the Fair Labor Standards Act of 1938, which not only bans interstate commerce in goods produced under sub-standard conditions but makes their production a penal offense against the United States if they are "intended" for interstate or foreign commerce. Speaking for the unanimous Court, Chief Justice Stone went straight back to Marshall's opinions in *McCulloch* v. *Maryland* and *Gibbons* v. *Ogden,* extracting from the former his latitudinarian construction of the "necessary and proper" clause and from both cases his uncompromising application of the "supremacy" clause.[29]

Today neither the State Police Power nor the concept of Federal Equilibrium is any "ingredient of national legislative power," whether as respects subject-matter to be governed, or the choice of objectives or of means for its exercise.

V.

Lastly, we come to the question whether the two centers of government ought to be regarded as standing in a competitive or cooperative relation to each other. The question first emerged at the executive and judicial levels. In Article VI, paragraph 3 the requirement is laid down that members of the State legislatures, their execu-

[26] See Corwin, *Commerce Power Versus Status Rights* 175–209 (1936).

[27] 301 U. S. 1, 57 Sup. Ct. 615, 81 L. Ed. 893 (1937).

[28] 312 U. S. 100, 61 Sup. Ct. 451, 85 L. Ed. 609 (1941).

[29] *Ibid.* See also *United States* v. *Carolene Products Co.,* 304 U.S. 144, 58 Sup. Ct. 778, 82 L. Ed. 1234 (1938); *Mulford* v. *Smith,* 307 U. S. 38, 59 Sup. Ct. 648, 83 L. Ed. 1092 (1939).

tive and judicial officers shall take an oath, or make affirmation, to support the Constitution, thus testifying, as Hamilton points out in *Federalist* 27, to the expectation that these functionaries would be "incorporated into the operations of the National Government," in the exercise of its constitutional powers. In much early legislation, furthermore, this expectation was realized. The Judiciary Act of 1789 left the State courts in exclusive possession of some categories of national jurisdiction and shared some others with it. The Act of 1793 entrusted the rendition of fugitive slaves in part to national officials and in part to State officials, and the rendition of fugitives from justice from one State to another exclusively to the State executives. Certain later acts empowered State courts to entertain criminal prosecutions for forging paper of the Bank of the United States and for counterfeiting coin of the United States; while still others conferred on State judges authority to admit aliens to national citizenship and provided penalties in case such judges should utter false certificates of naturalization—provisions which are still on the statute books.[30]

The subsequent rise, however, of the States Rights sentiment presently overcast this point of view with heavy clouds of doubt. From the nationalist angle Marshall stigmatized the efforts of Virginia and those who thought her way to "confederatize the Union"; and asserting in *McCulloch* v. *Maryland* the administrative independence of the National Government, he there laid down a sweeping rule prohibiting the States from taxing even to the slightest extent national instrumentalities on their operations. "The power to tax is the power to destroy," said he; and whatever a State may do at all it may do to the utmost extent.[31]

But when a few years later the Taney Court took over, the shoe was on the other foot. In 1842, the State of Pennsylvania was sustained by the Court, speaking by Marshall's apostle Story, in refusing to permit its magistrates to aid in enforcing the fugitive slave provisions of the Act of 1793. Said Story:

> . . . the national government, in the absence of all positive provisions to the contrary, is bound through its own proper departments,

[30] For references, see Corwin, *Court Over Constitution* 135–36 and notes (1938).

[31] See 4 Wheat. 316, 427–31, 4 L. Ed. 579, 606–7 (U. S. 1819); *Brown* v. *Maryland,* 12 Wheat. 419, 439, 6 L. Ed. 678, 685 (U. S. 1827).

legislative, executive, or judiciary, as the case may require, to carry into effect all the rights and duties imposed upon it by the Constitution.[32]

And in *Kentucky* v. *Dennison,* decided on the eve of the Civil War, the "duty" imposed by this same act on State governors to render up fugitives from justice on the demand of the executives of sister States, was watered down to a judicially unenforcible "moral duty." Said the Chief Justice: " . . . we think it clear, that the Federal Government, under the Constitution, has no power to impose on a State officer, as such, any duty whatever, and compel him to perform it; . . . "[33]

Nor was even this the end, for as late as 1871 the Court laid down the converse of Marshall's doctrine in *McCulloch* v. *Maryland,* holding that, since the States enjoyed equal constitutional status with the National Government, what was sauce for the one was sauce for the other too, and that therefore a national income tax could not be constitutionally applied to State official salaries.[34]

The doctrine of tax exemption was the climactic expression of the competitive theory of Federalism, and is today largely moribund in consequence of the emergence of the *cooperative* conception. According to this conception, the National Government and the States are mutually complementary parts of a *single* governmental mechanism all of whose powers are intended to realize the current purposes of government according to their applicability to the problem in hand. It is thus closely intertwined with the multiple-purpose conception of national power and with recent enlarged theories of the function of government generally. Here we are principally interested in two forms of joint action by the National Government and the States which have developed within recent years, primarily through the *legislative* powers of the two centers.

Thus in the first place the National Government has brought its augmented powers over interstate commerce and communications to the support of local policies of the States in the exercise of their reserved powers. By the doctrine that Congress's power to regulate "commerce among the States" is "exclusive," a State is frequently

[32] *Prigg* v. *Commonwealth of Pennsylvania,* 16 Peters 539, 616, 10 L. Ed. 1060, 1089 (U. S. 1842).

[33] 24 How. 66, 107, 16 L. Ed. 717, 729 (U. S. 1861).

[34] *Collector* v. *Day,* 11 Wall. 113, 20 L. Ed. 122 (U. S. 1871).

unable to stop the flow of commerce from sister States even when it threatens to undermine local legislation. In consequence Congress has within recent years come to the assistance of the police powers of the States by making certain crimes against them, like theft, racketeering, kidnapping, crimes also against the National Government whenever the offender extends his activities beyond state boundary lines.[35]

Justifying such legislation, the Court has said:

> Our dual form of government has its perplexities, state and Nation having different spheres of jurisdiction . . . but it must be kept in mind that we are one people; and the powers reserved to the states and those conferred on the nation are adapted to be exercised, whether independently or concurrently, to promote the general welfare, material and moral.[36]

It is true that in the *Child Labor* case of 1918 this postulate of constitutional interpretation seemed to have been discarded, but the logic of *United States* v. *Darby* restores it in full force.

Secondly, the National Government has held out inducements, primarily of a pecuniary kind, to the States—the so-called "grants-in-aid"—to use their reserved powers to support certain objectives of national policy in the field of expenditure. In other words, the greater financial strength of the National Government is joined to the wider coercive powers of the States. Thus since 1911, Congress has voted money to subsidize forest-protection, education in agricultural and industrial subjects and in home economics, vocational rehabilitation and education, the maintenance of nautical schools, experimentation in reforestation and highway construction in the States; in return for which cooperating States have appropriated equal sums for the same purposes, and have brought their further powers to the support thereof along lines laid down by Congress.[37]

The culmination of this type of National-State cooperation to date, however, is reached in The Social Security Act of August 14, 1935. The Act brings the national tax-spending power to the support of such States as desire to cooperate in the maintenance of

[35] For references, see Corwin, *Court Over Constitution* 148–50 and notes (1938).

[36] *Hoke* v. *United States,* 227 U. S. 308, 322, 33 Sup. Ct. 281, 284, 57 L. Ed. 523, 527 (1913).

[37] Corwin, *op. cit. supra* note 35, at 157–63.

old-age pensions, unemployment insurance, maternal welfare work, vocational rehabilitation, and public health work, and in financial assistance to impoverished old age, dependent children, and the blind. Such legislation is, as we have seen, within the national taxing-spending power. What, however, of the objection that it "coerced" complying States into "abdicating" their powers? Speaking to this point in the *Social Security Act* cases, the Court has said: "The . . . contention confuses motive with coercion . . . . To hold that motive or temptation is equivalent to coercion is to plunge the law in endless difficulties."[38] And again: "The United States and the state of Alabama are not alien governments. They co-exist within the same territory. Unemployment is their common concern. Together the two statutes before us [the Act of Congress and the Alabama Act] embody a cooperative legislative effort by state and national governments, for carrying out a public purpose common to both, which neither could fully achieve without the cooperation of the other. The Constitution does not prohibit such cooperation."[39]

It has been argued, to be sure, that the cooperative conception of the federal relationship, especially as it is realized in the policy of the "grants-in-aid," tends to break down State initiative and to devitalize State policies. Actually, its effect has often been the contrary, and for the reason pointed out by Justice Cardozo in *Helvering* v. *Davis*,[40] also decided in 1937; namely, that the States, competing as they do with one another to attract investors, have not been able to embark separately upon expensive programs of relief and social insurance.

The other great objection to Cooperative Federalism is more difficult to meet, if indeed it can be met. This is, that "Cooperative Federalism" spells further aggrandizement of national power. Unquestionably it does, for when two cooperate it is the stronger member of the combination who calls the tunes. Resting as it does primarily on the superior fiscal resources of the National Government, Cooperative Federalism has been, to date, a short expression for a constantly increasing concentration of power at Washington in the instigation and supervision of local policies.

[38] *Steward Machine Co.* v. *Davis,* 301 U. S. 548, 589, 57 Sup. Ct. 883, 892, 81 L. Ed. 1279, 1292 (1937).

[39] *Carmichael* v. *Southern Coal & Coke Co.,* 301 U. S. 495, 526, 57 Sup. Ct. 868, 880, 81 L. Ed. 1245, 1262 (1937).

[40] 301 U. S. 619, 57 Sup. Ct. 904, 81 L. Ed. 1307 (1937).

VI.

But the story of American federalism may also be surveyed from the angle of the diverse interests which the federal "contrivance"—to use Dicey's apt word—has served. Federalism's first achievement was to enable the American people to secure the benefits of national union without imperilling their republican institutions. In a passage in his *Spirit of the Laws* which Hamilton quotes in *The Federalist,* Montesquieu had anticipated this possibility in general terms. He said:

> It is very probable that mankind would have been obliged at length to live constantly under the government of a single person, had they not contrived a kind of constitution that has all the internal advantages of a republican, together with the external force of a monarchical government. I mean a Confederate Republic.[41]

In fact, the founders of the American Federal System for the first time in history ranged the power of a potentially great state on the side of institutions which had hitherto been confined to small states. Even the republicanism of Rome had stopped at the Eternal City's walls.

Then in the century following, American federalism served the great enterprise of appropriating the North American continent to western civilization. For one of the greatest lures to the westward movement of population was the possibility which federalism held out to the advancing settlers of establishing their own undictated political institutions, and endowing them with generous powers of government for local use. Federalism thus became the instrument of a new, *a democratic, imperialism,* one extending over an "Empire of liberty," in Jefferson's striking phrase.

Then, about 1890, just as the frontier was disappearing from the map, federalism became, through judicial review, an instrument of the current *laissez faire* conception of the function of government and a force promoting the rise of Big Business. Adopting the theory that the reason why Congress had been given the power to regulate "commerce among the several states" was to prevent the states from doing so, rather than to enable the National Government to pursue

[41] *The Federalist,* No. 9 at 48 (Lodge ed. 1888).

social policies of its own through exerting a positive control over commerce, the Court at one time created a realm of no-power, "a twilight zone," "a no-man's land" in which corporate enterprise was free to roam largely unchecked. While the economic unification of the nation was undoubtedly aided by this type of Constitutional Law, the benefit was handsomely paid for in the social detriments which attended it, as became clear when the Great Depression descended on the country.

Finally, by the constitutional revolution which once went by the name of the "New Deal" but now wears the label "Fair Deal," American federalism has been converted into an instrument for the achievement of peace abroad and economic security for "the common man" at home. In the process of remolding the Federal System for these purposes, however, the instrument has been overwhelmed and submerged in the objectives sought, so that today the question faces us whether the constituent States of the System can be saved for any useful purpose, and thereby saved as the vital cells that they have been heretofore of democratic sentiment, impulse, and action.

And it was probably with some such doubt in mind that Justice Frankfurter wrote a few years ago, in an opinion for the Court:

> The interpenetrations of modern society have not wiped out state lines. It is not for us to make inroads upon our federal system either by indifference to its maintenance or excessive regard for the unifying forces of modern technology. Scholastic reasoning may prove that no activity is isolated within the boundaries of a single State, but that cannot justify absorption of legislative power by the United States over every activity.[42]

These be brave words. Are they likely to determine the course of future history any more than Madison's similar utterance—130 years ago—has done to date?

[42] *Polish National Alliance* v. *NLRB*, 322 U. S. 643, 650, 64 Sup. Ct. 1196, 1200, 86 L. Ed. 1509, 1516 (1944).

★ XI ★

Bowing Out "Clear and Present Danger"*

By treating the formula as authorizing it to weigh the substantive good protected by the statute against the "clear and present" danger requirement, the court rids itself from the tyranny of a phrase.

"Every institution," wrote Emerson, "is the lengthened shadow of one man." The observation is nowhere borne out more strikingly than in judicial doctrines, which often exert an influence truly institutional in scope. An outstanding example in the field of American public law is Chief Justice Marshall's famous dictum that "the power to tax is the power to destroy."[1] Reflecting the lesson that Marshall drew from his experience as a young soldier under a government whose activities were repeatedly balked by local selfishness, this dictum came ultimately, through his dominant agency, to furnish the core of an important chapter of our constitutional law. A comparable instance in recent times is afforded by Justice Holmes' personal responsibility for the "clear and present danger" formula, a formula which illustrates a facet of its distinguished author's education and habit of mind.

Mr. Biddle tells in his little book on Holmes how, when the Justice was a lad, his father, the once celebrated "Autocrat of the Breakfast Table," was accustomed to reward "Wendell" with an extra dab of marmalade "for saying what the Governor [the Autocrat]

* 27 *Notre Dame Lawyer* (Spring, 1952) 325.

[1] *McCulloch* v. *Maryland,* 4 Wheat. 316, 431, 4 L. Ed. 579 (U. S. 1819).

thought was worth saying. . . ."[2] The result of this matutinal drill in the making of bright remarks was a pronounced turn for epigram, which sometimes indeed took on the more portentous tone of oracle. Was the "clear and present danger" formula, we may ask, one of Holmes' more fortunate or one of his less fortunate ventures in epigram-making? As we shall see, the Justice himself appeared at first to take his brain-child very casually, until, as we may surmise, somebody alerted him to its possibilities, thereby converting a biographical detail into constitutional history.

I.

As it finally matured into a doctrine of constitutional law, the "clear and present danger" formula became a measure of legislative power in the choice of values which may be protected against unrestricted speech and publication. Before an utterance could be punished by government, it must have occurred in such circumstances or have been of such a nature as (1) to create a "clear and present danger" that (2) it would bring about "substantive evils" within the constitutional power of government in the United States to combat; and on both these points the Supreme Court of the United States was, by virtue of the protection which is today thrown about freedom of speech and press by the First and Fourteenth Amendments, the final judge.

The phrase "clear and present danger" first appeared in Holmes' opinion for a unanimous Court in *Schenck* v. *United States,*[3] which was decided March 3, 1919. Four years prior the same Justice had written the opinion, also for a unanimous Court, in *Fox* v. *Washington,*[4] where the question at issue was the constitutionality of a Washington statute which made it unlawful to publish or circulate any matter "advocating, encouraging or inciting, or having a tendency to encourage or incite the commission of any crime. . . ."[5] The defendant had been convicted of publishing an article which was sharply critical of those who opposed nudism. According to Justice Holmes, this article "by indirection but unmistakably . . . encourages and incites a persistence in what we must assume would be a breach of the state laws against indecent exposure; and the

[2] Biddle, *Mr. Justice Holmes,* 27 (1942).
[3] 249 U. S. 47, 39 S. Ct. 247, 63 L. Ed. 470 (1919).
[4] 236 U. S. 273, 35 S. Ct. 383, 59 L. Ed. 573 (1915).
[5] As quoted in *id.,* 236 U. S. at 275.

jury so found."[6] Stating further that "We understand the state court by implication at least to have read the statute as confined to encouraging an actual breach of the law,"[7] he brushed aside the argument that it infringed the constitutional guarantee of freedom of speech. Nothing was said about the degree of danger that breach of the law would result from the publication; nor was the question raised whether appearance in public in a decent minimum of clothing is a "substantive" value which government in the United States is entitled to protect. The plain implication is that incitement to crime or encouragement thereof is sufficient, without reference to its actual consequences.[8]

Did the Court, or did Justice Holmes himself, intend to depart

[6] *Id.,* 236 U. S. at 277.

[7] *Ibid.*

[8] In *Davis* v. *Beason,* 133 U. S. 333, 10 S. Ct. 299, 33 L. Ed. 637 (1890), the question at issue was the constitutionality of a statute of the Territory of Idaho, providing that "no person who is a bigamist or polygamist, or who teaches, advises, counsels or encourages any person or persons to become bigamists or polygamists or to commit any other crime defined by law, or to enter into what is known as plural or celestial marriage, or who is a member of any order, organization or association which teaches, advises, counsels or encourages its members or devotees or any other person to commit the crime of bigamy or polygamy, or any other crime defined by law, either as a rite or ceremony of such order, organization or association, or otherwise, is permitted to vote at any election, or to hold any position or office of honor, trust or profit within this Territory."

A unanimous Court held this enactment to be within the legislative powers which Congress had conferred on the Territory and not to be open to any constitutional objection. Said Justice Field for the Court:

"Bigamy and polygamy are crimes by the laws of all civilized and Christian countries. They are crimes by the laws of the United States, and they are crimes by the laws of Idaho. They tend to destroy the purity of the marriage relation, to disturb the peace of families, to degrade woman and to debase man. Few crimes are more pernicious to the best interests of society and receive more general or more deserved punishment. To extend exemption from punishment for such crimes would be to shock the moral judgment of the community. To call their advocacy a tenet of religion is to offend the common sense of mankind. If they are crimes, then to teach, advise and counsel their practice is to aid in their commission, and such teaching and counseling are themselves criminal and proper subjects of punishment, as aiding and abetting crime are in all other cases." 133 U. S. at 341–2.

There was no talk about the necessity for showing that the prohibited teaching, counselling, advising, etc., must be shown to have occurred in circumstances creating a "clear and present danger" of its being followed; or of monogamy being a value which government in the United States is authorized to protect.

from these *Fox* views in the *Schenck* case? Read out of context, the following passage,[9] in which the words "clear and present danger" were first used, suggests an affirmative answer:

> We admit that in many places and in ordinary times the defendants in saying all that was said in the circular would have been within their constitutional rights. But the character of every act depends upon the circumstances in which it is done. . . . The most stringent protection of free speech would not protect a man in falsely shouting fire in a theatre and causing a panic. It does not even protect a man from an injunction against uttering words that may have all the effect of force. *Gompers* v. *Buck's Stove & Range Co.*, 221 U. S. 418, 439. . . . The question in every case is whether the words used are used in such circumstances and are of such a nature as to create a clear and present danger that they will bring about the substantive evils that Congress has a right to prevent. It is a question of proximity and degree. When a nation is at war many things that might be said in time of peace are such a hindrance to its effort that their utterance will not be endured so long as men fight and that no Court could regard them as protected by any constitutional right.

Reading these sentences, however, in light of the facts of the case and of other portions of the same opinion, we reach a different conclusion, as did the overwhelming majority of the Court itself as soon as its doing so became determinative. Defendants in *Schenck* had been convicted of a conspiracy to violate the Espionage Act of 1917[10] by attempting to cause insubordination in the armed forces and to obstruct recruiting. Pursuant to that conspiracy they had mailed to members of the armed forces circulars which criticized conscription in strong language and exhorted readers to assert and support their rights. Apparently these circulars did not in express terms counsel insubordination or obstruction to recruiting, nor was that result proved. Indeed, so far as the opinion discloses, no evidence was presented as to their possible or probable effect apart

[9] 249 U. S. 47, 52, 39 S. Ct. 247, 63 L. Ed. 470 (1919). It should be observed in passing that advocates of "clear and present danger" always quote the part about "shouting fire in a theatre," but usually omit the reference to the *Gompers* case where speech was held restrainable in enforcement of an anti-labor injunction.

[10] 40 *Stat.* 217 (1917). This statute is now substantially embodied in 18 U. S. C. § 793 (Supp. 1951).

from their contents and the fact of their publication. This circumstance, however, did not trouble Justice Holmes who disposed of the point by saying:

Of course the document would not have been sent unless it had been intended to have some effect, and we do not see what effect it could be expected to have upon persons subject to the draft except in influence them to obstruct the carrying of it out.[11]

And he later added: "If the act (speaking, or circulating a paper), its tendency and the intent with which it is done are the same, we perceive no ground for saying that success alone warrants making the act a crime."[12] In the final analysis the doctrine announced in the *Schenck* case is indistinguishable from that presented in *Fox*.

Within the next two weeks, two more convictions under the Espionage Act were also unanimously upheld in opinions written by Justice Holmes. These two pronouncements went far to dispel whatever impression may have been created by the earlier opinion that there is a constitutional requirement that "clear and present danger" of some "substantive evil" be proved where intent to incite a crime is found to exist. In *Frohwerk* v. *United States*,[13] the defendant was convicted of conspiriing to violate the Espionage Act and of attempting to cause disloyalty, mutiny and refusal of duty in the armed forces by the publication of twelve newspaper articles criticizing this country's entry into the war and the conscription of men for service overseas. The claim of privilege under the First Amendment Justice Holmes brusquely rejected:

With regard to that argument we think it necessary to add to what has been said in *Schenck* v. *United States* . . . only that the First Amendment while prohibiting legislation against free speech as such cannot have been, and obviously was not, intended to give immunity for every possible use of language. . . . We venture to believe that neither Hamilton nor Madison, nor any other competent person then or later, ever supposed that to make criminal the counselling of a murder within the jurisdiction of Congress would be an unconstitutional interference with free speech.[14]

[11] 249 U. S. 47, 51, 39 S. Ct. 247, 63 L. Ed. 470 (1919).
[12] *Id.* 249 U. S. at 52.
[13] 249 U. S. 204, 39 S. Ct. 249, 63 L. Ed. 561 (1919).
[14] *Id.*, 249 U. S. at 206.

Of significance, too, in view of some things said later in the *Dennis* case,[15] is the following passage from the same opinion:

It is said that the first count is bad because it does not allege the means by which the conspiracy was to be carried out. But a conspiracy to obstruct recruiting would be criminal even if no means were agreed upon specifically by which to accomplish the intent. It is enough if the parties agreed to set to work for that common purpose. That purpose could be accomplished or aided by persuasion as well as by false statements, and there was no need to allege that false reports were intended to be made, or made. It is argued that there is no sufficient allegation of intent, but intent to accomplish an object cannot be alleged more clearly than by stating that parties conspired to accomplish it.[16]

On the same day Justice Holmes also delivered the opinion in *Debs* v. *United States*,[17] sustaining a conviction for the same kind of offense. The charge arose out of a speech delivered by the defendant in which he extolled socialism and criticized the participation of the United States in World War I. As in the preceding cases there was no explicit exhortation to any criminal offense. The principal points at issue concerned the weight and admissibility of evidence bearing upon the unlawful intent of Debs' address. The Court held that the jury was warranted

. . . in finding that one purpose of the speech, whether incidental or not does not matter, was to oppose not only war in general but this war, and that the opposition was so expressed that its natural and intended effect would be to obstruct recruiting. If that was intended and if, in all the circumstances, that would be its probable effect, it would not be protected by reason of its being part of a general program and expressions of a general and conscientious belief.[18]

In short, we find three cases, decided within a period of two weeks, in which convictions for violation of the Espionage Act were

[15] *Dennis* v. *United States,* 341 U. S. 494, 71 S. Ct. 857, 95 L. Ed. 1137 (1951).

[16] *Frohwerk* v. *United States,* 249 U. S. 204, 209, 39 S. Ct. 249, 63 L. Ed. 561 (1919).

[17] 249 U. S. 211, 39 S. Ct. 252, 63 L. Ed. 566 (1919).

[18] *Id.,* 249 U. S. at 214–5.

unanimously sustained for utterances of such general nature that they might all have borne innocent interpretations if made in other circumstances, but which were deemed to be unlawful because the circumstances warranted the finding that their probable and intended effect would be to obstruct the war effort. Furthermore, in the last two of these three cases we hear not a word about "clear and present danger."

Eight months later, however, the apparently forgotten phrase leaps suddenly into prominence in the dissenting opinion of Justice Holmes for himself and Justice Brandeis in *Abrams* v. *United States*.[19] The defendants were Russian sympathizers who called upon workers to stop producing munitions which, they asserted, were being used against Russia as well as Germany. The majority held that even though defendants' primary purpose was to prevent injury to the Russian cause, they were accountable for the easily foreseeable effects which their utterances were likely to produce in the way of obstructing the war effort against Germany.

The intention of Justice Holmes' dissent is ambiguous. At first he seemed to be basing his case on the statute alone. Thus he said:

> I am aware of course that the word "intent" as vaguely used in ordinary legal discussion means no more than knowledge at the time of the act that the consequences said to be intended will ensue. . . . But, when words are used exactly, a deed is not done with intent to produce a consequence unless that consequence is the aim of the deed. . . . It seems to me that this statute must be taken to use its words in a strict and accurate sense.[20]

But he soon transferred the discussion to the First Amendment, as to the bearing of which on the case he wrote:

> I do not doubt for a moment that by the same reasoning that would justify punishing persuasion to murder, the United States constitutionally may punish speech that produces or is intended to produce a clear and imminent danger that it will bring about forthwith certain substantive evils that the United States constitutionally may seek to prevent. . . . It is only the present danger of immediate evil or an intent to bring it about that warrants Congress in setting a limit to the expression of opinion where private rights are

[19] 250 U. S. 616, 40 S. Ct. 17, 63 L. Ed. 1173 (1919).
[20] *Id.*, 250 U. S. at 626–7.

not concerned. Congress certainly cannot forbid all effort to change the mind of the country. Now nobody can suppose that the surreptitious publishing of a silly leaflet by an unknown man, without more, would present any immediate danger that its opinions would hinder the success of the government arms or have any appreciable tendency to do so. Publishing those opinions for the very purpose of obstructing, however, might indicate a greater danger and at any rate would have the quality of an attempt. So I assume that the second leaflet if published for the purposes alleged in the fourth count might be punishable.[21]

And being now in the full flood of composition, the Justice concluded his opinion with an appeal to history, as follows:

Persecution for the expression of opinions seems to me perfectly logical. . . . But when men have realized that time has upset many fighting faiths, they may come to believe even more than they believe the very foundations of their own conduct that the ultimate good desired is better reached by free trade in ideas—that the best test of truth is the power of the thought to get itself accepted in the competition of the market, and that truth is the only ground upon which their wishes safely can be carried out. That at any rate is the theory of our Constitution. It is an experiment, as all life is an experiment.[22]

Certain questions arise: Did Justice Holmes, when he spoke of "persuation to murder," mean successful persuasion? This is obviously something quite different from the "counselling of murder" which he said, in his *Frohwerk* opinion, that Hamilton and Madison never supposed could not be constitutionally punished. And was it his intention to assert it as a rule of constitutional law that the Court should disallow any act of Congress which is interpretable as punishing utterances that do not in its opinion produce a "clear and present danger" to an interest which it thinks of sufficient importance to deserve such protection? If so, how could he have said the *Frohwerk* and *Debs* cases were in his opinion correctly decided? And what did he mean by his suggestion that utterances which have "the quality of an attempt," to wit, of acts done for the purpose of committing a crime, but falling short of it, may be constitutionally punished? Was the suggestion intended to narrow still further the category of constitutionally restrainable utterances?

[21] *Id.,* 250 U. S. at 627–8.
[22] *Id.,* 250 U. S. at 630.

Coming then to the hortatory portion of the opinion—that concerning "fighting faiths"—did Justice Holmes mean that faiths are entitled to survive only so long as they don't fight, and that "the ultimate good desired" has always prevailed of its own inherent qualities without anybody fighting for it? And if so, how does this teaching square with the belief expressed by its author elsewhere that the "proximate test of excellence" is "correspondence to the actual equilibrium of forces in the community—that is, conformity to the wishes of the dominant power"?[23] The answer is perhaps supplied in the following passage from the same Justice's dissent in the *Gitlow* case,[24] five years later: "If in the long run the beliefs expressed in proletarian dictatorship are destined to be accepted by the dominant forces of the community, the only meaning of free speech is that they should be given their chance and have their way."

In short, the "ultimate good desired" and the triumph of destiny are one and the same thing, and the function of freedom of speech is to forward this triumph, not to block it, although just why destiny needs an assist does not quite appear. That the Constitution is an "experiment" need not be questioned; unquestionable too is the fact that its maintenance has not been achieved without a certain amount of fighting at times, in some of which the youthful Holmes himself bore a gallant part.

It should be noted that in his correspondence with Sir Frederick Pollock about *Abrams,* Holmes justified his dissent solely by reference to his reading of the word "intent" as used in the statute.[25] As to the "clear and present danger" formula he said not a word.

Between *Abrams* and Justice Holmes' retirement from the Bench, twelve years elapsed. In this interval he succeeded in enrolling only one other Justice under his banner, his fellow Bostonian and fellow graduate from Harvard Law School, Justice Brandeis, whose initial contribution to the discussion occurs in 1920 in connection with *Schaefer* v. *United States*.[26] Sustaining here a conviction based upon the publication of a series of newspaper articles which criticized the Government in its conduct of the war, the majority used language

23 Holmes, *Collected Legal Papers* 258 (1920).

24 *Gitlow* v. *New York,* 268 U. S. 652, 673, 45 S. Ct. 625, 69 L. Ed. 1138 (1925).

25 2 *Holmes-Pollock Letters* 29–45 (Howe ed. 1941).

26 251 U. S. 466, 40 S. Ct. 259, 64 L. Ed. 360 (1920).

quite similar to that employed by Holmes in the *Schenck* case. With respect to the contents of the articles, the Court, speaking by Justice McKenna, chanted the following answer:

> Coarse indeed, this was, and vulgar to us; but it was expected to produce, and it may be did produce, a different effect upon its readers. To them its derisive contempt may have been truly descriptive of American feebleness and inability to combat Germany's prowess, and thereby chill and check the ardency of patriotism and make it despair of success, and in hopelessness relax energy both in preparation and action. If it and the other articles . . . had not that purpose, what purpose had they? . . . Their effect or the persons affected could not be shown, nor was it necessary. The tendency of the articles and their efficacy were enough for offense—their "intent" and "attempt," for those are the words of the law—and to have required more would have made the law useless. It was passed in precaution. The incidence of its violation might not be immediately seen, evil appearing only in disaster, the result of the disloyalty engendered and the spirit of mutiny.[27]

Justice Brandeis' *riposte* for himself and Holmes is launched from the latter's dictum in *Schenck*. This is asserted to be a "rule of reason" and the measure, as "declared by a unanimous Court," of the power of Congress to "interfere with free speech." The opinion continues:

> Correctly applied, it will preserve the right of free speech both from suppression by tyrannous, well-meaning majorities, and from abuse by irresponsible, fanatical minorities. Like many other rules for human conduct, it can be applied correctly only by the exercise of good judgment; and to the exercise of good judgment calmness is, in times of deep feeling and on subjects which excite passion, as essential as fearlessness and honesty. The question whether in a particular instance the words spoken or written fall within the permissible curtailment of free speech is, under the rule enunciated by this court, one of degree; and because it is a question of degree the field in which the jury may exercise its judgment is necessarily a wide one. But its field is not unlimited. The trial provided for is one by judge *and* jury, and the judge may not abdicate his function. If the words were of such a nature and were used under such circumstances that men, judging in calmness, could not reasonably say

[27] *Id.*, 251 U. S. at 478–9.

that they created a clear and present danger that they would bring about the evil which Congress sought and had a right to prevent, then it is the duty of the trial judge to withdraw the case from the consideration of the jury; and, if he fails to do so, it is the duty of the appellate court to correct the error. In my opinion, no jury acting in calmness could reasonably say that any of the publications set forth in the indictment was of such a character or was made under such circumstances as to create a clear and present danger, either that they would obstruct recruiting or that they would promote the success of the enemies of the United States.[28]

What follows is a critical examination of the incriminating documents which seems to prove their gross misuse by the prosecution, effected with the aid and consent of the trial court. The necessity of invoking the "clear and present danger" formula to meet this situation is, however, left obscure. Justice Clarke also dissented, but on the ground that the proceedings constituted "a case of flagrant mistrial." He refused to concede that "the disposition of this case involves a great peril either to the maintenance of law and order and governmental authority on one hand, or to the freedom of the press on the other."[29]

II.

In 1925 occurred *Gitlow* v. *New York,*[30] a pivotal case for two reasons. In the first place, the Court adopted, as it had in the *Fox* case, the assumption that the Fourteenth Amendment was intended to render the restraints imposed by the First Amendment on Congress available also against the states so far as freedom of speech and press are concerned. In the second place, the case involved the first peacetime prosecution for criminal anarchy. The New York criminal anarchy statute made it a felony for any person to advise or teach the duty, necessity or propriety of overthrowing or overturning organized government by force and violence. The defendant had participated in the publication of a left wing manifesto advocating "revolutionary mass action" for the purpose of conquering and destroying the parliamentary State and establishing Commu-

[28] *Id.,* 251 U. S. at 482–3.
[29] *Id.,* 251 U. S. at 501.
[30] 268 U. S. 652, 45 S. Ct. 625, 69 L. Ed. 1138 (1925).

nism in its place. Since, according to the majority opinion, there was no evidence of any effect resulting from the publication and circulation of the manifesto, the jury's verdict of guilty imported a finding that the defendant had acted with unlawful intent in teaching and advocating unlawful acts for the purpose of overthrowing the government. So interpreted and applied, the statute was sustained by the Court, seven to two. Said Justice Sanford for the majority:

> It is a fundamental principle, long established, that the freedom of speech and of the press which is secured by the Constitution, does not confer an absolute right to speak or publish, without responsibility, whatever one may choose, or an unrestricted and unbridled license that gives immunity for every possible use of language and prevents the punishment of those who abuse this freedom.[31]

The Court accepted the soundness of the rule that a state, in the exercise of its police power, may punish one who abuses the freedom of speech by utterances tending to corrupt public morals, incite to crime or disturb the peace.[32] All the more then may it punish utterances endangering the foundations of organized government:

> It [freedom of speech and press] does not protect publications prompting the overthrow of government by force; the punishment of those who publish articles which tend to destroy organized society being essential to the security of freedom and the stability of the State. . . . And a State may penalize utterances which openly advocate the overthrow of the representative and constitutional form of government of the United States and the several States, by violence or other unlawful means. . . . In short this freedom does not deprive a State of the primary and essential right of self preservation; which, so long as human governments endure, they cannot be denied.[33]

Justice Sanford pointed out that the state, by enacting the statute, has determined that utterances advocating the overthrow of organized government by force and violence are so inimical to the

[31] *Id.,* 268 U. S. at 666.

[32] *Patterson* v. *Colorado,* 205 U. S. 454, 27 S. Ct. 556, 51 L. Ed. 879 (1907); *Robertson* v. *Baldwin,* 165 U. S. 275, 17 S. Ct. 326, 41 L. Ed. 715 (1897).

[33] *Gitlow* v. *New York,* 268 U. S. 652, 668, 45 S. Ct. 625, 69 L. Ed. 1138 (1925).

general welfare and involve such danger of substantive evil that they may be penalized under the police power. That determination, he added, "must be given great weight. Every presumption is to be indulged in favor of the validity of the statute."[34] He then continued:

That utterances inciting to the overthrow of organized government by unlawful means, present a sufficient danger of substantive evil to bring their punishment within the range of legislative discretion, is clear. Such utterances, by their very nature, involve danger to the public peace and to the security of the State. They threaten breaches of the peace and ultimate revolution. And the immediate danger is none the less real and substantial, because the effect of a given utterance cannot be accurately foreseen. The State cannot reasonably be required to measure the danger from every such utterance in the nice balance of a jeweler's scale. A single revolutionary spark may kindle a fire that, smouldering for a time, may burst into a sweeping and destructive conflagration. It cannot be said that the State is acting arbitrarily or unreasonably when in the exercise of its judgment as to the measures necessary to protect the public peace and safety, it seeks to extinguish the spark without waiting until it has enkindled the flame or blazed into the conflagration. It cannot reasonably be required to defer the adoption of measures for its own peace and safety until the revolutionary utterances lead to actual disturbances of the public peace or imminent and immediate danger of its own destruction; but it may, in the exercise of its judgment, suppress the threatened danger in its incipiency.[35]

Moreover, the statute's validity being settled,

. . . it may be applied to every utterance—not too trivial to be beneath the notice of the law—which is of such a character and used with such intent and purpose as to bring it within the prohibition of the statute. . . . In other words, when the legislative body has determined generally, in the constitutional exercise of its discretion, that utterances of a certain kind involve such danger of substantive evil that they may be punished, the question whether any specific utterance coming within the prohibited class is likely, in and of itself, to bring about the substantive evil, is not open to con-

[34] *Ibid.* The Court also cited as authority *Mugler* v. *Kansas,* 123 U. S. 623, 8 S. Ct. 273, 31 L. Ed. 205 (1887).

[35] 268 U. S. 652, 669, 45 S. Ct. 625, 69 L. Ed. 1138 (1925).

sideration. It is sufficient that the statute itself be constitutional and that the use of the language comes within its prohibition.[36]

The *Schenck* case Justice Sanford distinguished with the assertion that its "general statement" concerning "clear and present danger" had been intended to apply only to cases where the statute merely prohibits certain acts involving the danger of substantive evil, without any reference to language itself, and had no application where the legislative body itself had "previously determined the danger of substantive evil arising from utterances of a specified character."[37]

Speaking for himself and Justice Brandeis, Justice Holmes dissented in an opinion of which the following passage is the material one:

If what I think the correct test is applied, it is manifest that there was no present danger of an attempt to overthrow the government by force on the part of the admitedly small minority who shared the defendant's views. It is said that this manifesto was more than a theory, that it was an incitement. Every idea is an incitement. It offers itself for belief and if believed it is acted on unless some other belief outweighs it or some failure of energy stifles the movement at its birth. The only difference between the expression of an opinion and an incitement in the narrower sense is the speaker's enthusiasm for the result. Eloquence may set fire to reason. But whatever may be thought of the redundant discourse before us it had no chance of starting a present conflagration.[38]

One comment is quite inevitable. The assertion that "every idea is an incitement" is manifestly irrelevant to the question whether incitement in the sense of an utterance counselling or encouraging the commission of a crime may be punished by the state. It is in fact no better than a pun, which another master of oracular discourse, the late Dr. Samuel Johnson, pronounced the "lowest form of wit." Certainly it is not impressive when appearing in the context of a judicial opinion, even as exhortation.

And again we find Justice Holmes singularly reticent on the subject of "clear and present danger" when discussing the case

[36] *Id.,* 268 U. S. at 670.
[37] *Id.,* 268 U. S. at 671.
[38] *Id.,* 268 U. S. at 673.

with Sir Frederick Pollock. In a letter written a week before the opinion was announced Holmes confessed:

I am bothered by a case in which conscience and judgment are a little in doubt concerning the constitutionality under the 14th amendment of a State law punishing the publication of a manifesto advocating the forcible overthrow of government. . . . Such is the effect of putting a doubt into words that I turned aside from this letter and wrote my views which are now waiting to go to the printer. The theme is one on which I have written majority and minority opinions heretofore and to which I thought I could add about ten words to what I have said before.[39]

His next letter to Pollock underscored the fact that his dissent was prompted largely by the impression that the publication was utterly futile. "My last performance during the term," he wrote, "was a dissent (in which Brandeis joined) in favor of the rights of an anarchist (so-called) to talk drool in favor of the proletarian dictatorship."[40] "Drool"—the publication was intrinsically contemptible, and beneath the notice of the law. Evidently *"de minimis,"* not "clear and present danger," was the root-stem of this dissent. Justice Stone, consistent champion of personal liberty, joined in the judgment of the Court.

Two years later occurred *Whitney* v. *California*.[41] Here the defendant had been found guilty of violating the California Criminal Syndicalism Act by wilfully assisting in organizing and becoming a member of a group organized to "advocate, teach or aid and abet criminal syndicalism."[42] It was not denied that the evidence warranted the jury in finding that the accused assisted in organizing the Communist Labor Party of California and that this party was organized to advocate and abet criminal syndicalism. She insisted, however, that the conviction was invalid because there was no showing of a specific intent on her part to join in the forbidden purpose. Holding that this was a question of fact foreclosed by the verdict of the jury, and consequently not open to review, the Supreme Court sustained the conviction. Its decision was unani-

[39] 2 *Holmes-Pollock Letters* 162 (Howe ed. 1941).
[40] *Id.* at 163.
[41] 274 U. S. 357, 47 S. Ct. 641, 71 L. Ed. 1095 (1927).
[42] As quoted in *id.,* 274 U. S. at 360.

mous, but Justice Brandeis wrote a separate concurring opinion in which Justice Holmes joined. A material passage reads as follows:

> Every denunciation of existing law tends in some measure to increase the probability that there will be violation of it. Condonation of a breach enhances the probability. Expressions of approval add to the probability. Propagation of the criminal state of mind by teaching syndicalism increases it. Advocacy of law-breaking heightens it still further. But even advocacy of violation, however reprehensible morally, is not a justification for denying free speech where the advocacy falls short of incitement and there is nothing to indicate that the advocacy would be immediately acted on. The wide difference between advocacy and incitement, between preparation and attempt, between assembling and conspiracy, must be borne in mind. In order to support a finding of clear and present danger it must be shown either that immediate serious violence was to be expected or was advocated, or that the past conduct furnished reason to believe that such advocacy was then contemplated.[43]

It is somewhat hazardous to assess this collocation of sentences for its bearing on the topic here under discussion, but apparently there are two ideas present: First, that there is a "wide difference between advocacy and incitement"—that is, of or to illegal action—a proposition for which not one iota of supporting authority is offered and which is refuted again and again by the *usus loquendi* of the Court in the entire line of decisions reviewed above; secondly, that no utterance which the Court chooses to label "advocacy" may be constitutionally punished unless it was of immediate serious violence or unless the utterer was known to have a predilection for violence.

The opinion then proceeds:

> To courageous, self-reliant men, with confidence in the power of free and fearless reasoning applied through the processes of popular government, no danger flowing from speech can be deemed clear and present, unless the incidence of the evil apprehended is so imminent that it may befall before there is opportunity for full discussion. If there be time to expose through discussion the falsehood and fallacies, to avert the evil by the processes of education, the remedy to be applied is more speech, not enforced silence.[44]

[43] *Id.,* 274 U. S. at 376.
[44] *Id.,* 274 U. S. at 377.

Indulging the assumption that this passage was not written merely as exhortation, but with the serious intention of proposing a rule of constitutional law, we may well ask what it means? Apparently, it means that the ultimate test of the constitutionality of legislation restricting freedom of utterance is whether there is still sufficient time to educate the utterers out of their mistaken frame of mind, and the final say on this necessarily recondite matter rests with the Supreme Court!

Four years later, in *Stromberg* v. *California*,[45] both Justices Holmes and Brandeis joined in a decision which held the California Red Flag Law unconstitutional in so far as it prohibited display of such a flag as a symbol of peaceful and orderly opposition to government by legal means and within constitutional limitations, but expressly found the statute valid in prohibiting display of a red flag as a stimulus to anarchistic action or as an aid to propaganda which amounted to advocacy of force or violence in overthrowing the government of a state. During the same period two other state court convictions for subversive utterances were reversed for lack of evidence proving that the defendant had actually advocated criminal conduct to effect industrial or political change.[46] But after the *Whitney* case, no talk about "clear and present danger" was heard for a full decade.

III.

The formula achieved a second resurrection in 1937, in *Herndon* v. *Lowry*,[47] and at last in a majority opinion! The role which it played on this occasion was, however, a minor and quite dispensable one. Here a conviction under state statute for an attempt to "incite insurrection" was reversed by a closely divided Court, on the ground that as construed by the state courts the act set up an unascertainable standard of guilt and thereby offended the Due Process Clause of the Fourteenth Amendment. Said Justice Roberts:

> The Act does not prohibit incitement to violent interference with any given activity or operation of the state. By force of it, as construed, the judge and jury trying an alleged offender cannot appraise

[45] 283 U. S. 359, 51 S. Ct. 532, 75 L. Ed. 1117 (1931).

[46] *De Jonge* v. *Oregon*, 299 U. S. 353, 57 S. Ct. 255, 81 L. Ed. 278 (1937); *Fiske* v. *Kansas*, 274 U. S. 380, 47 S. Ct. 655, 71 L. Ed. 1108 (1927).

[47] 301 U. S. 242, 57 S. Ct. 732, 81 L. Ed. 1066 (1937).

the circumstances and character of the defendant's utterances or activities as begetting a clear and present danger of forcible obstruction of a particular state function.[48]

Nor was any specified conduct or utterance of the accused made an offense. In short, the "clear and present danger" formula is one of several elements which, independently of each other, will satisfy the constitutional requirement of certainty in defining an offense. In his 1951 Oliver Wendell Holmes Lectures at Harvard Law School,[49] former Justice Roberts does not mention *Herndon* v. *Lowry*.

Nevertheless, beginning with *Thornhill* v. *Alabama,*[50] decided in 1940, a majority of the Court frequently invoked the "clear and present danger" formula in nullifying state action, in fields unrelated to the advocacy of forbidden conduct: *e.g.,* laws prohibiting picketing, restricting the use of public places for propagating religious beliefs,[51] or requiring registration of labor organizers,[52] and judgments imposing sentences for contempt of court for criticism of judicial action.[53] The interest of these cases in the present connection is twofold: first, in many of them the Court reversed convictions on the ground that the interest which the state was endeavoring to protect was "too insubstantial to warrant restriction of speech,"[54] thus suggesting the converse tactic employed by the Chief Justice in his opinions in *American Communications Assn.* v. *Douds*[55] and in the *Dennis* case;[56] and secondly, they show a widening rift among the Justices touching the scope and constitutional basis of the "clear and present danger" doctrine prior to the case of the Eleven Communists.

[48] *Id.,* 301 U. S. at 261.

[49] Roberts, *The Court and The Constitution* (1951).

[50] 310 U. S. 88, 60 S. Ct. 736, 84 L. Ed. 1093 (1940).

[51] *Cantwell* v. *Connecticut,* 310 U. S. 296, 60 S. Ct. 900, 84 L. Ed. 1213 (1940).

[52] *Thomas* v. *Collins,* 323 U. S. 516, 65 S. Ct. 315, 89 L. Ed. 430 (1945).

[53] *Craig* v. *Harney,* 331 U. S. 367, 67 S. Ct. 1249, 91 L. Ed. 1546 (1947); *Pennekamp* v. *Florida,* 328 U. S. 331, 66 S. Ct. 1029, 90 L. Ed. 1295 (1946); *Bridges* v. *California,* 314 U. S. 252, 62 S. Ct. 190, 86 L. Ed. 192 (1941).

[54] *Dennis* v. *United States,* 341 U. S. 494, 508, 71 S. Ct. 857, 95 L. Ed. 1137 (1951).

[55] 339 U. S. 382, 70 S. Ct. 674, 94 L. Ed. 925 (1950).

[56] *Dennis* v. *United States,* 341 U. S. 494, 71 S. Ct. 857, 95 L. Ed. 1137 (1951).

This diversity of opinion among the Justices concerned the following three closely related topics: first, the restrictive force of the test; second, the constitutional status of freedom of speech and press; third, the kind of speech which the Constitution is concerned to protect. On the first point the following passage from Justice Black's opinion in *Bridges* v. *California* is pertinent:

> What finally emerges from the "clear and present danger" cases is a working principle that the substantive evil must be extremely serious and the degree of imminence extremely high before utterances can be punished. Those cases do not purport to mark the furthermost constitutional boundaries of protected expression, nor do we here. They do no more than recognize a minimum compulsion of the Bill of Rights. For the First Amendment does not speak equivocally. It prohibits any law "abridging the freedom of speech, or of the press." It must be taken as a command of the broadest scope that explicit language, read in the context of a liberty-loving society, will allow.[57]

With this should be compared the following words from Justice Frankfurter's concurring opinion in *Pennekamp* v. *Florida*,[58] which involved an issue closely related to the one dealt with in the *Bridges* case:

> "Clear and present danger" was never used by Mr. Justice Holmes to express a technical legal doctrine or to convey a formula for adjudicating cases. It was a literary phrase not to be distorted by being taken from its context. In its setting it served to indicate the importance of freedom of speech to a free society but also to emphasize that its exercise must be compatible with the preservation of other freedoms essential to a democracy and guaranteed by our Constitution. When those other attributes of a democracy are threatened by speech, the Constitution does not deny power to the States to curb it.[59]

The second question, in more definite terms, is whether freedom of speech and press occupies a "preferred position" in the constitutional hierarchy of values so that legislation restrictive of it is pre-

[57] 314 U. S. 252, 263, 62 S. Ct. 190, 86 L. Ed. 192 (1941).
[58] 328 U. S. 331, 66 S. Ct. 1029, 90 L. Ed. 1295 (1946).
[59] *Id.;* 328 U. S. at 353.

sumptively unconstitutional. An important contribution to the affirmative view on this point is the following dictum written by Justice Cardozo in 1937:

> . . . one may say that it is the matrix, the indispensable condition, of nearly every other form of freedom. . . . So it has come about that the domain of liberty, withdrawn by the Fourteenth Amendment from encroachment by the states, has been enlarged by latter-day judgments to include liberty of the mind as well as liberty of action. The extension became, indeed, a logical imperative when once it was recognized, as long ago it was, that liberty is something more than exemption from physical restraint, and that even in the field of substantive rights and duties the legislative judgment, if oppressive and arbitrary, may be overriden by the courts.[60]

Touching on the same subject a few months later, Chief Justice Stone suggested a narrow scope for the operation of the presumption of constitutionality when legislation appears to be within a specific prohibition of the Constitution, "such as those of the first ten amendments, which are deemed equally specific when held to be embraced within the Fourteenth."[61] Developing this theme, the Chief Justice continued:

> It is unnecessary to consider now whether legislation which restricts those political processes which can ordinarily be expected to bring about repeal of undesirable legislation, is to be subjected to more exacting judicial scrutiny under the general prohibitions of the Fourteenth Amendment than are most other types of legislation.[62]

But the most confident assertion of this position occurs in Justice Rutledge's opinion for a sharply divided Court in *Thomas* v. *Collins,* where it is said:

> The case confronts us again with the duty our system places on this Court to say where the individual's freedom ends and the State's power begins. Choice on that border, now as always delicate, is perhaps more so where the usual presumption supporting legislation is

[60] *Palko* v. *Connecticut,* 302 U. S. 319, 327, 58 S. Ct. 149, 82 L. Ed. 288 (1937).

[61] *United States* v. *Carolene Products Co.,* 304 U. S. 144, 152 n.4, 58 S. Ct. 778, 82 L. Ed. 1234 (1938).

[62] *Ibid.*

balanced by the preferred place given in our scheme to the great, the indispensable democratic freedoms secured by the First Amendment. . . . That priority gives these liberties a sanctity and a sanction not permitting dubious intrusions. And it is the character of the right, not of the limitation, which determines what standard governs the choice. . . .

For these reasons any attempt to restrict those liberties must be justified by clear public interest, threatened not doubtfully or remotely, but by clear and present danger. The rational connection between the remedy provided and the evil to be curbed, which in other contexts might support legislation against attack on due process grounds, will not suffice. These rights rest on firmer foundation. Accordingly, whatever occasion would restrain orderly discussion and persuasion at appropriate time and place, must have clear support in public danger, actual or impending. Only the gravest abuses, endangering paramount interests, give occasion for permissible limitation.[63]

This was 1945. Four years later a majority of the Court, in sustaining a local ordinance, endorsed a considerably less latitudinarian appraisal of freedom of speech and press.[64] Thus while alluding to "the preferred position of freedom of speech in a society that cherishes liberty for all," Justice Reed went on to say that this "does not require legislators to be insensible to claims by citizens to comfort and convenience. To enforce freedom of speech in disregard of the rights of others would be harsh and arbitrary in itself."[65] And Justice Frankfurter flatly denied the propriety of the phrase "preferred position," saying:

This is a phrase that has uncritically crept into some recent opinions of this Court. I deem it a mischievous phrase, if it carries the thought, which it may subtly imply, that any law touching communication is infected with presumptive invalidity. It is not the first time in the history of constitutional adjudication that such a doctrinaire attitude has disregarded the admonition most to be observed in exercising the Court's reviewing power over legislation, "that it is *a constitution* we are expounding," *M'Culloch* v. *Maryland,* 4 Wheat. 316, 407. I say the phrase is mischievous because it radiates a constitutional doctrine without avowing it. Clarity and candor in

63 323 U. S. 516, 529–30, 65 S. Ct. 315, 89 L. Ed. 430 (1945).

64 *Kovacs* v. *Cooper,* 336 U. S. 77, 69 S. Ct. 448, 93 L. Ed. 513 (1949).

65 *Id.,* 336 U. S. at 88.

these matters, so as to avoid gliding unwittingly into error, make it appropriate to trace the history of the phrase "preferred position."[66]

—which Justice Frankfurter then proceeded to do.

The third question concerns the quality and purpose of the speech which the Constitution aims to protect. In 1949 Justice Douglas, speaking for a sharply divided Court, returned the following robustious answer to this question:

. . . a function of free speech under our system of government is to invite dispute. It may indeed best serve its high purpose when it induces a condition of unrest, creates dissatisfaction with conditions as they are, or even stirs people to anger. Speech is often provocative and challenging. It may strike at prejudices and preconceptions and have profound unsettling effects as it presses for acceptance of an idea. That is why freedom of speech though not absolute . . . is nevertheless protected against censorship or punishment, unless shown likely to produce a clear and present danger of a serious substantive evil that arises far above public inconvenience, annoyance, or unrest.[67]

But early in 1951 Justice Jackson, in a dissenting opinion urged the Court to review its entire position in the light of the proposition that "the purpose of constitutional protection of freedom of speech is to foster peaceful interchange of all manner of thoughts, information and ideas," and that "its policy is rooted in faith in the force of reason."[68] He considered that the Court had been striking blindly at permit systems which indirectly may affect First Amendment freedoms. He said:

Cities throughout the country have adopted permit requirements to control private activities on public streets and for other purposes. The universality of this type of regulation demonstrates a need and indicates widespread opinion in the profession that it is not necessarily incompatible with our constitutional freedoms. Is everybody out of step but this Court?[69]

[66] *Id.,* 336 U. S. at 90.

[67] *Terminiello* v. *Chicago,* 337 U. S. 1, 4, 69 S. Ct. 894, 93 L. Ed. 1131 (1949).

[68] *Kunz* v. *New York,* 340 U. S. 290, 295, 302, 71 S. Ct. 312, 95 L. Ed. 28 (1951).

[69] *Id.,* 340 U. S. at 305–6.

He was of the opinion that the Court was assuming a hypercritical position in invalidating local laws for want of standards when the Court itself had set down no particular standard. He would leave a large measure of discretion to the local community or state in dealing with speech which is outside the immunity of the Constitution. He also "venture[d] to predict" that the Court "will not apply, to federal statutes the standard that they are unconstitutional if it is possible that they may be unconstitutionally applied,"[70] —a prophecy soon verified by event.

IV.

The immediate precursors of the *Dennis* case are two cases decided under the Taft-Hartley Act[71] a year earlier. That law requires, as a condition of a union's utilizing the opportunities afforded by the Act, each of its officers to file an affidavit with the National Labor Relations Board (1) that he is not a member of the Communist Party or affiliated with such party, and (2) that he does not believe in, and is not a member of any organization that believes in or teaches the overthrow of the United States Government by force or by any illegal or unconstitutional methods. In *American Communications Association* v. *Douds,*[72] five of the six Justices participating sustained the first requirement and an evenly divided Court sustained the second against the objection that the Act exceeded the power of Congress over interstate commerce and infringed freedom of speech and the rights of petition and assembly. And in *Osman* v. *Douds*[73] the same result was reached by a Court in which only Justice Clark did not participate. In the end only Justice Black condemned the first requirement while the Court was evenly divided as to the second. In the course of his opinion for the controlling wing of the Court in the *American Communications* case, Chief Justice Vinson said:

> . . . the attempt to apply the term, "clear and present danger," as a mechanical test in every case touching First Amendment freedoms,

[70] *Id.,* 340 U. S. at 304.

[71] 61 *Stat.* 146 (1947), 29 U.S.C. § 159 (h) (Supp. 1951).

[72] 339 U. S. 382, 70 S. Ct. 674, 94 L. Ed. 925 (1950).

[73] 339 U. S. 846, 70 S. Ct. 901, 94 L. Ed. 1328 (1950).

without regard to the context of its application, mistakes the form in which an idea was cast for the substance of the idea.[74]

The question with which the Court was dealing, he asserted, was not the same one that Justices Holmes and Brandeis had considered in terms of "clear and present danger," since the Government's interest in *American Communications* was in protecting the free flow of commerce from what Congress considered to be substantial evils of conduct rather than in preventing dissemination of Communist doctrine or the holding of particular beliefs because of a fear that unlawful conduct might result therefrom.[75] Applying that distinction, the Chief Justice recited:

> The contention of petitioner . . . that this Court must find that political strikes create a clear and present danger to the security of the Nation or of widespread industrial strife in order to sustain § 9(h) similarly misconceives the purpose that phrase was intended to serve. In that view, not the relative certainty that evil conduct will result from speech in the immediate future, but the extent and gravity of the substantive evil must be measured by the "test" laid down in the *Schenck* case.[76]

In thus balancing the gravity of the interest protected by legislation from harmful speech against the demands of the "clear and present danger" rule, the Court paved a feasible way for its decision a year later in *Dennis* v. *United States*.[77]

And undoubtedly it was Chief Justice Vinson's initial inclination, in his opinion for himself and Justices Reed, Burton and Minton, to rest decision in *Dennis* on a like calculation. Thus emphasizing the substantial character of the Government's interest in preventing its own overthrow by force, he said this was the ultimate value of any society, for if a society cannot protect itself from internal attack, "it must follow that no subordinate value can be protected."[78] The opinion continues:

> If, then, this interest may be protected, the literal problem which is presented is what has been meant by the use of the phrase "clear

[74] *American Communications Assn.* v. *Douds,* 339 U. S. 382, 394, 70 S. Ct. 674, 94 L. Ed. 925 (1950).

[75] *Id.,* 339 U. S. at 396.

[76] *Id.,* 339 U. S. at 397.

[77] 341 U. S. 494, 71 S. Ct. 857, 95 L. Ed. 1137 (1951)

[78] *Id.,* 341 U. S. at 509.

and present danger" of the utterances bringing about the evil within the power of Congress to punish.

Obviously, the words cannot mean that before the Government may act, it must wait until the *putsch* is about to be executed, the plans have been laid and the signal is awaited. If Government is aware that a group aiming at its overthrow is attempting to indoctrinate its members and to commit them to a course whereby they will strike when the leaders feel the circumstances permit, action by the Government is required. The argument that there is no need for Government to concern itself, for Government is strong, it possesses ample powers to put down a rebellion, it may defeat the revolution with ease needs no answer. For that is not the question. Certainly an attempt to overthrow the Government by force, even though doomed from the outset because of inadequate numbers or power of the revolutionists, is a sufficient evil for Congress to prevent. The damage which such attempts create both physically and politically to a nation makes it impossible to measure the validity in terms of the probability of success, or the immediacy of a successful attempt.[79]

The Chief Justice concluded this part of his opinion by quoting from Chief Judge Learned Hand's opinion for the circuit court of appeals in the same case, as follows: " 'In each case [courts] must ask whether the gravity of the 'evil,' discounted by its improbability, justifies such invasion of free speech as is necessary to avoid the danger.' "[80] On this he commented:

We adopt this statement of the rule. As articulated by Chief Judge Hand, it is as succinct and inclusive as any other we might devise at this time. It takes into consideration those factors which we deem relevant, and relates their significance. More we cannot expect from words.[81]

That is to say, if the evil legislated against is serious enough, advocacy of it does not, in order to be punishable, have to be attended by a "clear and present danger" of success.

But at this point the Chief Justice, as if recoiling from this abrupt dismissal of the "clear and present danger" formula, makes

[79] *Ibid.*
[80] *Id.*, 341 U. S. at 510.
[81] *Ibid.*

a last-moment effort to rescue the babe that he has so incontinently tossed out with the bath, stating that the Court was in accord with the circuit court, which affirmed a finding by the trial court that the requisite danger actually existed, and noting particularly that the "highly organized conspiracy . . . coupled with the inflammable nature of world conditions . . . convince us that their convictions were justified on this score."[82]

His final position seems to be that the question is one for judicial discretion, unbound by formulas, for he recites:

> When facts are found that establish the violation of a statute, the protection against conviction afforded by the First Amendment is a matter of law. The doctrine that there must be a clear and present danger of a substantive evil that Congress has a right to prevent is a judicial rule to be applied as a matter of law by the courts.[83]

In short, "clear and present danger" is informed that *the Court, not it, is on top.*

Justice Frankfurter's lengthy concurring opinion premises the "right of a government to maintain its existence—self-preservation . . . [as] the most pervasive aspect of sovereignty."[84] At the same time he admitted that there are competing interests to be assessed, but asked which agency of government is to do the job:

> Full responsibility for the choice cannot be given to the courts. Courts are not representative bodies. They are not designed to be a good reflex of a democratic society. Their judgment is best informed, and therefore most dependable, within narrow limits. Their essential quality is detachment, founded on independence. History teaches that the independence of the judiciary is jeopardized when courts become embroiled in the passions of the day and assume primary responsibility in choosing between competing political, economic and social pressures.
>
> Primary responsibility for adjusting the interests which compete in the situation before us of necessity belongs to the Congress. The nature of the power to be exercised by this Court has been delineated in decisions not charged with the emotional appeal of situations such

[82] *Id.,* 341 U. S. at 511.
[83] *Id.,* 341 U. S. at 513.
[84] *Id.,* 341 U. S. at 519.

as that now before us. We are to set aside the judgment of those whose duty it is to legislate only if there is no reasonable basis for it.[85]

But a difficulty seems to exist in the "clear and present danger" doctrine, for Justice Frankfurter admitted that defendants' argument could not be met by reinterpreting the phrase. He also was of the opinion that defendants' argument could not be met by citing isolated cases, but that their convictions should "be tested against the entire body of our relevant decisions."[86]

Turning then to an examination of the cases he exclaims at last: "I must leave to others the ungrateful task of trying to reconcile all these decisions."[87] The nearest precedent was the *Gitlow* case. Here "we put our respect for the legislative judgment in terms which, if they were accepted here, would make decision easy. . . . But it would be disingenuous to deny that the dissent in *Gitlow* has been treated with the respect usually accorded to a decision."[88] He concludes with a homily on the limitations which the nature of judicial power imposes on the power of judicial review:

> To make validity of legislation depend on judicial reading of events still in the womb of time—a forecast, that is, of the outcome of forces at best appreciated only with knowledge of the topmost secrets of nations—is to charge the judiciary with duties beyond its equipment. We do not expect courts to pronounce historic verdicts on bygone events. Even historians have conflicting views to this day on the origins and conduct of the French Revolution. . . . It is as absurd to be confident that we can measure the present clash of forces and their outcome as to ask us to read history still enveloped in clouds of controversy.[89]

Not without some justification has Justice Frankfurter's opinion been called "an interesting study in ambivalence."[90]

Justice Jackson's opinion underscores the conspiratorial element of the case, and is flat-footed in rejecting the "clear and present danger" formula for this type of case. He writes:

[85] *Id.*, 341 U. S. at 525.
[86] *Id.*, 341 U. S. at 528.
[87] *Id.*, 341 U. S. at 539.
[88] *Id.*, 341 U. S. at 541.
[89] *Id.*, 341 U. S. at 551–2.
[90] Woolsey, *The Supreme Court: 1951–52*, *Fortune*, Oct. 1951, p. 119, 162.

The test applies and has meaning where a conviction is sought to be based on a speech or writing which does not directly or explicitly advocate a crime but to which such tendency is sought to be attributed by construction or by implication from external circumstances. The formula in such cases favors freedoms that are vital to our society, and, even if sometimes applied too generously, the consequences cannot be grave. But its recent expansion has extended, in particular to Communists, unprecedented immunities. Unless we are to hold our Government captive in a judge-made verbal trap, we must approach the problem of a well-organized, nationwide conspiracy, such as I have described, as realistically as our predecessors faced the trivialities that were being prosecuted until they were checked with a rule of reason.[91]

He emphasizes that the Constitution does not make conspiracy a civil right and that the Court has consistently refused to do so on previous occasions and should so continue, whether the conspiracy be one to disturb interstate commerce or to undermine the Government. He disposes of the dissenters' contention that some overt act was necessary to support the convictions in the following words:

. . . no overt act is or need be required. The Court, in antitrust cases, early upheld the power of Congress to adopt the ancient common law that makes conspiracy itself a crime. Through Mr. Justice Holmes, it said: "Coming next to the objection that no overt act is laid, the answer is that the Sherman Act punishes the conspiracies at which it is aimed on the common law footing—that is to say, it does not make the doing of any act other than the act of conspiring a condition of liability." . . . It is not to be supposed that the power of Congress to protect the Nation's existence is more limited than its power to protect interstate commerce.

I do not suggest that Congress could punish conspiracy to advocate something, the doing of which it may not punish. Advocacy or exposition of the doctrine of communal property ownership, or any political philosophy unassociated with advocacy of its imposition by force or seizure of government by unlawful means could not be reached through conspiracy prosecution. But it is not forbidden to put down force or violence, it is not forbidden to punish its teaching or advocacy, and the end being punishable, there is no doubt of the power to punish conspiracy for the purpose.[92]

[91] *Dennis* v. *United States,* 341 U. S. 494, 568, 71 S. Ct. 857, 95 L. Ed. 1137 (1951).

[92] *Id.,* 341 U. S. at 574–5.

It would be "weird legal reasoning," he opined, for the Court to hold that conspiracy is one crime and its consummation another and then further hold that "Congress could punish the one only if there was 'clear and present danger' of the second."[93]

The dissenting opinions of Justices Black and Douglas indicate that they would not only apply the "clear and present danger" test to this type of case, but that they would give it the same broad reach which they had claimed for it in cases where the speech involved was not intended to induce violation of law. Justice Black reiterates his previously expressed opinion that:

> At least as to speech in the realm of public matters, I believe that the "clear and present danger" test does not "mark the furthermost constitutional boundaries of protected expression" but does "no more than recognize a minimum compulsion of the Bill of Rights." *Bridges* v. *California,* 314 U.S. 252, 263. [Justice Black is here quoting Justice Black.][94]

And Justice Douglas italicized Justice Brandeis' dictum in the *Whitney* case: "*'If there be time to expose through discussion the falsehood and fallacies, to avert the evil by the processes of education, the remedy to be applied is more speech, not enforced silence.'*"[95] The answer is that education had not in fact prevented the formation of the conspiracy for which the eleven defendants were convicted. If that be deemed a danger at all, it was certainly a "clear and present" one. Both dissenters, in fact, ignore the conspiracy element, although Justice Holmes had not done so in *Frohwerk,* nor had Justice Brandeis in *Whitney.*

CONCLUSION

"It is one of the misfortunes of the law," wrote Justice Holmes in 1912, "that ideas become encysted in phrases and thereafter for a long time cease to provoke further analysis."[96] No better confirmation of this observation could be asked than that which is afforded

[93] *Id.,* 341 U. S. at 576.

[94] *Id.,* 341 U. S. at 580.

[95] *Id.,* 341 U. S. at 586.

[96] *Hyde* v. *United States,* 225 U. S. 347, 390, 32 S. Ct. 793, 56 L. Ed. 1114 (1912).

by the remarkable extension of the influence of the "clear and present danger" formula both with courts and commentators in the decade just ended. To sum up the history reviewed above: The phrase had its origin in 1919 in a dictum tossed off by Holmes himself in an opinion sustaining a conviction under the Espionage Act of 1917,[97] but was soon thereafter invoked by its author and by Justice Brandeis in opinions dissenting from similar judgments. Not till nearly twenty years later, and after Holmes' death, did the formula find its way into a majority opinion of the Court[98] which reversed a judgment of conviction, and here it was invoked against the application of the statute to the facts of the case, not directly against the statute itself. Frequent repetition since 1940 in cases presenting problems entirely different from those raised by espionage and criminal anarchy statutes, or by incitements to breach of the law, had, however, by 1951, established the authority of this cliché so firmly that in *Dennis* v. *United States* five Justices of the Court wrote separate opinions variously construing it, three conceding its application in some sense or other. What effect does the judgment in *Dennis,* considered in the light shed by these opinions, have on the formula? How far does *Dennis* go in supplying the analysis that Justice Holmes would presumably have welcomed, or otherwise?

The writer of this article is inclined to the opinion that the Court would have done quite as well to have based its holding in *Dennis* on the *Gitlow* case, as the Solicitor General invited it to do. As the preceding pages amply demonstrate, not a single precedent would have had to be overturned to reach such a result. Furthermore, the Chief Justice's acceptance[99] of the explanation given by the Court in *Gitlow* of the reason why the "clear and present danger" formula had appeared in the *Schenck* case, smoothed the way to an unqualified reiteration of the *Gitlow* decision, which had had the support of seven of the nine Justices. That this course was not adopted was due in part, no doubt, to the fact that "the Case of the Eleven Communists" had been inflated by propaganda far beyond its strictly legal significance, and to the feeling of the Court, in consequence, that it must deal with the case at respectful length,

[97] 40 *Stat.* 217 (1917).

[98] *Herndon* v. *Lowry,* 301 U. S. 242, 57 S. Ct. 732, 81 L. Ed. 1066 (1937).

[99] *Dennis* v. *United States,* 341 U. S. 494, 505–6, 71 S. Ct. 857, 95 L. Ed. 1137 (1951).

and of course "significantly." But an even more important factor may have been the Court's habitual reluctance to cast aside at one fell swoop any formula or doctrine which lends its umpirage support and promises it an available "out" against undesired legislation—*i.e.*, undesired by the Court. It prefers the tactics of the rear guard action to those of outright retreat.

Taken, then, in the context of the opinions which support it, what conclusions does the decision suggest as to the future of "clear and present danger?" The outstanding result of the holding, undoubtedly, is that of *a declaration of independence by the Court from the tyranny of a phrase.* As expounded in the dissenting opinions of Justices Black and Douglas, the "clear and present danger" formula is a kind of slide rule whereby all cases involving the issue of free speech simply decide themselves automatically. By treating the formula as authorizing it to weigh the substantive good protected by a statute against the "clear and present danger" requirement, the Court rids itself of this absurd "heads-off" automatism and converts the rule, for the first time, into a real "rule of reason."

At the same time, the range of the rule's applicability has undoubtedly been curtailed, though just how greatly is not at present altogether apparent. It can be safely said that never again will the rule be successfully invoked in behalf of persons shown to have conspired to incite to a breach of federal law. On the other hand, as Justice Jackson suggests in effect, the "clear and present danger" test may still be applicable: (1) in cases essentially trivial; (2) in cases where the intent of the speaker is lawful, but circumstances create a danger of violence or other substantive evils which government has a right to prevent; (3) in cases where the speech is ambiguous and the evil purpose of the speaker can be reasonably inferred only from the "clear and present danger" of evil which the utterance engenders. But the common law, properly charged, would probably do just as well in such cases without any assistance from the formula.

Moreover, the vast majority of such cases arise under state and municipal legislation. Indeed, since the Court is apt to favor easily discernible boundaries, "clear and present danger" may "just fade away" in the field of congressional power. Such a result could be justified both on logical and on practical grounds. Thus it would take account of the well recognized rule of legal interpretation that the general yields to the specific. From this point of view it may well be held that freedom of speech and press stand in a different relation to enumerated powers of Congress than they do to the vague, undefined residual powers of the states. And that the protection of the larger interests of our ever more closely integrated society gravitates more and more to the National Government is a proposition that nobody is apt to contest.

★ XII ★

The Supreme Court as a National School Board*

Justice Rutledge sold his brethren a bill of goods when he persuaded them that the 'establishment of religion' clause of the First Amendment was intended to rule out all governmental "aid to all *religions."*

As a student at the University of Michigan a half century ago I had frequent occasion to attend convocations, lectures, and concerts in University Hall. Each time my eyes were confronted with the words, emblazoned on the wall over the great organ, "Religion, morality, and knowledge, being necessary to good government and the happiness of mankind, schools and the means of education shall forever be encouraged." These words are from the famous Northwest Ordinance which was enacted in 1787 by the last Congress of the Confederation,[1] and which from the provision it makes for the establishment of public schools is the matrix of the public school system of a great part of the United States. Two years later many of the same men, representatives of the same people, sitting as the first Congress under the Constitution, proposed the following amendment to the Constitution: "Congress shall make no law respecting an establishment of religion, or prohibiting the free exercise thereof. . . ." Do these words represent a fundamental change in attitude on the part of the American people on the question of what

* 14 *Law and Contemporary Problems* (Winter, 1949) 3.

[1] July 13, 1787, I Stat. 51, n., Art. III.

relation should subsist between public education and the teaching of religion? Prima facie it seems doubtful,[2] but that it is so, nevertheless, is the implication of the decision on March 8, 1948, of the United States Supreme Court in *Illinois* ex rel. *Vashti McCollum* v. *Board of Education of Champaign County*.[3] . . .

I.

People of the State of Illinois ex rel. *Vashti McCollum, Appellant* v. *Board of Education of School District No. 71, Champaign County* was welcomed by the Court with open arms, as affording it a grand opportunity to break a lance—or several of them—in behalf of the "constitutional principle"—as it is asserted to be—of Separation of Church and State. Actually, the Constitution does not mention this principle. In fact, it does not contain the word "church," nor yet the word "state" in the generic sense except in the Second Amendment, in which a "well regulated militia" is asserted to be "necessary to the security of a free state"; even the word "separation" fails to put in an appearance. These singular omissions—singular, if what the Framers wanted was "Separation of Church and State" in the Court's understanding of it—are now supplied by the Court by the interpretation which it affixes to the "establishment of religion" clause of the First Amendment. The Court's theory, which was stated in the first instance by Justice Black in his opinion for the Court in the *New Jersey Bus* case, is that, under this clause, supplemented by the word "liberty" of the Fourteenth Amendment, "Neither a state nor the Federal Government can [1] set up a church"; [2] "pass laws which aid one religion, [3] aid all religions, or [4] prefer one religion over another."[4] For this reading of the clause the Court relies primarily on historical data. *Do historical data, on the whole, sustain it?* The answer is, not in such a way or such a sense as to vindicate the *McCollum* decision.

So far as the *National Government* is concerned, the first of the above four propositions is true; originally, indeed, it came near being the whole truth; as to the *states* it is not, as we shall see, *necessarily* true even today. Of the remaining assertions, the second may be

[2] The doubt becomes doubly doubtful when we recall that Congress reenacted the Northwest Ordinance in 1791!

[3] 333 U. S. 203 (1948).

[4] *Everson* v. *Board of Education,* 330 U. S. 1 (1947).

ignored as ambiguous; the third is untrue historically; the fourth is true. In a word, what the "establishment of religion" clause of the First Amendment does, and *all that it does, is to forbid Congress to give any religious faith, sect, or denomination a preferred status;* and the Fourteenth Amendment, in making the clause applicable to the states, does not add to it, but *logically* curtails it.

Where, then, did Justice Black get his confident reading of the "establishment of religion" clause? He got it from Justice Rutledge's dissenting opinion in the *New Jersey Bus* case, which in turn is based largely on James Madison's *Memorial and Remonstrance Against Religious Assessments* of 1785.[5] At that time—four years *before* the First Amendment was framed—a proposal was pending in the Virginia Assembly to levy a tax for the benefit of "teachers of the Christian religion." The father of the measure was Patrick Henry, but it was also supported outside the Assembly by Washington, Marshall, and other great names. Madison, on the other hand, with the recent successful fight for the disestablishment of the Episcopal Church in mind, fought the measure tooth and nail, fearing that if it was enacted that body would have its foot in the stirrup for a fresh leap into the saddle. The keynote of the *Remonstrance,* which summed up his opposition, is sounded in the following passage:

> Who does not see that the same authority which can establish Christianity, in exclusion of all other Religions, may establish with the same ease any particular sect of Christians, in exclusion of all other Sects? That the same authority which can force a citizen to contribute three pence only of his property for the support of any one establishment, may force him to conform to any other establishment in all cases whatsover?[6]

As those very words show, however, Madison's conception of an "establishment of religion" in 1785 was precisely that which I have set forth above—*a religion enjoying a preferred status.* The same conception, moreover, underlies the state constitutions of the day,

[5] *Id.* at 63 ff, quoting II *The Writings of James Madison* 183–191 (Hunt ed. 1901).

[6] Justice Rutledge's dissenting opinion in *Everson* v. *Board of Education, supra* note 4, at 65–66, quoting II *The Writings of James Madison* 183, 186 (Hunt ed. 1901).

when they deal with the subject.[7] It also underlies all but one of the proposals from the states which led to the framing of the First Amendment in the first Congress. Thus Virginia proposed that "no particular religious sect or society ought to be favored or established, by law, in preference to others"—a formula which North Carolina reiterated word for word, and which New York reiterated save for the word "particular." Only New Hampshire, concerned for her own "establishment," wanted a broader prohibition, one that would keep Congress out of the field of religion entirely.[8]

But, it may well be asked, what bearing do the views which Madison advanced in 1785 in a local political fight regarding the subject of religious liberty in Virginia have on the question of the meaning of the First Amendment? Justice Rutledge's theory is (1) that Madison was the author of the First Amendment, and (2) that he must have intended by the ban which is there imposed on Congress's legislating "respecting an establishment of religion" to rule out the kind of legislation which he had opposed in Virginia four years earlier. Neither of these positions is correct.

As originally introduced into the House of Representatives by Madison, the proposal from which the religion clauses of the First Amendment finally issued read as follows:

> The civil rights of none shall be abridged on account of religious belief or worship, nor shall any national religion be established, nor shall the full and equal rights of conscience be in any manner, or on any pretext, infringed.[9]

These words Madison later elucidated thus:

> . . . he apprehended the meaning of the words to be, that Congress should not establish a religion, and enforce the legal observation of it by law, nor compel men to worship God in any manner contrary

[7] See I Francis Newton Thorpe, *The Federal and State Constitutions, Colonial Charters, and Other Organic Laws of the States, Territories, and Colonies Now or Hereafter Forming the United States of America* 567 (Dela.); Ill *id.* 1890 (Mass.); IV *id.* 2454 (N. H.); V *id.* 2597 (N. J.), 2636 (N. Y.), 2793 (N. C.); VI *id.* 3255 (S. C.).

[8] III *The Debates in the Several State Conventions on the Adoption of the Federal Constitution* 659 (Jonathan Elliott ed. 1836); I *id.* 326; IV *id.* 244, 251. See also II *id.* 553.

[9] I *Annals of Cong.* 434 (1789–1791).

to their conscience . . . if the word "national" was inserted before religion, it would satisfy the minds of honorable gentlemen. He believed that the people feared one sect might obtain a pre-eminence, or two combine together, and establish a religion to which they would compel others to conform. He thought if the word "national" was introduced, it would point the amendment directly to the object it was intended to prevent.[10]

In short, "to establish" a religion was to give it a preferred status, a pre-eminence, carrying with it even the right to compel others to conform. But in fact, before Madison's proposal was passed by the House and went to the Senate it had been changed to read: "Congress shall make no law establishing religion, or to prevent the free exercise thereof, or to infringe the rights of conscience"; and in the Senate this proposal was replaced by the following formula: "Congress shall make no law establishing articles of faith or a mode of worship or prohibiting the free exercise of religion."[11] That is, Congress should not prescribe a national faith, a possibility which those states with establishments of their own—Massachusetts, New Hampshire, Connecticut, Maryland, and South Carolina—probably regarded with fully as much concern as those which had gotten rid of their establishments. And the final form of the First Amendment, which came from a committee of conference between the two houses, appears to reflect this concern. The point turns on the significance

[10] *Id.* at 730–731.

[11] *Records of the United States Senate,* September 9, 1789, United States National Archives, cited in Appellees' Brief (Messrs. Franklin, Peterson, Rall, and Fisk) in the *McCollum* case, *supra* note 3. Here attention is drawn to the fact that the Virginia legislature postponed ratification of the third proposed amendment (Amendment I of the first ten amendments) until December 15, 1791 (III *Annals of Cong.* 54), by which time they had already received the approval of the required three-fourths of the state legislatures. The leaders in opposition to the First Amendment voiced their objections in the following terms: ". . . although it goes to restrain Congress from passing laws establishing any national religion, they might, notwithstanding, levy taxes to any amount for the support of religion or its preachers; and any particular denomination of Christians might be so favored and supported by the general government, as to give it a decided advantage over the others, and in the process of time render it powerful and dangerous as if it was established as the national religion of the country." Evidently, as Appellees' Brief remarks, Virginians, who, after all, were the ones most familiar with the Virginia concept of religious freedom, did not interpret the First Amendment as living up to the spirit or the letter of the Virginia Bill for Establishing Religious Freedom. Brief, pp. 53–54.

to be attached to the word "respecting," a two-edged word, which bans any law *disfavoring* as well as any law *favoring* an establishment of religion. As will be seen in a moment, Story's reading of the First Amendment makes "respecting" the pivotal word of the "no establishment" clause.

To come back for a moment to Madison. Thanks to his exertions, Henry's bill was defeated, and unquestionably his *Remonstrance* should be given considerable credit for this result. But political management also played a role, and no unimportant one. The great problem was to overcome the tremendous influence which Henry's oratory exerted in the Virginia Assembly. Writing Madison at this time from Paris, Jefferson said: "What we have to do, I think, is devotedly to pray for his death." Madison, however, had a better scheme. Relying on Henry's vanity, he concocted a movement to make him Governor, and Henry took the bait, hook, line, and sinker, thus automatically removing himself from the Assembly and destroying his brain-child.[12]

Yet it is probably due to his part in this fight that in his later years Madison carried the principle of separation of church and state to pedantic lengths, just as he did the principle of the separation of powers. In his essay on *Monopolies,* which was written after he left the presidency (probably long after), he put himself on record as opposed to the exemption of houses of worship from taxation, against the incorporation of ecclesiastical bodies with the faculty of acquiring property, against the houses of Congress having the right to choose chaplains to be paid out of national taxes, which, said he, "is a palpable violation of equal rights, as well as of Constitutional principles,"[13] and also against chaplains in the Army and the Navy. He states, indeed, that as President he was averse to issuing proclamations calling for days of thanksgiving or prayer, but was in some instances prevailed upon to affix his name to proclamations of this character at the request of the houses of Congress.[14] In all these respects, of course, Madison has been steadily overruled by the verdict of practice under the Constitution, as the data assembled by Justice Reed in his dissenting opinion show.[15]

[12] Irving Brant, *James Madison, The Nationalist* 345–346 (1948).

[13] Fleet, *Madison's "Detached* [sic] *Memoranda,"* 3 *William and Mary Q.* 534, 558 (3d Ser.) (1946).

[14] *Id.* at 551–562.

[15] *McCollum* v. *Board of Education, supra* note 3, at 253–255.

To conclude this—the Madisonian—phase of our subject: the importance attached by Justice Rutledge in the *School Bus* case to Madison's *Memorial and Remonstrance* of 1785 as interpretive of the First Amendment is obviously excessive. First, the *Remonstrance* antedated the framing of the amendment by four years; second, Madison himself never offered it as an interpretation of the amendment; third, he was not the author of the amendment in the form in which it was proposed to the state legislatures for ratification; fourth, even had he been, the *Remonstrance* itself is excellent evidence that "an establishment of religion" meant in 1785 a religion, sect, or denomination enjoying a privileged legal position; finally, Madison himself asserted repeatedly as to the Constitution as a whole that "the legitimate meaning of the Instrument must be derived from the text itself."[16] Rejecting in a recent case the proposition that the Fourteenth Amendment, but more particularly the "due process" clause thereof, was intended to impose upon the States all of "the various explicit provisions of the first eight Amendments," Justice Frankfurter said: "Remarks of a particular proponent of the Amendment no matter how influential are not to be deemed part of the Amendment. What was submitted for ratification was his proposal, not his speech."[17] And Madison was not even the proponent of the First Amendment in its final form!

But Justice Rutledge, and the Court also, urge the authority of Jefferson as an interpreter of the First Amendment, although, being in Paris at the time, Jefferson had no hand in framing it. The reason for the Court's deference to the third president is that in 1802 he wrote a letter to a group of Baptists in Danbury, Connecticut, in which he declared that it was the purpose of the First Amendment to build "a wall of separation between church and state."[18] What, then, was Jefferson's idea of such a wall? So far as it bears on the question of religion in the schools, it certainly does not support the position of the Court in the *McCollum* case. Dealing with the subject with respect to his own recently established University of Virginia, Jefferson wrote in 1822:

It was not, however, to be understood that instruction in religious opinion and duties was meant to be precluded by the public authori-

[16] III *The Works of James Madison* 228, 552 (Phila. 1867).

[17] *Adamson* v. *California,* 332 U. S. 46, 64 (1947).

[18] Saul K. Padover, *The Complete Jefferson* 518–519 (1943).

ties, as indifferent to the interests of society. On the contrary, the relations which exist between man and his Maker, and the duties resulting from those relations, are the most interesting and important to every human being, and most incumbent on his study and investigation. The want of instruction in the various creeds of religious faith existing among our citizens presents, therefore, a chasm in a general institution of the useful sciences. . . . A remedy, however, has been suggested of promising aspect, which, while it excludes the public authorities from the domain of religious freedom, will give to the sectarian schools of divinity the full benefit the public provisions made for instruction in the other branches of science. . . . It has, therefore, been in contemplation, and suggested by some pious individuals, who perceive the advantages of associating other studies with those of religion, to establish their religious schools on the confines of the University, so as to give to their students ready and convenient access and attendance on the scientific lectures of the University; and to maintain, by that means, those destined for the religious professions on as high a standing of science, and of personal weight and respectability, as may be obtained by others from the benefits of the University. . . . Such an arrangement would complete the circle of the useful sciences embraced by this institution, and would fill the chasm now existing, on principles which would leave inviolate the constitutional freedom of religion, the most inalienable and sacred of all human rights, over which the people and authorities of this state, individually and publicly, have ever manifested the most watchful jealousy; and could this jealousy be now alarmed, in the opinion of the legislature, by what is here suggested, the idea will be relinquished on any surmise of disapprobation which they might think proper to express.[19]

And again:

. . . by bringing the sects together, and mixing them with the mass of other students, we shall soften their asperities, liberalize and neutralize their prejudices, and make the general religion a religion of peace, reason, and morality.[20]

The eager crusaders on the Court make too much of Jefferson's Danbury letter, which was not improbably motivated by an impish

[19] *Id.* at 957–958.

[20] 12 *The Works of Thomas Jefferson* 272 (Ford ed. 1905). These passages are both quoted by Justice Reed in a footnote, 333 U. S. 203, 245, 246 n. 11.

desire to heave a brick at the Congregationalist-Federalist hierarchy of Connecticut, whose leading members had denounced him two years before as an "infidel" and "atheist." A more deliberate, more carefully considered evaluation by Jefferson of the religious clauses of the First Amendment is that which occurs in his Second Inaugural: "In matters of religion, I have considered that its free exercise is placed by the constitution independent of the powers of the general government."[21] In short, the principal importance of the amendment lay in the separation which it effected between the respective jurisdictions of state and nation regarding religion, rather than in its bearing on the question of the separation of church and state. For the rest, it is not irrelevant to the major subject opened up by the Court's decision to note that Jefferson regarded religion as "a supplement to law in the government of men," as "the alpha and omega of the moral law"—an attitude closely akin to that voiced in the Northwest Ordinance.[22]

Finally, I wish to adduce the evidence afforded by some important systematic works on the subject of constitutional interpretation, as to the meaning of the term "an establishment of religion." The first of these, although the Court seems to have overlooked it entirely in its researches on the present occasion, carried vast authority a century ago, especially north of the Potomac. I refer to Story's *Commentaries on the Constitution*. Interestingly enough, with one important exception, Story's hard-bitten New England views are quite in line in this instance with those of the Virginians. The exception is that according to Story, while the "no establishment" clause inhibited Congress from giving preference to any sect or denomination of the Christian faith, it was not intended thus to withdraw the Christian religion as a whole from the protection of Congress. Thus he wrote:

> Probably at the time of the adoption of the Constitution, and of the amendment to it, now under consideration, the general, if not the universal sentiment in America was, that christianity ought to receive encouragement from the state, so far as was not in-

[21] I *Messages and Papers of the Presidents* 379 (Richardson ed. 1896).

[22] 7 *The Writings of Thomas Jefferson* 339 (H. A. Washington ed. 1854); I *id.* at 545. For the latter reference, I am indebted to J. M. O'Neill, *Religion and Education Under the Constitution*. This work, now in press, is a devastating assault upon the *McCollum* decision from several angles.

compatible with the private rights of conscience and the freedom of religious worship. An attempt to level all religions, and to make it a matter of state policy to hold all in utter indifference, would have created universal disapprobation if not universal indignation.[23]

Nor was it the purpose of the Amendment to discredit state establishments of religion, but simply "to exclude from the National Government all power to act on the subject."

The situation . . . of the different states equally proclaimed the policy, as well as the necessity of such an exclusion. In some of the states, Episcopalians constituted the predominant sect; in others, Presbyterians; in others, Congregationalists; in others, Quakers; and in others again, there was a close numerical rivalry among contending sects. It was impossible, that there should not arise perpetual strife and perpetual jealousy on the subject of ecclesiastical ascendency, if the national government were left free to create a religious establishment. The only security was in extirpating the power. But this alone would have been an imperfect security, if it had not been followed up by a declaration of the right of the free exercise of religion, and a prohibition (as we have seen) of all religious tests. Thus, the whole power over the subject of religion is left exclusively to the state governments, to be acted upon according to their own sense of justice, and the state constitutions; and the Catholic and the Protestant, the Calvinist and the Arminian, the Jew and the Infidel, may sit down at the common table of the national councils, without any inquisition into their faith, or mode of worship.[24]

A generation later Cooley's famous work on *Constitutional Limitations* appeared, the province of which is the constitutional restraints imposed by the state constitutions of that date on the state legislatures. In striking contrast to the passage just quoted from Story, Cooley's work records the disappearance of religious establishments from the state constitutions. His conception of "an establishment of religion" is, however, still the same as that of Story, Madison, and Jefferson, *viz.*, "a sect . . . favored by the State and given an advantage by law over other sects."[25] And in his later *Principles of Constitutional Law,* Cooley is more explicit: "By

[23] Joseph Story, *Commentaries on the Constitution* § 1874 (1833).
[24] *Id.* § 1879.
[25] Cooley, *Constitutional Limitations* 469 (2d ed. 1871).

establishment of religion is meant the setting up or recognition of a state church, or at least the conferring upon one church of special favors and advantages which are denied to others [citing 1 *Tuck. Bl. Comm.*, App. 296; 2 *id.*, App. Note G.]. It was never intended by the Constitution that the Government should be prohibited from recognizing religion—where it might be done without drawing any invidious distinctions between different religious beliefs, organizations, or sects."[26]

II.

All in all, it is fairly evident that Justice Rutledge sold his brethren a bill of goods when he persuaded them that the "establishment of religion" clause of the First Amendment was intended to rule out all governmental "aid to *all* religions." However, the First Amendment, taken by itself, is binding only on Congress; and the legislation involved in the *McCollum* case was state legislation. The *immediate* basis of the decision in this case was, in fact, the "due process" clause of the Fourteenth Amendment; or more strictly speaking, the word "liberty" there. In other words, the theory of the case is that the Fourteenth Amendment renders the ban of the First Amendment on an establishment of religion applicable also to the states? Whence came this theory; and to what, logically, does it lead?

I shall deal with these questions in a moment. But first I wish to comment briefly on Justice Frankfurter's supplemental opinion in the *McCollum* case, in which he is joined by three other justices. For while the opinion throws no additional light on the meaning of the "establishment of religion" clause, it does have bearing on the broader subject of religion in the schools.

The opinion is a well-documented sketch of the secularization of public school education in the United States, a reform effected—so far as it has been effected—purely by the political process, unaided up to this point by the Supreme Court. An outstanding figure in the fight on *sectarianism* in the schools was Horace Mann, who lived

[26] Cooley, *Principles of Constitutional Law* 224–225 (3d ed. 1898). It is perhaps worth noting that it is in Tucker's *Blackstone* (1803) that Madison's and Jefferson's Virginia and Kentucky Resolutions were first elevated to the rank of an authoritative gloss on the Constitution.

and wrought in Massachusetts in the second quarter of the last century. Of him Justice Frankfurter writes:

> In Massachusetts, largely through the efforts of Horace Mann, all sectarian teachings were barred from the common school to save it from being rent by denominational conflict. The upshot of these controversies, often long and fierce, is fairly summarized by saying that long before the Fourteenth Amendment subjected the States to new limitations, the prohibition of furtherance by the State of religious instruction became the guiding principle, in law and feeling, of the American people.[27]

This account of things requires some amplifying. Any implication that he was totally opposed to religious instruction in the schools Mann himself would have denied vehemently. Summing the matter up, Culver writes in his authoritative work on the subject:

> It is true that Mr. Mann stood strongly for a "type of school with instruction adapted to democratic and national ends." But it is not quite just to him to contrast this type of school with the school adapted to religious ends, without defining terms. Horace Mann was opposed to sectarian doctrinal instruction in the schools, but he repeatedly urged the teaching of the elements of religion common to all of the Christian sects. He took a firm stand against the idea of a purely secular education, and on one occasion said he was in favor of religious instruction "to the extremest verge to which it can be carried without invading those rights of conscience which are established by the laws of God, and guaranteed to us by the Constitution of the State." At another time he said that he regarded hostility to religion in the schools as the greatest crime he could commit. Lest his name should go down in history as that of one who had attempted to drive religious instruction from the schools, he devoted several pages in his final Report—the twelfth—to a statement in which he denied the charges of his enemies.[28]

At another point, Justice Frankfurter quotes President Grant's "famous remarks" in 1875 to a convention of the Army of Tennessee, and his message to Congress of the same year, asking for a constitutional amendment which, among other things, would forbid

[27] *McCollum* v. *Board of Education, supra* note 4, at 215.

[28] Raymond B. Culver, *Horace Mann and Religion in the Massachusetts Public Schools* 235 (1929).

the use of public funds for sectarian education, and attacking the exemption of church property from taxation.[29] Acting on these suggestions James G. Blaine introduced a resolution providing that "no State shall make any law respecting an establishment of religion" and prohibiting any appropriation of public school money by any state to sectarian schools. The proposal was adopted by the House overwhelmingly, but was lost in the Senate.[30] Down to 1929 it had been reintroduced some twenty times, without result. The proposal assumes, of course, that it was necessary in order to fill a gap in the Constitution. Conversely, the Court's reading of the "due process" clause of the Fourteenth Amendment in the *McCollum* case assumes that any such amendment would be superfluous.

That the Fourteenth Amendment would make the Bill of Rights applicable to the states was frequently asserted in the congressional debates on the former, but this circumstance lends little if any support to the holding in the *McCollum* case. For one thing, the Court can hardly rely on it and at the same time reject the conception of the "establishment of religion" clause which prevailed in 1868. If history is to be followed on the one point, it cannot fairly be abandoned on the other. Again, the expectations of its framers regarding the operation of the amendment rested mainly on two ideas, both of which were early discredited by the Court itself. The first of these was that the "privileges and immunities of citizens of the United States" protected by the amendment covered the whole realm of civil rights; the second was that Congress's legislative power under Section V of the amendment would be equally extensive. Thus the application of the Bill of Rights to the states would be effected by congressional action; the notion that the Court would have any hand in the business was not widely entertained.[31]

[29] *McCollum* v. *Board of Education, supra* note 4, at 218.

[30] M. A. Musmanno, *Proposed Amendments to the Constitution* 182 (1929).

[31] In his dissenting opinion in *Adamson* v. *California,* 332 U. S. 46, 68ff. (1947), Justice Black argues that the Fourteenth Amendment adopts the Bill of Rights in toto and quotes from the congressional debates on the former to prove the point, relying especially on speeches by Representative Bingham of Ohio and Senator Howard of Michigan. He overlooks the fact that both these high authorities expected that the application of the Bill of Rights to the states would be effected by congressional legislation. See the Appendix compiled by Justice Black to his opinion, 332 U. S. 92–123, especially at pp. 93, 94, 95, 97, 98, 101, 106, 107, 110, 112, 114, 115, 117, and 118.

The Court itself, however, had different ideas. In the famous *Slaughter House Cases*[32] of 1873 it adopted a conception of "privileges and immunities of citizens of the United States" which extruded all "fundamental" rights from the term. In the *Civil Rights Cases*[33] ten years later it pared down Congress's powers under the fifth section of the amendment to the bare disallowance of state legislation violative of the first section—a function better left to the processes of judicial review. The subsequent judicial history of the Fourteenth Amendment has in the main been the history of the Court's interpretation of the due process clause; but of this history the only phase of interest in the present connection is that which involves the word "liberty" in that clause. In 1898, thirty years after the adoption of the amendment, the Court, responding to the pressure of preponderant legal opinion in the country, at last adopted a definition of "liberty" embracing "freedom of contract," and especially freedom of contract in the sphere of employer-employee relations.[34] More expansive conceptions of the term, on the other hand, it steadily repelled throughout the next quarter of a century.[35] Even as late as 1922 we find it using the following words:

> Neither the Fourteenth Amendment nor any other provision of the Constitution of the United States imposes upon the States any restrictions about "freedom of speech" or the "liberty of silence."[36]

Following the first World War, however, the Court began shifting its position; and in the notable case of *Pierce* v. *Society of Sisters*,[37] decided in 1925, it held that the word "liberty" in the Fourteenth Amendment protects the rights of parents to guide the education of their children, and hence the right to send them to parochial schools rather than the public schools, if they so choose. And on this basis, the Oregon compulsory school law, which made it impossible, practically, for children to attend parochial schools, was pronounced unconstitutional. As I shall point out in a moment, the

[32] *Slaughter House Cases*, 16 Wall. 36 (U. S. 1873).

[33] *Civil Rights Cases*, 109 U. S. 3 (1883).

[34] *Holden* v. *Hardy*, 169 U. S. 366 (1898).

[35] On this and the following paragraph, see my *Liberty Against Government* 134–168 (1948).

[36] *Prudential Insurance Co.* v. *Cheek*, 259 U. S. 530, 543 (1922).

[37] 268 U. S. 510 (1925).

holding in the *McCollum* case is logically incompatible with the decision just mentioned. Finally, in this same year, 1925, the Court, in the well-known *Gitlow* case,[38] tentatively adopted the thesis that the word "liberty" in the Fourteenth Amendment includes freedom of speech and press as recognized in the First Amendment; and this tentative thesis has since become a firm part of the Court's jurisprudence. In many recent cases, most of which involve Jehovah's Witnesses, the same doctrine has, moreover, been applied to religious liberty.[39]

That the Court was warranted by a considerable line of recent decisions in taking the position in the *McCollum* case that if the "released time" program there involved amounted to an invasion of anybody's freedom of religion it was unconstitutional, is clear. Indeed, whether the program did this or not was, properly speaking, the only question before the Court; and the talk about "an establishment of religion" was entirely beside the point *unless the "released time" program of the Champaign schools involved an establishment of religion of such a nature as to deprive the plaintiff in the case of freedom of religion.* That is to say, the Fourteenth Amendment does not authorize the Court to substitute the word "state" for "Congress" in the ban imposed by the First Amendment on laws "respecting an establishment of religion." *So far as the Fourteenth Amendment is concerned, states are entirely free to establish religions, provided they do not deprive anybody of religious liberty.* It is only *liberty* that the Fourteenth Amendment protects. And in this connection it should not be overlooked that contemporary England manages to maintain as complete freedom of religion as exists in this country alongside an establishment of religion, although originally that establishment involved a ban upon all other faiths.[40]

[38] *Gitlow* v. *New York,* 268 U. S. 652 (1925).

[39] *Cantwell* v. *Connecticut,* 310 U. S. 296 (1940); *West Virginia State Board of Education* v. *Barnette,* 319 U. S. 624 (1943), and cases there cited.

[40] In the *Cantwell* case, cited above, it is stated incidentally (p. 303) that the Fourteenth Amendment makes the "establishment of religion" clause of the First Amendment operate with the same force on the states as it does on Congress; but this statement is based on the idea that an establishment signifies "compulsion by law of the acceptance of . . . [a] creed or the practice of . . . [a] form of worship." *Ibid.* Story, on the other hand, holds that an ecclesiastical establishment may be perfectly compatible with full freedom of religion for all sects. Joseph Story, *Commentaries on the Constitution* § 1872 (1833).

Vital, therefore, to the Court's argument in the *McCollum* case is the proposition that such children in the Champaign schools as came under the program were *coerced* to do so by virtue of the fact that they were gathered there—"recruited" is the Court's word—in consequence of the state compulsory school law. The answer is that no children were admitted to the program unless their parents formally requested that they be, and the choice of the parent must be imputed to the child. There is still, of course, the coercion exercised by the parent, but it seems unlikely that the Court is out to emancipate children from their parents!

This is not to say, however, that there was no question of coercion involved in this case and involved in a very significant way, although one which appears to have escaped entirely the careful diligence of the Court. I recur to my reference a paragraph or two back to the decision in 1925 in *Pierce* v. *Society of Sisters*,[41] in which an Oregon compulsory school law was set aside as impairing the right of parents, who wished their children to attend parochial schools, to guide the education of their children. Two observations seem called for. In the first place, it is an inevitable implication of the case that compulsory school laws which *permit* attendance at parochial schools are constitutional, notwithstanding the compulsion which is thereby lent such schools in "recruiting" pupils. This compulsion is, in fact, immensely more evident than that which was put upon pupils to avail themselves of the Champaign "released time" program. In the second place, the parental right which was vindicated in the *Pierce* case, whatever else it is, must also be reckoned to be an *element of the right which the Constitution guarantees to all to "the free exercise" of their religion*. The question accordingly arises whether this right is confined to parents who can afford to send their children to parochial or other private schools; whether, in other words, parents who must for financial or other reasons send their children to the public schools have no right to guide their education to the extent of demanding that the education there available shall include some religious instruction, provided nobody's freedom of religion is thereby impaired? *All in all, it seems clear that the Court, by its decision in the* McCollum *case, has itself promulgated a law prohibiting "the free exercise" of religion, contrary to the express prohibition of the First Amendment!*

[41] See note 37 *supra*.

To summarize the argument against the decision in the *McCollum* case: In the first place, the justification for the Court's intervention was trivial and directly violative of restrictions hitherto existing on judicial review. In the second place, the decision is based, as Justice Reed rightly contends,[42] on "a figure of speech," the concept of "a wall of separation between Church and State." Thirdly, leaving this figure of speech to one side, the decision is seen to stem from an unhistorical conception of what is meant by "an establishment of religion" in the First Amendment. The historical record shows beyond peradventure that the core idea of "an establishment of religion" comprises the idea of *preference;* and that any act of public authority favorable to religion in general cannot, without manifest falsification of history, be brought under the ban of that phrase. Undoubtedly the Court has the right to make history, as it has often done in the past; but it has no right to *remake* it. In the fourth place, the prohibition on the establishment of religion by Congress is not convertible into a similar prohibition on the states, under the authorization of the Fourteenth Amendment, unless the term "establishment of religion" be given an application which carries with it invasion of somebody's freedom of religion, that is, of "liberty." Finally, the decision is accompanied by opinions and by a mandate which together have created great uncertainty in the minds of governing bodies of all public educational institutions. And, of course, as is always the case, the Court's intervention is purely negative. It is incapable of solving the complex problem with which forty-six states and 2,200 communities have been struggling by means of the "released time" expedient. With the utmost insouciance the Court overturns or casts under the shadow of unconstitutionality the "conscientious attempt" of hundreds of people to deal with what they have considered to be a pressing problem in a way that they have considered to be fair and just to all.

Finally, this question may be asked: Is the decision favorable to democracy? Primarily democracy is a system of ethical values, and that this system of values so far as the American people are concerned, is grounded in religion will not be denied by anybody who knows the historical record. And that the agencies by which this system of values has been transmitted in the past from generation

[42] *McCollum* v. *Board of Education,* at 247.

to generation—the family, the neighborhood, the church—have to-day become much impaired will not be seriously questioned by anybody who knows anything about contemporary conditions. But what this all adds up to is that *the work of transmission has been put more and more upon the shoulders of the public schools.* Can they, then, do the job without the assistance of religious instruction? At least, there seems to be a widely held opinion to the contrary.

I wonder just how the shade of Justice Holmes would comment on this decision. I can imagine the late Justice repeating some words which he used in a dissenting opinion in 1921:

> There is nothing that I more deprecate than the use of the Fourteenth Amendment beyond the absolute compulsion of its words to prevent the making of social experiments that an important part of the community desires, in the insulated chambers afforded by the several States, even though the experiments may seem futile or even noxious to me and to those whose judgment I most respect.[43]

Indeed, he might even feel called upon to repeat his gibe about judges being "naïf, simple-minded men"[44] one mark of naiveté being a preference for slogans over solutions.

And what would the Court answer? Perhaps it might adopt the words of Justice Jackson in a recent case:

> We [the Court] act in these matters not by the authority of our competence but by force of our commissions. We cannot, because of modest estimates of our competence in such specialties as public education, withhold the judgment that history authenticates as the function of this Court when liberty is infringed.[45]

This is a plea in confession and avoidance which can by no means be granted. It is not to be presumed that the Constitution puts burdens on the Court in the discharge of which with appropriate modesty it must still risk disaster for the country. The decision in the *McCollum* case, however, is not a "modest" decision. Instead

[43] *Traux* v. *Corrigan,* 257 U. S. 312, 244 (1921). The "watchfulness of state interests against exuberant judicial restrictions," which Holmes gave expression to in the passage just quoted, is praised by Justice Frankfurter with warm enthusiasm in his *Mr. Justice Holmes and the Supreme Court* 86–88 (1938). See also his recent opinion in *Adamson* v. *California* 332 U. S. 46, 59, 62.

[44] Holmes, *Collected Legal Papers* 295 (1921).

[45] *West Virginia State Board of Education* v. *Barnette, supra* note 39, at 640.

it is to be grouped with those high-flying *tours de force* in which the Court has occasionally indulged, to solve "forever" some teasing problem—slavery, for example, in the *Dred Scott* case[46]—or to correct, as in the *Pollock* case,[47] "a century of error."

In my opinion the Court would act wisely to make it clear at the first opportunity that it does not aspire to become, as Justice Jackson puts it, "a super board of education for every school district in the nation."[48]

[46] *Dred Scott* v. *Sandford,* 19 How. 393 (U. S. 1856).
[47] *Pollock* v. *Farmers Loan and Trust Co.,* 157 U. S. 429 (1895).
[48] *McCollum* v. *Board of Education, supra* note 3, at 237.

Writings of Edward S. Corwin

I. Books

National Supremacy (New York: Holt, 1913).

The Doctrine of Judicial Review and Other Essays (Princeton, 1914). First essay reprinted in part in I *Selected Essays on Constitutional Law*, '20.

War Dictionary (Washington: Committee on Public Information, 1917), E. S. Corwin and F. L. Paxson, eds.

French Policy and the American Alliance of 1778 (Princeton, 1916).

John Marshall and the Constitution (New Haven: Yale, 1919).

The Constitution and What It Means Today (Princeton, 1958). Earlier editions: 1920, 1921, 1924, 1930, 1937, 1938, 1941, 1946, 1947, 1948, 1954.

Woodrow Wilson, *Division and Reunion* (New York: Longmans, Green, 1921). Preface and revision by Edward S. Corwin.

The President's Removal Power Under the Constitution (New York: National Municipal League, 1927). Reprinted in part from "Tenure of Office and Removal Under the Constitution," 27 *Columbia Law Review* (April, 1927), 353.

The Democratic Dogma and Other Essays (Shanghai: Kelly and Walsh, 1930).

The Twilight of the Supreme Court (New Haven: Yale, 1934).

Commerce Power versus States Rights (Princeton, 1936).

Court over Constitution (Princeton, 1938).

The President: Office and Powers (New York: New York U., 1958). Other editions: 1940, 1941, 1948, 1956.

Constitutional Revolution, Ltd. (Claremont, Calif., 1941).

The Constitution and World Organization (Princeton, 1944).

Total War and the Constitution (New York: Knopf, 1947).

Liberty Against Government (Baton Rouge: Louisiana State, 1948).

A Constitution of Powers in a Secular State (Charlottesville: Michie, 1951).

The Constitution of the United States of America: Analysis and Interpretation, Edward S. Corwin, ed. (Washington: U.S. Government Printing Office, 1953).

Our Expendable Constitution (Urbana: Illinois, 1955).

The Presidency Today (New York: New York U., 1956), with Louis W. Koenig.

Understanding the Constitution (New York: Dryden, 1958), with Jack W. Peltason.

II. Articles

"The Supreme Court and Unconstitutional Acts of Congress," 4 *Michigan Law Review* (June, 1906), 616.

"The Supreme Court and the Fourteenth Amendment," 7 *Michigan Law Review* (June, 1909), 643.

"The Establishment of Judicial Review," 9 *Michigan Law Review* (December, 1910), pp. 102 ff. and (February, 1911), pp. 283 ff.

"The Doctrine of Due Process of Law Before the Civil War," I *Selected Essays on Constitutional Law,* 2. Reprinted from 24 *Harvard Law Review* (March, 1911), pp. 366 ff. and (April, 1911), pp. 460 ff.

"The Dred Scott Decision in the Light of Contemporary Legal Doctrine," 17 *American Hist. Review* (October, 1911), 52.

"National Power and State Interposition, 1787–1861," III *Selected Essays on Constitutional Law,* 1171. Reprinted from 10 *Michigan Law Review* (May, 1912), 535.

"Due Process," "Dred Scott Decision," "Fourteenth Amendment," "Internal Improvements," "*Trevett* v. *Weldon,*" in McLaughlin and Hart's *Cyclopedia of American Government* (New York: Appleton, 1914).

The Basic Doctrine of American Constitutional Law, Offprint from 12 *Michigan Law Review* (February, 1914), 247. 1 *Selected Essays on Constitutional Law,* 101.

"Marbury v. Madison and the Doctrine of Judicial Review," 12 *Michigan Law Review* (May, 1914), 538. Reprinted in part in *The Doctrine of Judicial Review and Other Essays,* Chapter I.

"The Treaty-Making Power: A Rejoinder," 199 *North American Review* (June, 1914), 893.

"Making Railroad Legislation National," 2 *New Republic* (February 27, 1915), 94.

"Is the British Embargo Lawful?" 4 *New Republic* (August 14, 1915), 37.

"French Objectives in the American Revolution," 21 *American Hist. Review* (October, 1915), 33.

"Rights of Aliens," 7 *New Republic* (May 20, 1916), 70.

"Game Protection and the Constitution," 14 *Michigan Law Review* (June, 1916), 613.

"Sea-Rights and Sea-Power: The British Embargo," 204 *North American Review* (October, 1916), 515.

"International Law Imperilled," in *The World Peril* (Princeton: Princeton, 1917).

"The Extension of Judicial Review in New York," 15 *Michigan Law Review* (February, 1917), 281.

"Right of Retaliation," 104 *Nation* (March, 1917), 233.

"Social Insurance and Constitutional Limitations," 26 *Yale Law Journal* (April, 1917), 431.

"War, the Constitution-Moulder," 11 *New Republic* (June 9, 1917), 153.

"Validity of the Child Labor Act," 12 *New Republic* (September 15, 1917), 186.

"Freedom of the Sea," 209 *North American Review* (January, 1919), 29.

"Freedom of the Seas—A Compromise," 108 *Nation* (March 8, 1919), 365.

"Examination of the Covenant," 1 *Weekly Review* (June 7, 1919), 77.

"Wilson and the Senate," 1 *Weekly Review* (July 26, 1919), 228.

"The Worship of the Constitution," 4 *Constitutional Review* (January, 1920), 1.

"Congress's Right to Declare Peace," 2 *Weekly Review* (April 17, 1920), 388.

"The Power of Congress to Declare Peace," 18 *Michigan Law Review* (May, 1920), 669.

"The League, the Constitution and Governor Cox," 3 *Weekly Review* (August 25, 1920), 165.

"An International Court of Justice," 3 *Weekly Review* (September 29, 1920), 265.

"The Permanent Court of International Justice," 3 *Weekly Review* (September 29, 1920), 265.

"Mr. McCall on the Senate," 3 *Weekly Review* (October 6, 1920), 287.

"The President's Defiance of Congress," 3 *Weekly Review* (October 6, 1920), 282.

"Constitutional Law in 1919–1920, I," 14 *American Political Science Review* (November, 1920), 635.

"Freedom of Speech and Press Under the First Amendment," 30 *Yale Law Journal* (November, 1920), 48. Reprinted in II *Selected Essays on Constitutional Law,* 1060.

"A Possible Way Out," 3 *Weekly Review* (December 22, 1920), 617.

"Constitutional Law in 1919–1920, II," 15 *American Political Science Review* (February, 1921), 52.

"Constitutional Law in 1920–1921, I," 16 *American Political Science Review* (February, 1922), 22.

"Constitutional Law in 1920–1921, II," 16 *American Political Science Review* (May, 1922), 228.

"The Child Labor Decisions," 31 *New Republic* (July 12, 1922), 177.

"Constitutional Law in 1921–1922," 16 *American Political Science Review* (November, 1922), 612.

"Pending Amendments to the Constitution," *Daily Princetonian* (February 21, 27, 1923).

"Spending Power of Congress," 36 *Harvard Law Review* (March, 1923), Reprinted in III *Selected Essays on Constitutional Law,* 565.

"Monroe Doctrine," 218 *North American Review* (December, 1923), 721.

"Constitutional Tax Exemption," 13 *National Municipal Review* (January, 1924), 50.

"Constitutional Law in 1922–1923," 18 *American Political Science Review* (February, 1924), 49.

"Public Law," 18 *American Political Science Review* (February, 1924), 148.

"The Presidency," 25 *Princeton Alumni Weekly* (October 22, 1924), 80.

"Judicial Review," *New York Law Journal* (January 21, 1925).

"The Power of the Supreme Court Over Legislation," 57 *Chicago Legal News* (February 5, 1925), 228.

"The Progress of Constitutional Theory from the Signing of the Declaration of Independence to the Meeting of the Philadelphia Convention," 30 *American Hist. Review* (April, 1925), 511.

"Constitution v. Constitutional Theory," 19 *American Political Science Review* (May, 1925), 290.

"Henry Jones Ford," 19 *American Political Science Review* (November, 1925), 813.

"Judicial Review in Action," 74 *U. of Pennsylvania Law Review* (May, 1926), 639. Reprinted in I *Selected Essays on Constitutional Law,* 449.

"The Lessons of the Colorado River Compact," 16 *National Municipal Review* (July, 1927), 459.

"Extraterritoriality: An American View," 48 *China Weekly Review* (1928), 154.

"The 'Higher Law' Background of American Constitutional Law," 42 *Harvard Law Review* (December–January, 1928–29), pp. 149 ff., 365 ff. Reprinted in I *Selected Essays on Constitutional Law,* 1 and in paperback book of same title (Cornell: Great Seal, 1959).

"The Democratic Dogma and the Future of Political Science," 23 *American* Political Science Review (August, 1929), 569. Reprinted in the *Democratic Dogma,* Chapter I.

"The Supreme Court's Construction of the Self-Incrimination Clause," 29 *Michigan Law Review* (November, 1960), 1. Reprinted in II *Selected Essays on Constitutional Law,* 1398.

"The Anti-Trust Acts and the Constitution," 18 *Virginia Law Review* (February, 1932), 355.

"Social Planning Under the Constitution—A Study in Perspectives," 26 *American Political Science Review* (February, 1932), 1. Reprinted in II *Selected Essays on Constitutional Law,* 131.

"Martial Law, Yesterday and Today," 47 *Political Science Quarterly* (March, 1932), 95.

"The Three Mile Limit," 70 *Forum* (September, 1932), 1880.

"The 'Full Faith and Credit Clause,'" 81 *U. of Pennsylvania Law Review* (February, 1933), 371. Reprinted in III *Selected Essays on Constitutional Law,* 1414.

"Congress' Power to Prohibit Commerce—A Crucial Constitutional Issue," 18 *Cornell Law Quarterly* (June, 1933), 477. Reprinted in III *Selected Essays on Constitutional Law,* 103.

"On Constitutionality of N.I.R.A.," *New York Times,* November 7, 1933, p. 3:5.

"The Bases of N.R.A.," *New York Times,* November 12, 1933, sec. IV, p. 4:7.

"Judicial Review," 8 *Encyclopedia of the Social Sciences,* 457.

"John Marshall," 10 *Encyclopedia of the Social Sciences,* 157.

"On Effects of N.I.R.A. on U.S. Constitutional System," *New York Times,* January 7, 1934, sec. II, p. 6:1.

"Some Probable Repercussions of Nira on our Constitutional System," 172 *Annals of the American Academy of Political and Social Sciences* (March, 1934), 139.

"Gold Clause Cases," *New York Times,* February 24, 1935, sec. II, p. 1:1.

"The President, Court and Constitution, I," *Christian Science Monitor,* July 3, 1935, p. 18:6.

"The President, Court and Constitution, II," *Christian Science Monitor,* July 5, 1935.

"The President, Court and Constitution, III," *Christian Science Monitor,* July 6, 1935.

"Constitutional Aspects of Federal Housing," 84 *U. of Pennsylvania Law Review* (December, 1935), 131.

"Curbing the Court," 2 *Vital Speeches* (March 9, 1936), 373.

"Curbing the Court," 185 *Annals of the American Academy of Political and Social Sciences* (May, 1936), 45.

"Curbing the Court," 26 *American Labor Legislation Review* (June, 1936), 85.

"President and Court: A Crucial Issue," *New York Times,* February 14, 1937, sec. VIII, p. 1.

"National-State Cooperation—Its Present Possibilities," III *Selected Essays on Constitutional Law,* 973. Reprinted from 46 *Yale Law Journal* (February, 1937), 599.

"Justices Pressed for Court Views," *New York Times,* March 18, 1937, p. 18:1.

"Sermon on the Supreme Court Issue," *New York Times,* April 5, 1937, p. 15:1.

"Speech on the Constitution," *New York Times,* May 10, 1937, p. 39:1.

"Supreme Court Personnel," *New York Times,* May 30, 1937, sec. IV, p. 8:7.

"Standpoint in Constitutional Law," 17 *Boston University Law Review* (June, 1937), 510. Reprinted in part in *Court Over Constitution,* Chapter II.

"The Court Sees a New Light," 91 *New Republic* (August 4, 1937), 354.

Part II, Hearings Before the Committee on the Judiciary, U. S. Senate, 75th Congress, 1st Session, on S. 1392 (The Roosevelt "Court-Packing Bill") Washington: U. S. Government Printing Office, 1937.

"Portrait," 32 *American Political Science Review* (December, 1938), 1057.

"The President as Administrative Chief," 1 *Journal of Politics* (February, 1939), 17.

"The Posthumous Career of James Madison as Lawyer," 25 *American Bar Ass'n. Journal* (October, 1939), 821.

"Statesmanship on the Supreme Court," 9 *American Scholar* (Spring, 1940), 159.

"Fifty Destroyers versus the Constitution: A Criticism of the Attorney General's Opinion of August 28, 1940," *New York Times,* October 13, 1940, sec. IV, p. 6:5.

"The War and the Constitution: President and Congress," 37 *American Political Science Review* (February, 1943), 18.

"Notice: *The Third Term Tradition,* Charles W. Stein," 38 *American Political Science Review* (February, 1944), 185.

"Out-Haddocking Haddock," 93 *U. of Pennsylvania Law Review* (June, 1945), 341.

"Departmental Colleague," W. S. Meyers, Ed., *Woodrow Wilson: Some Princeton Memories* (Princeton: Princeton, 1946), 19.

"How Executive Power Has Increased," 26 *Congressional Digest* (January, 1947), 5.

"Our Constitutional Revolution and How to Round It Out," 19 *Pennsylvania Bar Ass'n Quarterly* (April, 1948), 261.

"Wanted: A New Type Cabinet," *New York Times,* October 10, 1948, sec. VI, p. 10.

"The Supreme Court as a National School Board," 14 *Law and Contemporary Problems* (Winter, 1949), 3. Reprinted in *A Constitution of Powers in a Secular State,* Chapter IV.

"The Natural Law and Constitutional Law," III *Proceedings of the Natural Law Institute* (Notre Dame: Notre Dame, College of Law, 1950), 47.

"The Passing of Dual Federalism," 36 *Virginia Law Review* (February, 1950), 1. Reprinted in *A Constitution of Powers in a Secular State,* Chapter I.

"The Debt of American Constitutional Law to Natural Law Concepts," 25 *Notre Dame Lawyer* (Winter, 1950), 258.

"The President's Power," 124 *New Republic* (January 29, 1951), 15.

"The Constitutional Law of Constitutional Amendment," 26 *Notre Dame Lawyer* (Winter, 1951), 185, with Mary Louise Ramsay.

"James Madison: Layman, Publicist and Exegete," 27 *New York U. Law Review* (April, 1952), 277.

"Bowing Out 'Clear and Present Danger,' " 27 *Notre Dame Lawyer* (Spring, 1952), 325.

"The Steel Seizure Case: A Judicial Brick Without Straw," 53 *Columbia Law Review* (June, 1953), 53.

"The Dissolving Structure of our Constitutional Law," 20 *Washington Law Review* (November, 1954), 185.

"State of the Nation," 94 *America* (October 1, 1955), 20.

"John Marshall, Revolutionist *Malgré Lui*," 104 *U. of Pennsylvania Law Review* (October, 1955), 9.

"Leader and Party," 95 *America* (September 22, 1956), 95.

"Woodrow Wilson and the Presidency," 42 *Virginia Law Review* (October, 1956), 761.

"Limiting the Judiciary: Letter to the Times," *New York Times*, March 16, 1958, sec. IV, p. 10:6.

"Congress and the Judiciary: Letter to the Times," *New York Times*, April 19, 1958, p. 20:6.

III. Reviews

"*The American Nation*, vols. 16–19," 2 *American Political Science Review* (November, 1907), 110.

"*The Assassination of Lincoln and its Expiation*, David M. DeWitt," 14 *American Hist. Review* (July, 1909), 880.

"*Social Reform and the Constitution*, Frank J. Goodnow," 6 *American Political Science Review* (May, 1912), 270.

"*Our Judicial Oligarchy*, Gilbert E. Roe," 6 *American Political Science Review* (November, 1912), 654.

"*The Power of the Federal Judiciary Over Legislation*, J. Hampden Dougherty, and *The Supreme Court and the Constitution*, Charles A. Beard," 7 *American Political Science Review* (May, 1913), 329.

"*The Fourteenth Amendment and the States*, Charles W. Collins," 28 *Political Science Quarterly* (June, 1913), 334.

"*History of the Supreme Court of the United States,* Gustavus Meyers," 7 *American Political Science Review* (August, 1913), 500.

"*An Economic Interpretation of the Constitution,* Charles A. Beard," 5 *History Teachers Magazine* (February, 1914), 65.

"*Notes on the Science of Government and the Relations of the States to the United States,* Raleigh C. Minor," 8 *American Political Science Review* (February, 1914), 144.

"*The Supreme Court of the United States and Its Appellate Powers Under the Constitution,* Edwin Countryman," 8 *American Political Science Review* (August, 1914), 503.

"*The Validity of Rate Regulation, State and Federal,* Robert P. Reeder," 9 *American Political Science Review* (February, 1915), 161.

"*The Postal Power of Congress, A Study in Constitutional Expansion,* Lindsay Rogers," 10 *American Political Science Review* (August, 1916), 773.

"*Life of John Marshall,* Albert J. Beveridge," 4 *Mississippi Valley Hist. Review* (June, 1917), 116.

"*Miscellaneous Addresses,* Elihu Root," 24 *American Hist. Review* (October, 1918), 132.

"*Beaumarchais and the War of American Independence,* Elizabeth S. Kite," 24 *American Hist. Review* (January, 1919), 293.

"*The Obligation of Contract Clause of the United States Constitution,* Warren B. Hastings," 14 *American Political Science Review* (November, 1920), 719.

"*The Degradation of the Democratic Dogma,* Henry Adams," 14 *American Political Science Review* (August, 1920), 507.

"*Woodrow Wilson and His Work,* William E. Dodd," 27 *American Hist. Review* (January, 1922), 334.

"*The Constitution at the Crossroads,* Edward A. Harrison," 21 *American Political Science Review* (February, 1922), 194.

"*War Powers of the Executive in the United States,* Clarence A. Berdahl," 16 *American Political Science Review* (August, 1922), 511.

"*Supreme Court in United States History,* Charles Warren," 28 *American Hist. Review* (October, 1922), 134.

"*Cases on International Law,* James Brown Scott," 71 *U. of Pennsylvania Law Review* (January, 1923), 197.

"*The Control of Foreign Relations,* Quincy Wright," 36 *Harvard Law Review* (February, 1923), 499.

"*The Constitution of the United States,* James M. Beck," *Literary Review, New York Evening Post,* March 24, 1923.

"*Life of Roger Brooke Taney,* Bernard C. Steiner," 28 *American Hist. Review* (April, 1923), 556.

"*The Law of the American Constitution,* Charles K. Burdick," 22 *Michigan Law Review* (November, 1923), 84.

"*Diplomatic Portraits,* Cresson," *Literary Review, New York Evening Post,* January 26, 1924.

"*The American Revolution: A Constitutional Interpretation,* C. H. McIlwain," 29 *American Hist. Review* (July, 1924), 775.

"*The Elements of Jurisprudence,* Thomas Holland," 24 *Columbia Law Review* (December, 1924), 936.

"*Congress, The Constitution and the Supreme Court,* Charles Warren," 12 *American Bar Ass'n Journal* (March, 1926), 170.

"*The Usages of the American Constitution,* Hubert W. Horwill," 20 *American Political Science Review* (May, 1926), 436.

"*Constitutional Problems Under Lincoln,* James G. Randall," 21 *American Political Science Review* (May, 1927), 429.

"*The State as Party Litigant,* Robert Dorsey Watkins," 42 *Political Science Quarterly* (June, 1927), 308.

"*An Introduction to the Study of the American Constitution,* Charles E. Martin," 32 *American Hist. Review* (July, 1927), 929.

"*The United States and France,* James Brown Scott," 42 *Political Science Quarterly* (September, 1927), 482.

"*The Living Constitution: A Consideration of the Realities and Legends of Our Fundamental Law,*" 22 *American Political Science Review* (May, 1928), 461.

"*The Business of the Supreme Court: A Study in the Federal Judicial System,* Felix Frankfurter and James Landis," 43 *Political Science Quarterly* (June, 1928), 272.

"*American Citizenship as Distinguished from Alien Status,* Frederick A. Cleveland," 17 *National Municipal Review* (July, 1928), 420.

"*The Worker Looks at Government,* Arthur W. Calhoun," 23 *American Political Science Review* (May, 1929), 504.

"*Some Lessons From Our Legal History,* William Searle Holdsworth," 36 *American Hist. Review* (October, 1929), 98.

"*Principles of Judicial Administration,* W. F. Willoughby," 23 *American Political Science Review* (November, 1929), 1007.

"*The Supreme Court of the United States,* Charles Evans Hughes," 39 *Yale Law Journal* (December, 1929), 295.

"*A Review of the Work of the Supreme Court . . . for October Term, 1928,* Gregory and Charlotte A. Hankin," 78 *U. of Pennsylvania Law Review* (May, 1930), 926.

"*The Dissenting Opinions of Mr. Justice Holmes,*" 24 *American Political Science Review* (August, 1930), 780.

"*A Selection of Cases and Authorities on Constitutional Law,* Oliver P. Field," 25 *American Political Science Review* (May, 1931), 459.

"*Tenure of Office Under the Constitution,* James Hart," 20 *National Municipal Review* (February, 1931), 96.

"*The Public and its Government,* Felix Frankfurter," 47 *Political Science Quarterly* (March, 1932), 105.

"*American Interpretations of Natural Law,* Benjamin F. Wright," 32 *Columbia Law Review* (April, 1932), 764.

"*Our Wonderland of Bureaucracy,* James M. Beck," 81 *U. of Pennsylvania Law Review* (November, 1932), 99.

"*Constitutional Law,* E. C. S. Wade and C. Godfrey Phillips," 18 *Virginia Law Review* (June, 1932), 917.

"*Cases on Constitutional Law,* Walter F. Dodd," 2 *Mercer Beasley Law Review* (January, 1933), 166.

"*Legislative Regulation,* Ernst Freund," 33 *Columbia Law Review* (March, 1933), 554.

"*Government by Judiciary,* Louis D. Boudin," 27 *American Political Science Review* (June, 1933), 473.

"*Parliamentary Opinion of Delegated Legislation,* Chih-Mai Chen," 82 *U. of Pennsylvania Law Review* (April, 1934), 677.

"*The Challenge to Liberty,* Herbert Hoover; *New Frontiers,* Henry A. Wallace; *Liberty Under Law and Administration,* Homer Cummings; *The House of Adam Smith,* Eli Ginzberg," 44 *Yale Law Journal* (January, 1935), 546.

"*Administrative Legislation and Adjudication,* Frederick F. Blachly and Miriam E. Oatman, and *Principles of Legislative Organization and Administration,* W. F. Willoughby," 83 *U. of Pennsylvania Law Review* (May, 1935), 933.

"*Proceedings of the Maryland Court of Appeals,* Carrol T. Bond and Richard B. Morris, eds., 50 *Political Science Quarterly* (June, 1935), 312.

"*World Politics and Personal Insecurity,* Harold D. Lasswell," 181 *Annals of the American Academy of Political and Social Sciences* (September, 1935), 188.

"*The Need for Constitutional Reform,* William Yandell Elliott," 54 *Yale Law Journal* (November, 1935), 185.

"*The Effect of an Unconstitutional Statute,* Oliver P. Field," 21 *Cornell Law Quarterly* (December, 1935), 197.

"*Declaratory Judgements,* Edwin M. Borchard," 1 *U. of Toronto Law Journal* (Lent, 1936), 402.

"*Roger Brooke Taney,* Carl Brent Swisher, and *Roger B. Taney, Jacksonian Jurist,* Charles W. Smith, Jr.," 30 *American Political Science Review* (April, 1936), 372.

"*Storm Over the Constitution,* Irving Brant; *Fifty Five Men,* Fred Rodell; *Whose Constitution?,* Henry A. Wallace," 88 *New Republic* (September, 1936), 135.

"*Storm Over the Constitution,* Irving Brant, and *Whose Constitution?* and *Inquiry Into the General Welfare,* Henry A. Wallace," 30 *American Political Science Review* (October, 1936), 981.

"*State Interests in American Treaties,* Nichols Pendleton Mitchell," 6 *Brooklyn Law Review* (October, 1936), 126.

"*Nine Old Men,* Drew Pearson and Robert S. Allen," 26 *Survey Graphic* (March, 1937), 156.

"*Brandeis,* Alfred Leif," 26 *Yale Review* (Spring, 1937), 590.

"*Neither Purse Nor Sword,* James M. Beck and Merle Thorpe," 191 *Annals of the American Academy of Political and Social Sciences* (May, 1937), 244.

"*The Power to Govern,* Walton H. Hamilton and Douglass Adair," 21 *American Political Science Review* (December, 1937), 1147.

"*State and National Power Over Commerce,* Frederick D. G. Ribble," 23 *Washington University Law Quarterly* (December, 1937), 142.

"*The Influence of the American Bar Association,* M. Louise Rutherford," 2 *Public Opinion Quarterly* (January, 1938), 153.

"*Interpreting the Constitution,* William Draper Lewis," 24 *American Bar Ass'n Journal* (August, 1938), 655.

"*The Folklore of Capitalism,* Thurman Arnold," 32 *American Political Science Review* (August, 1938), 745.

"*Mr. Justice Holmes and the Supreme Court,* Felix Frankfurter," 52 *Harvard Law Review* (December, 1938), 346.

"*The Constitution of Canada, 1534–1937,* W. P. M. Kennedy," 19 *Canadian Hist. Review* (December, 1938), 414.

"*The Rise of the New Federalism,* Jane Perry Clark," 27 *Survey Graphic* (December, 1938), 618.

"*The Contract Clause of the Constitution,* Benjamin F. Wright," 202 *Annals of the American Academy of Political and Social Sciences* (March, 1939), 217.

"*Lectures on the American Constitution,* Maurice Sheldon Amos," 202 *Annals of the American Academy of Political and Social Sciences* (March, 1939), 216.

"*Our Eleven Chief Justices,* Kenneth B. Umbreit," 28 *Survey Graphic* (March, 1939), 241.

"*The Constitution Reconsidered,* Conyers Read, ed.," 16 *New York U. Law* Law Quarterly Review (May, 1939), 674.

"*Taxation of Government Bondholders and Employees,* Dept. of Justice," 87 *U. of Pennsylvania Law Review* (May, 1939), 883.

"*Power: A New Social Analysis,* Bertrand Russell," 25 *American Bar Ass'n Journal* (July, 1939), 569.

"*Handbook of American Constitutional Law,* Henry Rottschaeffer," 49 *Yale Law Journal* (April, 1940), 1143.

"*Constitutionalism: Ancient and Modern* and *Constitutionalism and the Changing World,* Charles Howard McIlwain," 54 *Harvard Law Review* (January, 1941), 533. Reprinted in *Liberty Against Government,* pp. 184 ff.

"*The Constitutional History of the United States,* Homer Carey Hockett," 36 *American Political Science Review* (October, 1942), 954.

"*The Growth of American Constitutional Law,* Benjamin F. Wright," 56 *Harvard Law Review* (November, 1942), 484.

"*Federal Cooperation With the States Under the Commerce Clause,* Joseph E. Kallenbach," 5 *U. of Toronto Law Journal* (Lent, 1943), 195.

"*Amending the Federal Constitution,* Lester B. Orefield," 5 *U. of Toronto Law Journal* (Lent, 1943), 195.

"*The Republic,* Charles A. Beard," 44 *Columbia Law Review* (March, 1944), 283.

"*The Role of the Supreme Court in American Government and Politics,* Charles Grove Haines," 54 *Yale Law Journal* (December, 1944), 168.

"*Our Civil Liberties,* Osmond K. Fraenkel," 38 *American Political Science Review* (December, 1944), 1216.

"*The Constitution and Civil Rights,* Milton R. Konvitz," 42 *American Political Science Review* (February, 1948), 117.

"*A Declaration of Legal Faith,* Wiley Rutledge," 96 *U. of Pennsylvania Law Review* (June, 1948), 910.

"*The Court and the Constitution,* Owen J. Roberts," 65 *Harvard Law Review* (June, 1952), 1471.

"*The Declaration of Independence and What It Means Today,* Edward Dumbauld," 37 *Cornell Law Quarterly* (Winter, 1952), 342.

Table of Cases

Index

Revised August, 1964

HARPER TORCHBOOKS

HUMANITIES AND SOCIAL SCIENCES

American Studies

JOHN R. ALDEN: The American Revolution, 1775-1783.† *Illus.* TB/3011

RAY STANNARD BAKER: Following the Color Line: *American Negro Citizenship in the Progressive Era.‡ Illus. Edited by Dewey W. Grantham, Jr.* TB/3053

RAY A. BILLINGTON: The Far Western Frontier, 1830-1860.† *Illus.* TB/3012

JOSEPH L. BLAU, Ed.: Cornerstones of Religious Freedom in America. *Selected Basic Documents, Court Decisions and Public Statements. Enlarged and revised edition with new Intro. by Editor* TB/118

RANDOLPH S. BOURNE: War and the Intellectuals: *Collected Essays, 1915-1919.‡ Edited by Carl Resek* TB/3043

A. RUSSELL BUCHANAN: The United States and World War II. † *Illus.* Volume I TB/3044, Volume II TB/3045

ABRAHAM CAHAN: The Rise of David Levinsky: *a novel. Introduction by John Higham* TB/1028

JOSEPH CHARLES: The Origins of the American Party System TB/1049

THOMAS C. COCHRAN: The Inner Revolution: *Essays on the Social Sciences in History* TB/1140

T. C. COCHRAN & WILLIAM MILLER: The Age of Enterprise: *A Social History of Industrial America* TB/1054

EDWARD S. CORWIN: American Constitutional History: *Essays edited by Alpheus T. Mason and Gerald Garvey* TB/1136

FOSTER RHEA DULLES: America's Rise to World Power, 1898-1954.† *Illus.* TB/3021

W. A. DUNNING: Reconstruction, Political and Economic, 1865-1877 TB/1073

A. HUNTER DUPREE: Science in the Federal Government: *A History of Policies and Activities to 1940* TB/573

CLEMENT EATON: The Growth of Southern Civilization, 1790-1860.† *Illus.* TB/3040

HAROLD U. FAULKNER: Politics, Reform and Expansion, 1890-1900.† *Illus.* TB/3020

LOUIS FILLER: The Crusade against Slavery, 1830-1860.† *Illus.* TB/3029

EDITORS OF FORTUNE: America in the Sixties: *the Economy and the Society. Two-color charts* TB/1015

LAWRENCE HENRY GIPSON: The Coming of the Revolution, 1763-1775.† *Illus.* TB/3007

FRANCIS J. GRUND: Aristocracy in America: *Jacksonian Democracy* TB/1001

ALEXANDER HAMILTON: The Reports of Alexander Hamilton.‡ *Edited by Jacob E. Cooke* TB/3060

OSCAR HANDLIN, Editor: This Was America: *As Recorded by European Travelers to the Western Shore in the Eighteenth, Nineteenth, and Twentieth Cenuries. Illus.* TB/1119

MARCUS LEE HANSEN: The Atlantic Migration: 1607-1860. *Edited by Arthur M. Schlesinger; Introduction by Oscar Handlin* TB/1052

MARCUS LEE HANSEN: The Immigrant in American History. *Edited with a Foreword by Arthur Schlesinger, Sr.* TB/1120

JOHN D. HICKS: Republican Ascendancy, 1921-1933.† *Illus.* TB/3041

JOHN HIGHAM, Ed.: The Reconstruction of American History TB/1068

DANIEL R. HUNDLEY: Social Relations in our Southern States.‡ *Edited by William R. Taylor* TB/3058

ROBERT H. JACKSON: The Supreme Court in the American System of Government TB/1106

THOMAS JEFFERSON: Notes on the State of Virginia.‡ *Edited by Thomas Perkins Abernethy* TB/3052

WILLIAM L. LANGER & S. EVERETT GLEASON: The Challenge to Isolation: *The World Crisis of 1937-1940 and American Foreign Policy* Volume I TB/3054, Volume II TB/3055

WILLIAM E. LEUCHTENBURG: Franklin D. Roosevelt and the New Deal, 1932-1940.† *Illus.* TB/3025

LEONARD W. LEVY: Freedom of Speech and Press in Early American History: *Legacy of Suppression* TB/1109

ARTHUR S. LINK: Woodrow Wilson and the Progressive Era, 1910-1917.† *Illus.* TB/3023

ROBERT GREEN McCLOSKEY: American Conservatism in the Age of Enterprise, 1865-1910 TB/1137

BERNARD MAYO: Myths and Men: *Patrick Henry, George Washington, Thomas Jefferson* TB/1108

JOHN C. MILLER: Alexander Hamilton and the Growth of the New Nation TB/3057

JOHN C. MILLER: The Federalist Era, 1789-1801.† *Illus.* TB/3027

† The New American Nation Series, edited by Henry Steele Commager and Richard B. Morris.

‡ American Perspectives series, edited by Bernard Wishy and William E. Leuchtenburg.

* The Rise of Modern Europe series, edited by William L. Langer.

‖ Researches in the Social, Cultural, and Behavioral Sciences, edited by Benjamin Nelson.

§ The Library of Religion and Culture, edited by Benjamin Nelson.

Σ Harper Modern Science Series, edited by James R. Newman.

° Not for sale in Canada.

PERRY MILLER: Errand into the Wilderness TB/1139

PERRY MILLER & T. H. JOHNSON, Editors: The Puritans: *A Sourcebook of Their Writings*
Volume I TB/1093
Volume II TB/1094

GEORGE E. MOWRY: The Era of Theodore Roosevelt and the Birth of Modern America, 1900-1912.† *Illus.* TB/3022

WALLACE NOTESTEIN: The English People on the Eve of Colonization, 1603-1630.† *Illus.* TB/3006

RUSSEL BLAINE NYE: The Cultural Life of the New Nation, 1776-1801.† *Illus.* TB/3026

RALPH BARTON PERRY: Puritanism and Democracy TB/1138

GEORGE E. PROBST, Ed.: The Happy Republic: *A Reader in Tocqueville's America* TB/1060

WALTER RAUSCHENBUSCH: Christianity and the Social Crisis.‡ *Edited by Robert D. Cross* TB/3059

FRANK THISTLETHWAITE: America and the Atlantic Community: *Anglo-American Aspects, 1790-1850* TB/1107

TWELVE SOUTHERNERS: I'll Take My Stand: *The South and the Agrarian Tradition. Introduction by Louis D. Rubin, Jr.; Biographical Essays by Virginia Rock* TB/1072

A. F. TYLER: Freedom's Ferment: *Phases of American Social History from the Revolution to the Outbreak of the Civil War. Illus.* TB/1074

GLYNDON G. VAN DEUSEN: The Jacksonian Era, 1828-1848.† *Illus.* TB/3028

WALTER E. WEYL: The New Democracy: *An Essay on Certain Political and Economic Tendencies in the United States.‡ Edited by Charles Forcey* TB/3042

LOUIS B. WRIGHT: The Cultural Life of the American Colonies, 1607-1763.† *Illus.* TB/3005

LOUIS B. WRIGHT: Culture on the Moving Frontier TB/1053

Anthropology & Sociology

BERNARD BERELSON, Ed.: The Behavioral Sciences Today TB/1127

JOSEPH B. CASAGRANDE, Ed.: In the Company of Man: *20 Portraits of Anthropological Informants. Illus.* TB/3047

W. E. LE GROS CLARK: The Antecedents of Man: *An Introduction to the Evolution of the Primates.*° *Illus.* TB/559

THOMAS C. COCHRAN: The Inner Revolution: *Essays on the Social Sciences in History* TB/1140

ALLISON DAVIS & JOHN DOLLARD: Children of Bondage: *The Personality Development of Negro Youth in the Urban South*‖ TB/3049

ST. CLAIR DRAKE & HORACE R. CAYTON: Black Metropolis: *A Study of Negro Life in a Northern City. Introduction by Everett C. Hughes. Tables, maps, charts and graphs*
Volume I TB/1086
Volume II TB/1087

CORA DU BOIS: The People of Alor. *New Preface by the author. Illus.*
Volume I TB/1042
Volume II TB/1043

LEON FESTINGER, HENRY W. RIECKEN & STANLEY SCHACHTER: When Prophecy Fails: *A Social and Psychological Account of a Modern Group that Predicted the Destruction of the World*‖ TB/1132

RAYMOND FIRTH, Ed.: Man and Culture: *An Evaluation of the Work of Bronislaw Malinowski*‖° TB/1133

L. S. B. LEAKEY: Adam's Ancestors: *The Evolution of Man and his Culture. Illus.* TB/1019

KURT LEWIN: Field Theory in Social Science: *Selected Theoretical Papers.*‖ *Edited with a Foreword by Dorwin Cartwright* TB/1135

ROBERT H. LOWIE: Primitive Society. *Introduction by Fred Eggan* TB/1056

BENJAMIN NELSON: Religious Traditions and the Spirit of Capitalism: *From the Church Fathers to Jeremy Bentham* TB/1130

TALCOTT PARSONS & EDWARD A. SHILS, Editors: Toward a General Theory of Action: *Theoretical Foundations for the Social Sciences* TB/1083

JOHN H. ROHRER & MUNRO S. EDMONSON, Eds.: The Eighth Generation Grows Up: *Cultures and Personalities of New Orleans Negroes*‖ TB/3050

ARNOLD ROSE: The Negro in America: *The Condensed Version of Gunnar Myrdal's* An American Dilemma. *New Introduction by the Author; Foreword by Gunnar Myrdal* TB/3048

KURT SAMUELSSON: Religion and Economic Action: *A Critique of Max Weber's* The Protestant Ethic and the Spirit of Capitalism.‖° *Trans. by E. G. French; Ed. with Intro. by D. C. Coleman* TB/1131

PITIRIM SOROKIN: Contemporary Sociological Theories: *Through the First Quarter of the Twentieth Century* TB/3046

MAURICE R. STEIN: The Eclipse of Community: *An Interpretation of American Studies. New Introduction by the Author* TB/1128

SIR EDWARD TYLOR: The Origins of Culture. *Part I of "Primitive Culture."*§ *Introduction by Paul Radin* TB/33

SIR EDWARD TYLOR: Religion in Primitive Culture. *Part II of "Primitive Culture."*§ *Introduction by Paul Radin* TB/34

W. LLOYD WARNER & Associates: Democracy in Jonesville: *A Study in Quality and Inequality*** TB/1129

W. LLOYD WARNER: A Black Civilization: *A Study of an Australian Tribe.*‖ *Illus.* TB/3056

W. LLOYD WARNER: Social Class in America: *The Evaluation of Status* TB/1013

Art and Art History

EMILE MÂLE: The Gothic Image: *Religious Art in France of the Thirteenth Century.*§ *190 illus.* TB/44

MILLARD MEISS: Painting in Florence and Siena after the Black Death. *169 illus.* TB/1148

ERWIN PANOFSKY: Studies in Iconology: *Humanistic Themes in the Art of the Renaissance. 180 illustrations* TB/1077

ALEXANDRE PIANKOFF: The Shrines of Tut-Ankh-Amon. *Edited by N. Rambova. 117 illus.* TB/2011

JEAN SEZNEC: The Survival of the Pagan Gods: *The Mythological Tradition and Its Place in Renaissance Humanism and Art. 108 illustrations* TB/2004

OTTO VON SIMSON: The Gothic Cathedral: *Origins of Gothic Architecture and the Medieval Concept of Order. 58 illus.* TB/2018

HEINRICH ZIMMER: Myths and Symbols in Indian Art and Civilization. *70 illustrations* TB/2005

Business, Economics & Economic History

REINHARD BENDIX: Work and Authority in Industry: *Ideologies of Management in the Course of Industrialization* TB/3035

THOMAS C. COCHRAN: The American Business System: *A Historical Perspective, 1900-1955* TB/1080

ROBERT DAHL & CHARLES E. LINDBLOM: Politics, Economics, and Welfare: *Planning and Politico-Economic Systems Resolved into Basic Social Processes* TB/3037

PETER F. DRUCKER: The New Society: *The Anatomy of Industrial Order* TB/1082

ROBERT L. HEILBRONER: The Great Ascent: *The Struggle for Economic Development in Our Time* TB/3030

ABBA P. LERNER: Everybody's Business: *A Re-examination of Current Assumptions in Economics and Public Policy* TB/3051

ROBERT GREEN McCLOSKEY: American Conservatism in the Age of Enterprise, 1865-1910 TB/1137

PAUL MANTOUX: The Industrial Revolution in the Eighteenth Century: *The Beginnings of the Modern Factory System in England*° TB/1079

WILLIAM MILLER, Ed.: Men in Business: *Essays on the Historical Role of the Entrepreneur* TB/1081

PERRIN STRYKER: The Character of the Executive: *Eleven Studies in Managerial Qualities* TB/1041

PIERRE URI: Partnership for Progress: *A Program for Transatlantic Action* TB/3036

Contemporary Culture

JACQUES BARZUN: The House of Intellect TB/1051

JOHN U. NEF: Cultural Foundations of Industrial Civilization TB/1024

PAUL VALÉRY: The Outlook for Intelligence TB/2016

History: General

L. CARRINGTON GOODRICH: A Short History of the Chinese People. *Illus.* TB/3015

BERNARD LEWIS: The Arabs in History TB/1029

SIR PERCY SYKES: A History of Exploration.° *Introduction by John K. Wright* TB/1046

History: Ancient and Medieval

A. ANDREWES: The Greek Tyrants TB/1103

P. BOISSONNADE: Life and Work in Medieval Europe.° *Preface by Lynn White, Jr.* TB/1141

HELEN CAM: England before Elizabeth TB/1026

NORMAN COHN: The Pursuit of the Millennium: *Revolutionary Messianism in medieval and Reformation Europe and its bearing on modern Leftist and Rightist totalitarian movements* TB/1037

G. G. COULTON: Medieval Village, Manor, and Monastery TB/1022

HEINRICH FICHTENAU: The Carolingian Empire: *The Age of Charlemagne* TB/1142

F. L. GANSHOF: Feudalism TB/1058

J. M. HUSSEY: The Byzantine World TB/1057

SAMUEL NOAH KRAMER: Sumerian Mythology TB/1055

FERDINAND LOT: The End of the Ancient World and the Beginnings of the Middle Ages. *Introduction by Glanville Downey* TB/1044

STEVEN RUNCIMAN: A History of the Crusades. Volume I: *The First Crusade and the Foundation of the Kingdom of Jerusalem. Illus.* TB/1143

HENRY OSBORN TAYLOR: The Classical Heritage of the Middle Ages. *Foreword and Biblio. by Kenneth M. Setton* [Formerly listed as TB/48 under the title *The Emergence of Christian Culture in the West*] TB/1117

J. M. WALLACE-HADRILL: The Barbarian West: *The Early Middle Ages, A.D. 400-1000* TB/1061

History: Renaissance & Reformation

R. R. BOLGAR: The Classical Heritage and Its Beneficiaries: *From the Carolingian Age to the End of the Renaissance* TB/1125

JACOB BURCKHARDT: The Civilization of the Renaissance in Italy. *Introduction by Benjamin Nelson and Charles Trinkaus. Illus.* Volume I TB/40; Volume II TB/41

ERNST CASSIRER: The Individual and the Cosmos in Renaissance Philosophy. *Translated with an Introduction by Mario Domandi* TB/1097

EDWARD P. CHEYNEY: The Dawn of a New Era, 1250-1453.* *Illus.* TB/3002

WALLACE K. FERGUSON, et al.: Facets of the Renaissance TB/1098

WALLACE K. FERGUSON, et al.: The Renaissance: *Six Essays. Illus.* TB/1084

MYRON P. GILMORE: The World of Humanism, 1453-1517.* *Illus.* TB/3003

JOHAN HUIZINGA: Erasmus and the Age of Reformation. *Illus.* TB/19

ULRICH VON HUTTEN, et al.: On the Eve of the Reformation: *"Letters of Obscure Men." Introduction by Hajo Holborn* TB/1124

PAUL O. KRISTELLER: Renaissance Thought: *The Classic, Scholastic, and Humanist Strains* TB/1048

NICCOLÒ MACHIAVELLI: History of Florence and of the Affairs of Italy: *from the earliest times to the death of Lorenzo the Magnificent. Introduction by Felix Gilbert* TB/1027

ALFRED VON MARTIN: Sociology of the Renaissance. *Introduction by Wallace K. Ferguson* TB/1099

MILLARD MEISS: Painting in Florence and Siena after the Black Death. *169 illus.* TB/1148

J. E. NEALE: The Age of Catherine de Medici° TB/1085

ERWIN PANOFSKY: Studies in Iconology: *Humanistic Themes in the Art of the Renaissance. 180 illustrations* TB/1077

J. H. PARRY: The Establishment of the European Hegemony: 1415-1715: *Trade and Exploration in the Age of the Renaissance* TB/1045

HENRI PIRENNE: Early Democracies in the Low Countries: *Urban Society and Political Conflict in the Middle Ages and the Renaissance. Introduction by John Mundy* TB/1110

FERDINAND SCHEVILL: The Medici. *Illus.* TB/1010

FERDINAND SCHEVILL: Medieval and Renaissance Florence. *Illus.* Volume I: *Medieval Florence* TB/1090 Volume II: *The Coming of Humanism and the Age of the Medici* TB/1091

G. M. TREVELYAN: England in the Age of Wycliffe, 1368-1520° TB/1112

VESPASIANO: Renaissance Princes, Popes, and Prelates: *The Vespasiano Memoirs: Lives of Illustrious Men of the XVth Century. Introduction by Myron P. Gilmore* TB/1111

History: Modern European

FREDERICK B. ARTZ: Reaction and Revolution, 1815-1832.* *Illus.* TB/3034

MAX BELOFF: The Age of Absolutism, 1660-1815 TB/1062

ROBERT C. BINKLEY: Realism and Nationalism, 1852-1871.* *Illus.* TB/3038

CRANE BRINTON: A Decade of Revolution, 1789-1799.* *Illus.* TB/3018

J. BRONOWSKI & BRUCE MAZLISH: The Western Intellectual Tradition: *From Leonardo to Hegel* TB/3001

GEOFFREY BRUUN: Europe and the French Imperium, 1799-1814.* *Illus.* TB/3033

ALAN BULLOCK: Hitler, A Study in Tyranny.° *Illus.* TB/1123

E. H. CARR: The Twenty Years' Crisis, 1919-1939: *An Introduction to the Study of International Relations*° TB/1122

WALTER L. DORN: Competition for Empire, 1740-1763.* *Illus.* TB/3032

CARL J. FRIEDRICH: The Age of the Baroque, 1610-1660.* *Illus.* TB/3004

LEO GERSHOY: From Despotism to Revolution, 1763-1789.* *Illus.* TB/3017

ALBERT GOODWIN: The French Revolution TB/1064

CARLTON J. H. HAYES: A Generation of Materialism, 1871-1900.* *Illus.* TB/3039

J. H. HEXTER: Reappraisals in History: *New Views on History and Society in Early Modern Europe* TB/1100

A. R. HUMPHREYS: The Augustan World: *Society, Thought, and Letters in Eighteenth Century England* TB/1105

HANS KOHN, Ed.: The Mind of Modern Russia: *Historical and Political Thought of Russia's Great Age* TB/1065

SIR LEWIS NAMIER: Vanished Supremacies: *Essays on European History, 1812-1918*° TB/1088

JOHN U. NEF: Western Civilization Since the Renaissance: *Peace, War, Industry, and the Arts* TB/1113

FREDERICK L. NUSSBAUM: The Triumph of Science and Reason, 1660-1685.* *Illus.* TB/3009

RAYMOND W. POSTGATE, Ed.: Revolution from 1789 to 1906: *Selected Documents* TB/1063

PENFIELD ROBERTS: The Quest for Security, 1715-1740.* *Illus.* TB/3016

PRISCILLA ROBERTSON: Revolutions of 1848: *A Social History* TB/1025

ALBERT SOREL: Europe Under the Old Regime. *Translated by Francis H. Herrick* TB/1121

N. N. SUKHANOV: The Russian Revolution, 1917: *Eyewitness Account. Edited by Joel Carmichael*
Volume I TB/1066
Volume II TB/1067

JOHN B. WOLF: The Emergence of the Great Powers, 1685-1715.* *Illus.* TB/3010

JOHN B. WOLF: France: 1814-1919: *The Rise of a Liberal-Democratic Society* TB/3019

Intellectual History

HERSCHEL BAKER: The Image of Man: *A Study of the Idea of Human Dignity in Classical Antiquity, the Middle Ages, and the Renaissance* TB/1047

J. BRONOWSKI & BRUCE MAZLISH: The Western Intellectual Tradition: *From Leonardo to Hegel* TB/3001

ERNST CASSIRER: The Individual and the Cosmos in Renaissance Philosophy. *Translated with an Introduction by Mario Domandi* TB/1097

NORMAN COHN: The Pursuit of the Millennium: *Revolutionary Messianism in medieval and Reformation Europe and its bearing on modern Leftist and Rightist totalitarian movements* TB/1037

ARTHUR O. LOVEJOY: The Great Chain of Being: *A Study of the History of an Idea* TB/1009

ROBERT PAYNE: Hubris: *A Study of Pride. Foreword by Sir Herbert Read* TB/1031

BRUNO SNELL: The Discovery of the Mind: *The Greek Origins of European Thought* TB/1018

ERNEST LEE TUVESON: Millennium and Utopia: *A Study in the Background of the Idea of Progress.*‖ *New Preface by Author* TB/1134

Literature, Poetry, The Novel & Criticism

JAMES BAIRD: Ishmael: *The Art of Melville in the Contexts of International Primitivism* TB/1023

JACQUES BARZUN: The House of Intellect TB/1051

W. J. BATE: From Classic to Romantic: *Premises of Taste in Eighteenth Century England* TB/1036

RACHEL BESPALOFF: On the Iliad TB/2006

R. P. BLACKMUR, et al.: Lectures in Criticism. *Introduction by Huntington Cairns* TB/2003

ABRAHAM CAHAN: The Rise of David Levinsky: *a novel. Introduction by John Higham* TB/1028

ERNST R. CURTIUS: European Literature and the Latin Middle Ages TB/2015

GEORGE ELIOT: Daniel Deronda: *a novel. Introduction by F. R. Leavis* TB/1039

ETIENNE GILSON: Dante and Philosophy TB/1089

ALFRED HARBAGE: As They Liked It: *A Study of Shakespeare's Moral Artistry* TB/1035

STANLEY R. HOPPER, Ed.: Spiritual Problems in Contemporary Literature§ TB/21

A. R. HUMPHREYS: The Augustan World: *Society, Thought, and Letters in Eighteenth Century England*° TB/1105

ALDOUS HUXLEY: Antic Hay & The Gioconda Smile.° *Introduction by Martin Green* TB/3503

ALDOUS HUXLEY: Brave New World & Brave New World Revisited.° *Introduction by C. P. Snow* TB/3501

ALDOUS HUXLEY: Point Counter Point.° *Introduction by C. P. Snow* TB/3502

HENRY JAMES: The Princess Casamassima: *a novel. Introduction by Clinton F. Oliver* TB/1005

HENRY JAMES: Roderick Hudson: *a novel. Introduction by Leon Edel* TB/1016

HENRY JAMES: The Tragic Muse: *a novel. Introduction by Leon Edel* TB/1017

ARNOLD KETTLE: An Introduction to the English Novel. Volume I: *Defoe to George Eliot* TB/1011
Volume II: *Henry James to the Present* TB/1012

JOHN STUART MILL: On Bentham and Coleridge. *Introduction by F. R. Leavis* TB/1070

PERRY MILLER & T. H. JOHNSON, Editors: The Puritans: *A Sourcebook of Their Writings*
Volume I TB/1093
Volume II TB/1094

KENNETH B. MURDOCK: Literature and Theology in Colonial New England TB/99

SAMUEL PEPYS: The Diary of Samuel Pepys.° *Edited by O. F. Morshead. Illustrations by Ernest Shepard* TB/1007

ST.-JOHN PERSE: Seamarks TB/2002

O. E. RÖLVAAG: Giants in the Earth. *Introduction by Einar Haugen* TB/3504

GEORGE SANTAYANA: Interpretations of Poetry and Religion§ TB/9

C. P. SNOW: Time of Hope: *a novel* TB/1040

DOROTHY VAN GHENT: The English Novel: *Form and Function* TB/1050

E. B. WHITE: One Man's Meat. *Introduction by Walter Blair* TB/3505

MORTON DAUWEN ZABEL, Editor: Literary Opinion in America Volume I TB/3013 Volume II TB/3014

Myth, Symbol & Folklore

JOSEPH CAMPBELL, Editor: Pagan and Christian Mysteries. *Illus.* TB/2013

MIRCEA ELIADE: Cosmos and History: *The Myth of the Eternal Return*§ TB/2050

C. G. JUNG & C. KERÉNYI: Essays on a Science of Mythology: *The Myths of the Divine Child and the Divine Maiden* TB/2014

ERWIN PANOFSKY: Studies in Iconology: *Humanistic Themes in the Art of the Renaissance. 180 illustrations* TB/1077

JEAN SEZNEC: The Survival of the Pagan Gods: *The Mythological Tradition and its Place in Renaissance Humanism and Art. 108 illustrations* TB/2004

HELLMUT WILHELM: Change: *Eight Lectures on the I Ching* TB/2019

HEINRICH ZIMMER: Myths and Symbols in Indian Art and Civilization. *70 illustrations* TB/2005

Philosophy

HENRI BERGSON: Time and Free Will: *An Essay on the Immediate Data of Consciousness*° TB/1021

H. J. BLACKHAM: Six Existentialist Thinkers: *Kierkegaard, Nietzsche, Jaspers, Marcel, Heidegger, Sartre*° TB/1002

ERNST CASSIRER: Rousseau, Kant and Goethe. *Introduction by Peter Gay* TB/1092

FREDERICK COPLESTON: Medieval Philosophy° TB/76

F. M. CORNFORD: From Religion to Philosophy: *A Study in the Origins of Western Speculation*§ TB/20

WILFRID DESAN: The Tragic Finale: *An Essay on the Philosophy of Jean-Paul Sartre* TB/1030

PAUL FRIEDLÄNDER: Plato: *An Introduction* TB/2017

ETIENNE GILSON: Dante and Philosophy TB/1089

WILLIAM CHASE GREENE: Moira: *Fate, Good, and Evil in Greek Thought* TB/1104

W. K. C. GUTHRIE: The Greek Philosophers: *From Thales to Aristotle*° TB/1008

F. H. HEINEMANN: Existentialism and the Modern Predicament TB/28

IMMANUEL KANT: The Doctrine of Virtue, *being Part II of The Metaphysic of Morals. Translated with Notes and Introduction by Mary J. Gregor. Foreword by H. J. Paton* TB/110

IMMANUEL KANT: Lectures on Ethics.§ *Introduction by Lewis W. Beck* TB/105

WILLARD VAN ORMAN QUINE: From a Logical Point of View: *Logico-Philosophical Essays* TB/566

BERTRAND RUSSELL et al.: The Philosophy of Bertrand Russell. *Edited by Paul Arthur Schilpp* Volume I TB/1095 Volume II TB/1096

L. S. STEBBING: A Modern Introduction to Logic TB/538

ALFRED NORTH WHITEHEAD: Process and Reality: *An Essay in Cosmology* TB/1033

WILHELM WINDELBAND: A History of Philosophy I: *Greek, Roman, Medieval* TB/38

WILHELM WINDELBAND: A History of Philosophy II: *Renaissance, Enlightenment, Modern* TB/39

Philosophy of History

NICOLAS BERDYAEV: The Beginning and the End§ TB/14

NICOLAS BERDYAEV: The Destiny of Man TB/61

WILHELM DILTHEY: Pattern and Meaning in History: *Thoughts on History and Society.*° *Edited with an Introduction by H. P. Rickman* TB/1075

RAYMOND KLIBANSKY & H. J. PATON, Eds.: Philosophy and History: *The Ernst Cassirer Festschrift. Illus.* TB/1115

JOSE ORTEGA Y GASSET: The Modern Theme. *Introduction by Jose Ferrater Mora* TB/1038

KARL R. POPPER: The Poverty of Historicism° TB/1126

W. H. WALSH: Philosophy of History: *An Introduction* TB/1020

Political Science & Government

JEREMY BENTHAM: The Handbook of Political Fallacies: *Introduction by Crane Brinton* TB/1069

KENNETH E. BOULDING: Conflict and Defense: *A General Theory* TB/3024

CRANE BRINTON: English Political Thought in the Nineteenth Century TB/1071

EDWARD S. CORWIN: American Constitutional History: *Essays edited by Alpheus T. Mason and Gerald Garvey* TB/1136

ROBERT DAHL & CHARLES E. LINDBLOM: Politics, Economics, and Welfare: *Planning and Politico-Economic Systems Resolved into Basic Social Processes* TB/3037

JOHN NEVILLE FIGGIS: Political Thought from Gerson to Grotius: 1414-1625: *Seven Studies. Introduction by Garrett Mattingly* TB/1032

F. L. GANSHOF: Feudalism TB/1058

G. P. GOOCH: English Democratic Ideas in the Seventeenth Century TB/1006

ROBERT H. JACKSON: The Supreme Court in the American System of Government TB/1106

DAN N. JACOBS, Ed.: The New Communist Manifesto *and Related Documents* TB/1078

DAN N. JACOBS & HANS BAERWALD, Eds.: Chinese Communism: *Selected Documents* TB/3031

ROBERT GREEN McCLOSKEY: American Conservatism in the Age of Enterprise, 1865-1910 TB/1137

KINGSLEY MARTIN: French Liberal Thought in the Eighteenth Century: *A Study of Political Ideas from Bayle to Condorcet* TB/1114

JOHN STUART MILL: On Bentham and Coleridge. *Introduction by F. R. Leavis* TB/1070

JOHN B. MORRALL: Political Thought in Medieval Times TB/1076

KARL R. POPPER: The Open Society and Its Enemies
Volume I: *The Spell of Plato* TB/1101
Volume II: *The High Tide of Prophecy: Hegel, Marx, and the Aftermath* TB/1102

JOSEPH A. SCHUMPETER: Capitalism, Socialism and Democracy TB/3008

Psychology

ALFRED ADLER: Problems of Neurosis. *Introduction by Heinz L. Ansbacher* TB/1145

ANTON T. BOISEN: The Exploration of the Inner World: *A Study of Mental Disorder and Religious Experience* TB/87

LEON FESTINGER, HENRY W. RIECKEN, STANLEY SCHACHTER: When Prophecy Fails: *A Social and Psychological Study of a Modern Group that Predicted the Destruction of the World* ‖ TB/1132

SIGMUND FREUD: On Creativity and the Unconscious: *Papers on the Psychology of Art, Literature, Love, Religion.*§ *Intro. by Benjamin Nelson* TB/45

C. JUDSON HERRICK: The Evolution of Human Nature TB/545

ALDOUS HUXLEY: The Devils of Loudun: *A Study in the Psychology of Power Politics and Mystical Religion in the France of Cardinal Richelieu*§° TB/60

WILLIAM JAMES: Psychology: *The Briefer Course. Edited with an Intro. by Gordon Allport* TB/1034

C. G. JUNG: Psychological Reflections. *Edited by Jolande Jacobi* TB/2001

C. G. JUNG: Symbols of Transformation: *An Analysis of the Prelude to a Case of Schizophrenia. Illus.*
Volume I TB/2009
Volume II TB/2010

C. G. JUNG & C. KERÉNYI: Essays on a Science of Mythology: *The Myths of the Divine Child and the Divine Maiden* TB/2014

SOREN KIERKEGAARD: Repetition: *An Essay in Experimental Psychology. Translated with Introduction & Notes by Walter Lowrie* TB/117

KARL MENNINGER: Theory of Psychoanalytic Technique TB/1144

ERICH NEUMANN: Amor and Psyche: *The Psychic Development of the Feminine* TB/2012

ERICH NEUMANN: The Origins and History of Consciousness Volume I *Illus.* TB/2007
Volume II TB/2008

C. P. OBERNDORF: A History of Psychoanalysis in America TB/1147

JEAN PIAGET, BÄRBEL INHELDER, & ALINA SZEMINSKA: The Child's Conception of Geometry TB/1146

RELIGION

Ancient & Classical

J. H. BREASTED: Development of Religion and Thought in Ancient Egypt. *Introduction by John A. Wilson* TB/57

HENRI FRANKFORT: Ancient Egyptian Religion: *An Interpretation* TB/77

WILLIAM CHASE GREENE: Moira: *Fate, Good and Evil in Greek Thought* TB/1104

G. RACHEL LEVY: Religious Conceptions of the Stone Age *and their Influence upon European Thought. Illus. Introduction by Henri Frankfort* TB/106

MARTIN P. NILSSON: Greek Folk Religion. *Foreword by Arthur Darby Nock* TB/78

ALEXANDRE PIANKOFF: The Shrines of Tut-Ankh-Amon. *Edited by N. Rambova. 117 illus.* TB/2011

H. J. ROSE: Religion in Greece and Rome TB/55

Biblical Thought & Literature

W. F. ALBRIGHT: The Biblical Period from Abraham to Ezra TB/102

C. K. BARRETT, Ed.: The New Testament Background: *Selected Documents* TB/86

C. H. DODD: The Authority of the Bible TB/43

M. S. ENSLIN: Christian Beginnings TB/5

M. S. ENSLIN: The Literature of the Christian Movement TB/6

H. E. FOSDICK: A Guide to Understanding the Bible TB/2

H. H. ROWLEY: The Growth of the Old Testament TB/107

D. WINTON THOMAS, Ed.: Documents from Old Testament Times TB/85

Christianity: Origins & Early Development

ADOLF DEISSMANN: Paul: *A Study in Social and Religious History* TB/15

EDWARD GIBBON: The Triumph of Christendom in the Roman Empire *(Chaps. XV-XX of "Decline and Fall," J. B. Bury edition).*§ *Illus.* TB/46

MAURICE GOGUEL: Jesus and the Origins of Christianity.° *Introduction by C. Leslie Mitton*
Volume I: *Prolegomena to the Life of Jesus* TB/65
Volume II: *The Life of Jesus* TB/66

EDGAR J. GOODSPEED: A Life of Jesus TB/1

ADOLF HARNACK: The Mission and Expansion of Christianity *in the First Three Centuries. Introduction by Jaroslav Pelikan* TB/92

R. K. HARRISON: The Dead Sea Scrolls: *An Introduction*° TB/84

EDWIN HATCH: The Influence of Greek Ideas on Christianity.§ *Introduction and Bibliography by Frederick C. Grant* TB /18

ARTHUR DARBY NOCK: Early Gentile Christianity and Its Hellenistic Background TB/111

ARTHUR DARBY NOCK: St. Paul° TB/104

JOHANNES WEISS: Earliest Christianity: *A History of the Period A.D. 30-150. Introduction and Bibilography by Frederick C. Grant* Volume I TB/53
Volume II TB/54

Christianity: The Middle Ages, The Reformation, and After

G. P. FEDOTOV: The Russian Religious Mind: *Kievan Christianity, the tenth to the thirteenth centuries* TB/70

ÉTIENNE GILSON: Dante and Philosophy TB/1089

WILLIAM HALLER: The Rise of Puritanism TB/22

JOHAN HUIZINGA: Erasmus and the Age of Reformation. *Illus.* TB/19

JOHN T. McNEILL: Makers of Christianity: *From Alfred the Great to Schleiermacher* TB/121

A. C. McGIFFERT: Protestant Thought Before Kant. *Preface by Jaroslav Pelikan* TB/93

KENNETH B. MURDOCK: Literature and Theology in Colonial New England TB/99

GORDON RUPP: Luther's Progress to the Diet of Worms° TB/120

Judaic Thought & Literature

MARTIN BUBER: Eclipse of God: *Studies in the Relation Between Religion and Philosophy* TB/12

MARTIN BUBER: Moses: *The Revelation and the Covenant* TB/27

MARTIN BUBER: Pointing the Way. *Introduction by Maurice S. Friedman* TB/103

MARTIN BUBER: The Prophetic Faith TB/73

MARTIN BUBER: Two Types of Faith: *the interpenetration of Judaism and Christianity*° TB/75

MAURICE S. FRIEDMAN: Martin Buber: *The Life of Dialogue* TB/64

FLAVIUS JOSEPHUS: The Great Roman-Jewish War, *with* The Life of Josephus. *Introduction by William R. Farmer* TB/74

T. J. MEEK: Hebrew Origins TB/69

Oriental Religions: Far Eastern, Near Eastern

TOR ANDRAE: Mohammed: *The Man and His Faith* TB/62

EDWARD CONZE: Buddhism: *Its Essence and Development.*° *Foreword by Arthur Waley* TB/58

EDWARD CONZE, et al., Editors: Buddhist Texts Through the Ages TB/113

ANANDA COOMARASWAMY: Buddha and the Gospel of Buddhism TB/119

H. G. CREEL: Confucius and the Chinese Way TB/63

FRANKLIN EDGERTON, Trans. & Ed.: The Bhagavad Gita TB/115

SWAMI NIKHILANANDA, Trans. & Ed.: The Upanishads: *A One-Volume Abridgment* TB/114

HELLMUT WILHELM: Change: *Eight Lectures on the I Ching* TB/2019

Philosophy of Religion

RUDOLF BULTMANN: History and Eschatology: *The Presence of Eternity* TB/91

RUDOLF BULTMANN AND FIVE CRITICS: Kerygma and Myth: *A Theological Debate* TB/80

RUDOLF BULTMANN and KARL KUNDSIN: Form Criticism: *Two Essays on New Testament Research. Translated by Frederick C. Grant* TB/96

MIRCEA ELIADE: The Sacred and the Profane TB/81

LUDWIG FEUERBACH: The Essence of Christianity.§ *Introduction by Karl Barth. Foreword by H. Richard Niebuhr* TB/11

ADOLF HARNACK: What is Christianity?§ *Introduction by Rudolf Bultmann* TB/17

FRIEDRICH HEGEL: On Christianity: *Early Theological Writings. Edited by Richard Kroner and T. M. Knox* TB/79

KARL HEIM: Christian Faith and Natural Science TB/16

IMMANUEL KANT: Religion Within the Limits of Reason Alone.§ *Introduction by Theodore M. Greene and John Silber* TB/67

PIERRE TEILHARD DE CHARDIN: The Phenomenon of Man° TB/83

Religion, Culture & Society

JOSEPH L. BLAU, Ed.: Cornerstones of Religious Freedom in America: *Selected Basic Documents, Court Decisions and Public Statements. Enlarged and revised edition, with new Introduction by the Editor* TB/118

C. C. GILLISPIE: Genesis and Geology: *The Decades before Darwin*§ TB/51

BENJAMIN NELSON: Religious Traditions and the Spirit of Capitalism: *From the Church Fathers to Jeremy Bentham* TB/1130

H. RICHARD NIEBUHR: Christ and Culture TB/3

H. RICHARD NIEBUHR: The Kingdom of God in America TB/49

RALPH BARTON PERRY: Puritanism and Democracy TB/1138

WALTER RAUSCHENBUSCH: Christianity and the Social Crisis.‡ *Edited by Robert D. Cross* TB/3059

KURT SAMUELSSON: Religion and Economic Action: *A Critique of Max Weber's* The Protestant Ethic and the Spirit of Capitalism.¶° *Trans. by E. G. French; Ed. with Intro. by D. C. Coleman* TB/1131

ERNST TROELTSCH: The Social Teaching of the Christian Churches.° *Introduction by H. Richard Niebuhr* Volume I TB/71, Volume II TB/72

Religious Thinkers & Traditions

AUGUSTINE: An Augustine Synthesis. *Edited by Erich Przywara* TB/35

KARL BARTH: Church Dogmatics: *A Selection. Introduction by H. Gollwitzer; Edited by G. W. Bromiley* TB/95

KARL BARTH: Dogmatics in Outline TB/56

KARL BARTH: The Word of God and the Word of Man TB/13

THOMAS CORBISHLEY, S. J.: Roman Catholicism TB/112

ADOLF DEISSMANN: Paul: *A Study in Social and Religious History* TB/15

JOHANNES ECKHART: Meister Eckhart: *A Modern Translation by R. B. Blakney* TB/8

WINTHROP HUDSON: The Great Tradition of the American Churches TB/98

SOREN KIERKEGAARD: Edifying Discourses. *Edited with an Introduction by Paul Holmer* TB/32

SOREN KIERKEGAARD: The Journals of Kierkegaard.° *Edited with an Introduction by Alexander Dru* TB/52

SOREN KIERKEGAARD: The Point of View for My Work as an Author: *A Report to History.*§ *Preface by Benjamin Nelson* TB/88

SOREN KIERKEGAARD: The Present Age.§ *Translated and edited by Alexander Dru. Introduction by Walter Kaufmann* TB/94

SOREN KIERKEGAARD: Purity of Heart. *Translated by Douglas Steere* TB/4

SOREN KIERKEGAARD: Repetition: *An Essay in Experimental Psychology. Translated with Introduction & Notes by Walter Lowrie* TB/117

SOREN KIERKEGAARD: Works of Love: *Some Christian Reflections in the Form of Discourses* TB/122

WALTER LOWRIE: Kierkegaard: *A Life*
Volume I TB/89
Volume II TB/90

GABRIEL MARCEL: Homo Viator: *Introduction to a Metaphysic of Hope* TB/97

PERRY MILLER: Errand into the Wilderness TB/1139

PERRY MILLER & T. H. JOHNSON, Editors: The Puritans: *A Sourcebook of Their Writings*
Volume I TB/1093
Volume II TB/1094

PAUL PFUETZE: Self, Society, Existence: *Human Nature and Dialogue in the Thought of George Herbert Mead and Martin Buber* TB/1059

F. SCHLEIERMACHER: The Christian Faith. *Introduction by Richard R. Niebuhr* Volume I TB/108
Volume II TB/109

F. SCHLEIERMACHER: On Religion: *Speeches to Its Cultured Despisers. Intro. by Rudolf Otto* TB/36

PAUL TILLICH: Dynamics of Faith TB/42

EVELYN UNDERHILL: Worship TB/10

G. VAN DER LEEUW: Religion in Essence and Manifestation: *A Study in Phenomenology. Appendices by Hans H. Penner* Volume I TB/100
Volume II TB/101

NATURAL SCIENCES AND MATHEMATICS

Biological Sciences

CHARLOTTE AUERBACH: The Science of Genetics Σ TB/568

A. BELLAIRS: Reptiles: *Life History, Evolution, and Structure. Illus.* TB/520

LUDWIG VON BERTALANFFY: Modern Theories of Development: *An Introduction to Theoretical Biology* TB/554

LUDWIG VON BERTALANFFY: Problems of Life: *An Evaluation of Modern Biological and Scientific Thought* TB/521

JOHN TYLER BONNER: The Ideas of Biology. Σ *Illus.* TB/570

HAROLD F. BLUM: Time's Arrow and Evolution TB/555

A. J. CAIN: Animal Species and their Evolution. *Illus.* TB/519

WALTER B. CANNON: Bodily Changes in Pain, Hunger, Fear and Rage. *Illus.* TB/562

W. E. LE GROS CLARK: The Antecedents of Man: *An Introduction to the Evolution of the Primates.*° *Illus.* TB/559

W. H. DOWDESWELL: Animal Ecology. *Illus.* TB/543

W. H. DOWDESWELL: The Mechanism of Evolution. *Illus.* TB/527

R. W. GERARD: Unresting Cells. *Illus.* TB/541

DAVID LACK: Darwin's Finches. *Illus.* TB/544

J. E. MORTON: Molluscs: *An Introduction to their Form and Functions. Illus.* TB/529

ADOLF PORTMANN: Animals as Social Beings.° *Illus.* TB/572

O. W. RICHARDS: The Social Insects. *Illus.* TB/542

P. M. SHEPPARD: Natural Selection and Heredity. *Illus.* TB/528

EDMUND W. SINNOTT: Cell and Psyche: *The Biology of Purpose* TB/546

C. H. WADDINGTON: How Animals Develop. *Illus.* TB/553

Chemistry

J. R. PARTINGTON: A Short History of Chemistry. *Illus.* TB/522

J. READ: A Direct Entry to Organic Chemistry. *Illus.* TB/523

J. READ: Through Alchemy to Chemistry. *Illus.* TB/561

Geography

R. E. COKER: This Great and Wide Sea: *An Introduction to Oceanography and Marine Biology. Illus.* TB/551

F. K. HARE: The Restless Atmosphere TB/560

History of Science

W. DAMPIER, Ed.: Readings in the Literature of Science. *Illus.* TB/512

A. HUNTER DUPREE: Science in the Federal Government: *A History of Policies and Activities to 1940* TB/573

ALEXANDRE KOYRÉ: From the Closed World to the Infinite Universe: *Copernicus, Kepler, Galileo, Newton, etc.* TB/31

A. G. VAN MELSEN: From Atomos to Atom: *A History of the Concept* Atom TB/517

O. NEUGEBAUER: The Exact Sciences in Antiquity TB/552

H. T. PLEDGE: Science Since 1500: *A Short History of Mathematics, Physics, Chemistry and Biology. Illus.* TB/506

GEORGE SARTON: Ancient Science and Modern Civilization TB/501

HANS THIRRING: Energy for Man: *From Windmills to Nuclear Power* TB/556

WILLIAM LAW WHYTE: Essay on Atomism: *From Democritus to 1960* TB/565

A. WOLF: A History of Science, Technology and Philosophy in the 16th and 17th Centuries.° *Illus.*
Volume I TB/508
Volume II TB/509

A. WOLF: A History of Science, Technology, and Philosophy in the Eighteenth Century.° *Illus.*
Volume I TB/539
Volume II TB/540

Mathematics

H. DAVENPORT: The Higher Arithmetic: *An Introduction to the Theory of Numbers* TB/526

H. G. FORDER: Geometry: *An Introduction* TB/548

GOTTLOB FREGE: The Foundations of Arithmetic: *A Logico-Mathematical Enquiry into the Concept of Number* TB/534

S. KÖRNER: The Philosophy of Mathematics: *An Introduction* TB/547

D. E. LITTLEWOOD: Skeleton Key of Mathematics: *A Simple Account of Complex Algebraic Problems* TB/525

GEORGE E. OWEN: Fundamentals of Scientific Mathematics TB/569

WILLARD VAN ORMAN QUINE: Mathematical Logic TB/558

O. G. SUTTON: Mathematics in Action.° *Foreword by James R. Newman. Illus.* TB/518

FREDERICK WAISMANN: Introduction to Mathematical Thinking. *Foreword by Karl Menger* TB/511

Philosophy of Science

R. B. BRAITHWAITE: Scientific Explanation TB/515

J. BRONOWSKI: Science and Human Values. *Illus.* TB/505

ALBERT EINSTEIN: Philosopher-Scientist. *Edited by Paul A. Schilpp* Volume I TB/502
Volume II TB/503

WERNER HEISENBERG: Physics and Philosophy: *The Revolution in Modern Science. Introduction by F. S. C. Northrop* TB/549

JOHN MAYNARD KEYNES: A Treatise on Probability.° *Introduction by N. R. Hanson* TB/557

STEPHEN TOULMIN: Foresight and Understanding: *An Enquiry into the Aims of Science. Foreword by Jacques Barzun* TB/564

STEPHEN TOULMIN: The Philosophy of Science: *An Introduction* TB/513

G. J. WHITROW: The Natural Philosophy of Time° TB/563

Physics and Cosmology

DAVID BOHM: Causality and Chance in Modern Physics. *Foreword by Louis de Broglie* TB/536

P. W. BRIDGMAN: The Nature of Thermodynamics TB/537

A. C. CROMBIE, Ed.: Turning Point in Physics TB/535

C. V. DURELL: Readable Relativity. *Foreword by Freeman J. Dyson* TB/530

ARTHUR EDDINGTON: Space, Time and Gravitation: *An outline of the General Relativity Theory* TB/510

GEORGE GAMOW: Biography of PhysicsΣ TB/567

MAX JAMMER: Concepts of Force: *A Study in the Foundation of Dynamics* TB/550

MAX JAMMER: Concepts of Mass *in Classical and Modern Physics* TB/571

MAX JAMMER: Concepts of Space: *The History of Theories of Space in Physics. Foreword by Albert Einstein* TB/533

EDMUND WHITTAKER: History of the Theories of Aether and Electricity
Volume I: *The Classical Theories* TB/531
Volume II: *The Modern Theories* TB/532

G. J. WHITROW: The Structure and Evolution of the Universe: *An Introduction to Cosmology. Illus.* TB/504

A LETTER TO THE READER

Overseas, there is considerable belief that we are a country of extreme conservatism and that we cannot accommodate to social change.

Books about America in the hands of readers abroad can help change those ideas.

The U. S. Information Agency cannot, by itself, meet the vast need for books about the United States.

You can help.

Harper Torchbooks provides three packets of books on American history, economics, sociology, literature and politics to help meet the need.

To send a packet of Torchbooks [*] overseas, all you need do is send your check for $7 (which includes cost of shipping) to Harper & Row. The U. S. Information Agency will distribute the books to libraries, schools, and other centers all over the world.

I ask every American to support this program, part of a worldwide BOOKS USA campaign.

I ask you to share in the opportunity to help tell others about America.

EDWARD R. MURROW
Director,
U. S. Information Agency

[*retailing at $10.85 to $12.00]

PACKET I: Twentieth Century America

Dulles/America's Rise to World Power, 1898-1954
Cochran/The American Business System, 1900-1955
Zabel, Editor/Literary Opinion in America (two volumes)
Drucker/The New Society: *The Anatomy of Industrial Order*
Fortune Editors/America in the Sixties: *The Economy and the Society*

PACKET II: American History

Billington/The Far Western Frontier, 1830-1860
Mowry/The Era of Theodore Roosevelt and the Birth of Modern America, 1900-1912
Faulkner/Politics, Reform, and Expansion, 1890-1900
Cochran & Miller/The Age of Enterprise: *A Social History of Industrial America*
Tyler/Freedom's Ferment: *American Social History from the Revolution to the Civil War*

PACKET III: American History

Hansen/The Atlantic Migration, 1607-1860
Degler/Out of Our Past: *The Forces that Shaped Modern America*
Probst, Editor/The Happy Republic: *A Reader in Tocqueville's America*
Alden/The American Revolution, 1775-1783
Wright/The Cultural Life of the American Colonies, 1607-1763

Your gift will be acknowledged directly to you by the overseas recipient. Simply fill out the coupon, detach and mail with your check or money order.

HARPER & ROW, PUBLISHERS • BOOKS USA DEPT.
49 East 33rd Street, New York 16, N. Y.

Packet I ☐ Packet II ☐ Packet III ☐

Please send the BOOKS USA library packet(s) indicated above, in my name, to the area checked below. Enclosed is my remittance in the amount of ____________ for ____________ packet(s) at $7.00 each.

_____ Africa _____ Latin America

_____ Far East _____ Near East

Name______________________________________

Address____________________________________

____

NOTE: This offer expires December 31, 1966.